# Globalization of Education

Continuing Joel Spring's reportage and analysis of the intersection of global forces and education, this text offers a comprehensive overview and synthesis of current research, theories, and models related to the topic. Spring introduces readers to the processes, institutions, and forces by which schooling has been globalized and examines the impact of these forces on schooling in local contexts.

*Globalization of Education: An Introduction*:
- Introduces readers to theories about the globalization of education and world models of education
- Analyzes the concept of the knowledge economy and its use by the World Bank to shape school systems in developing countries
- Surveys the educational influences of the United Nations and the OECD and the impact of the PISA and TIMSS international testing programs
- Looks at the global marketing of educational products and institutions, multinational learning and publishing corporations, assessment companies, and universities
- Discusses alternative educational models, such as progressive and indigenous forms, that compete for global attention with dominant educational discourses
- Addresses global religious models of education
- Examines educational responses to global migration, global language issues, and differences and conflicts resulting f~ ~he impact of global culture and migration on ethical val~~ ~al school systems
- Evaluates different theori~~ ~ucation in the context of complex thi~

Designed for courses on ~tional and comparative education, educa~ ~ucation, and educational policy, the text is ~rative style to engage readers in thoughtful consideratio~ ~s discussed. Each chapter includes "Key Points" that summarize the content and suggest issues and questions for critical analysis, discussion, and debate.

**Joel Spring** is Professor of Education, Queens College and the Graduate Center of the City University of New York

# Sociocultural, Political, and Historical Studies in Education

Joel Spring, Editor

For additional information on titles in the Sociocultural, Political, and Historical Studies in Education series visit **www.routledge.com**

# Globalization of Education

## An Introduction

## Joel Spring

Queens College and Graduate Center
City University of New York

Routledge
Taylor & Francis Group

NEW YORK AND LONDON

First published 2009
by Routledge
270 Madison Ave, New York, NY 10016

Simultaneously published in the UK
by Routledge
2 Park Square, Milton Park, Abingdon, Oxon OX14 4RN

Routledge is an imprint of the Taylor & Francis Group, an informa business

© 2009 Taylor & Francis

Typeset in Sabon and Gill Sans by EvS Communication Networx, Inc.
Printed and bound in the United States of America on acid-free paper by Walsworth
Publishing Company, Marceline, MO.

Library of Congress Cataloging in Publication Data
Spring, Joel H.
Globalization of education : an introduction / Joel Spring.
p. cm. — (Sociocultural, political, and historical studies in education)
Includes bibliographical references and index.
1. Education—Economic aspects. 2. Education and globalization. I. Title.
LC65.S67 2008
370—dc22
2008023483


ISBN 10: 0-415-98946-9 (hbk)
ISBN 10: 0-415-98947-7 (pbk)
ISBN 10: 0-203-88685-2 (ebk)

ISBN 13: 978-0-415-98946-6 (hbk)
ISBN 13: 978-0-415-98947-3 (pbk)
ISBN 13: 978-0-203-88685-4 (ebk)

To Ella, Max, Stella, and the Internet

# Contents

# Preface

This book is a synthesis of current research and theories about the globalization of education. Chapter 1 introduces readers to theories about the globalization of education and world models of education. The chapter provides a framework to guide the reader through the remainder of the book. Chapter 2 analyzes the concept of the knowledge economy and the efforts by the World Bank to use this concept to shape school systems in developing nations. In addition, the chapter examines the World Bank's global networks and their relationship to the globalization of education. The educational influence of the United Nations and the Organisation for Economic Co-operation and Development (OECD) are analyzed in chapter 3 along with the impact of OECDs international testing programs PISA and TIMSS. Chapter 4 looks at the global marketing of educational products and institutions by multinational learning and publishing corporations, international assessment companies, and universities. A discussion of the World Trade Organization and its General Agreement on Trade in Services serves as a background for discussing global educational marketing.

In chapter 5, I turn to a discussion of the interaction between the global and the local. Also, the chapter discusses alternative educational models, such as progressive and indigenous models, that are competing for global attention along with the dominant educational discourses of organizations like the World Bank and OECD. These alternative educational models, as I discuss in chapter 5, are often promoted by international nongovernment organizations, including human rights and environmental organizations. Chapter 6 examines the potential global clash of civilizations resulting from differing concepts about the nature of knowledge and religious beliefs. The chapter examines global religious models of education which are central to any discussion of the globalization of education.

Global migration is directly affecting national educational policies as populations move legally and illegally between nations and as national populations move from rural to urban centers. Chapter 7 examines the consequences of migration within the framework of the global knowledge economy including what has been called brain drain, brain gain, brain circulation, and brain waste. Global migration also creates national issues regarding multicultural and multilingual education policies. In addition, chapter 7 examines the range of global possibilities for educating multicultural and multilingual populations. In the final chapter 8, I evaluate the different theories about the globalization of education in the context of complex thinking and I review the major themes of the book.

# Chapter 1

# Globalization of Education

Globalization of education refers to the worldwide discussions, processes, and institutions affecting local educational practices and policies. The key in the previous statement is the word "worldwide." This means that events are happening on a global scale that affect national school systems. The image is that of global educational policies and practices existing in a superstructure above national and local schools. Nothing is static in this image. There is a constant dynamic of interaction: global ideas about school practices interact with local school systems while, through mutual interaction, both the local and the global are changed. In other the words, this global superstructure is constantly changing. Nations continue to independently control their school systems while being influenced by this superstructure of global education processes. Today, many nations choose to adopt policies from this global superstructure in order to compete in the global economy.

What comprises this global education superstructure? There are international organizations that directly and indirectly influence national school systems. There are multinational education corporations and schools. Government and professionals engage in global discussions about school policies. In the first issue of the journal *Globalisation, Societies and Education* (2003), the editors stated that globalization of education would be considered as an intertwined set of global processes affecting education, such as worldwide discourses on human capital, economic development, and multiculturalism; intergovernmental organizations; information and communication technology; nongovernment organizations; and multinational corporations.[1] Each of these aspects of the educational global superstructure is discussed in later chapters. For example, global discourses exist about the knowledge economy, lifelong learning, global migration and brain circulation, and neoliberalism. Illustrative of major global institutions affecting worldwide educational practices and policies are the World Bank, Organization for Economic Cooperation and Development (OECD), the World Trade Organization (WTO) and its General Agreement on Trade in Services (GATS), the United Nations, UNESCO and other intergovernmental organizations (IGOs) and nongovernment organizations (NGOs), such as human rights, environmental, and women's organizations. Another factor is the impact on local schools of the development of English as the language of global business. Explanations and analyzes of these aspects of educational globalization and their impact on national school systems comprise the major part of this book.

In this chapter I examine differing theoretical interpretations of the globalization of education, world models of educational practices, and the global borrowing and lending of educational ideas and practices. These interpretations and models establish the basic framework for analyzing in later chapters various aspects of educational globalization. In chapters 2 and 3, I discuss major discourses and global networks including the World Bank, the Organization for Economic Cooperation and Development, UNESCO, human capital concepts and the idea of a knowledge economy. Chapter 4 examines the marketing of education by multinational corporations, international testing organizations and higher education. Chapter 5 focuses on the global role of non-government organizations and progressive education. Alternatives to the dominant world educational paradigm are explored in chapter 6 through an examination of religion and indigenous education. In the summary chapter 7, I will expand on previous discussions about English as the language of educational globalization and consider the impact, particularly for differing forms of multiculturalism, of the world's migration of peoples. Chapter 8 provides an analysis of the various theoretical attempts to explain the globalization of education.

## Globalization of Education

The concept of globalized educational institutions and discourses developed after the term "globalization" was coined by the economist Theodore Levitt in 1985 to describe changes in global economics affecting production, consumption, and investment.[2] The term was quickly applied to political and cultural changes that affect in common ways large segments of the world's peoples. One of these common global phenomenon is schooling. As the opening editorial in the first edition of *Globalisation, Societies and Education*—the very founding of this journal indicates the growing importance of globalization and education as a field of study—states "formal education is the most commonly found institution and most commonly shared experience of all in the contemporary world."[3] However, globalization of education does not mean that all schools are the same as indicated by studies of differences between the local and the global.[4]

In the 1990s, the language of globalization entered discourses about schooling. Government and business groups began talking about the necessity of schools meeting the needs of the global economy. For example, the United States' organization Achieve Inc. formed in 1996 by the National Governors Associations and CEOs of major corporations for the purpose of school reform declared that "High school is now the front line in America's battle to remain competitive on the increasingly competitive international economic stage."[5] The organization provided the following definition of the global economy in a publication title that suggested the linkages made by politicians and business people between education and globalization: "America's High Schools: The Front Line in the Battle for Our Economic Future."

The integration of the world economy through low-cost information and communication technologies has an even more important implication than the dramatic expansion of both the volume of trade and what can be traded. Trade and technology are making all the nations of the world more alike. Together they can bring all of the world's companies the same resources—the same scientific research, the same capital, the same parts and components, the same business services, and the same skills.[6]

In the same fashion, the European Commission's document *Teaching and Learning: On Route to the Learning Society* describes three basic causes of globalization: "the advent of the information society, scientific and technical civilisation and the globalisation of the economy. All three contribute to the development of a learning society."[7]

The growth of worldwide educational discourses and institutions led to similar national educational agendas, particularly the concept that education should be viewed as an economic investment with the goal of developing human capital or better workers to promote economic growth. Consequently, educational discourses around the world often refer to human capital, lifelong learning for improving job skills, and economic development. Also, the global economy is sparking a mass migration of workers resulting in global discussions about multicultural education.

Intergovernmental organizations, such as the United Nations, OECD, and the World Bank, are promoting global educational agendas that reflect discourses about human capital, economic development, and multiculturalism. Information and communication technology is speeding the global flow of information and creating a library of world knowledges. Global nongovernment organizations, particularly those concerned with human rights and environmentalism, are trying to influence school curricula throughout the world. Multinational corporations, particularly those involved in publishing, information, testing, for-profit schooling, and computers, are marketing their products to governments, schools, and parents around the world.

Discussions of globalization often refer to societies in contrast to nation states as indicated by the journal title *Globalisation, Societies and Education*. This results in references to a global society or societies. The term "societies" is meant to encompass something broader than a nation by including economic and political organizations, civil society, and culture. It is meant to identify groups of peoples sharing similar characteristics who see themselves as connected across the national boundaries. In this definition nations do not disappear but they become subsets of societies. In other words, particular societies might be identified as having similar political forms such as democratic or totalitarian, similar economic organizations, such as market-driven or planned, or similar religions such as Islamic, Christian, Buddhist, or Hindu.

While the founders of *Globalisation, Societies and Education* use the word "societies" in their title in contrast to "nations" or "nation states," others have chosen the word "civilizations."[8] The term civilizations can be used for the categories of East and West and North and South. However, these terms are so broad that they defy any clear definition. In comparing the thinking of Asian and Western students, Nesbitt defined his concept of Asian civilization as one based on Confucian ethical values, such as those found in China, Korea, and Japan, while Western civilization is based on the early works of Greek thinkers like Plato and Aristotle.[8]

Samuel Huntington popularized the idea of clashes of civilizations. His vision is of a world divided by religious, cultural, and economic differences that override the boundaries of the nation state. His civilization categories include Western, Latin America, African, Islamic, Sinic (China and Korea), Hindu, Eastern Orthodox Christianity, and Japanese. In the future civilization clashes, he argues, will be between Western, Islamic, and Sinic civilizations.[9]

## Global and Comparative Education

How is the study of globalization and education different from the traditional field of comparative education? First, researchers on globalization and education are not drawn exclusively from comparative education though many of those studying globalization are identified with that field. As a new field of study, researchers into the processes and effects of globalization on educational practices and policies come from a variety of education disciplines, including anthropology, curriculum studies, economics, history, sociology, educational policy, comparative education, psychology, and instructional methodologies. For instance, the book *Globalizing Education: Policies, Pedagogies, & Politics* is edited by Michael Apple, a curriculum researcher, Jane Kenway, a sociology of education researcher, and Michael Singh, an educational policy researcher.[10] Consequently, at least in its initial stages, research in this new field tends to be interdisciplinary. This does not preclude the possibility that sometime in the future researchers in the field of globalization and education will be specialists educated in doctoral programs devoted to the topic.

Second, comparative education has traditionally focused on comparing the educational systems of nations. Referring to the "new world for comparative education," Dale wrote that with globalization the world "can no longer unproblematically be apprehended as made up of autonomous states, an assumption that had been fairly fundamental to much work in comparative education, indeed, the basis of the comparisons it undertook."[11] Or, as Carnoy and Rhoten asserted, "Before the 1950s, comparative education focused mainly on the philosophical and cultural origins of national education systems."[12] In an editorial in *Comparative Education*, Broadfoot wrote that the topic of globalization has had a positive effect on the historic swings in the perceived value of the field of comparative education: "At the present time we find ourselves at the latter extreme, with governments around the world anxious to learn about

---

## Key Points: The Components of Educational Globalization

1. The adoption by nations of similar educational practices, including curricula, school organizations, and pedagogies
2. Global discourses that are influencing local and national educational policymakers, school administrators, college faculties, and teachers
3. Intergovernmental and nongovernment organizations that influence national and local educational practices
4. Global networks and flow of ideas and practices
5. Multinational corporations that market educational products, such as tests, curricula, and school materials
6. Global marketing of higher education and educational services
7. Global information technology, e-learning and communications
8. The effect of the world migration of peoples on national and local school policies and practices regarding multiculturalism
9. The current effect of English as the global language of commerce on local school curricula and cultures
10. Global models of religious and Indigenous education

educational practices in other countries, as they scan the latest international league tables of school performance."[13] Researchers in the field of comparative education have logically turned their attention to the issue of globalization as indicated by articles appearing in the *Comparative Education* journal such as "Globalisation, Knowledge Economy and Comparative Education"[14] and "Meeting the Global Challenge? Comparing Recent Initiatives in School Science and Technology."[15]

In summary, the Key Components of Educational Globalization highlight its different aspects.

## Global Flows and Networks

I have suggested the image of global educational policies as part of a superstructure influencing national and local educational practices. Other images about the workings of this superstructure have been offered, such a global flows and networks. Arjun Appadurai introduced the image of global flows of ideas, practices, institutions, and people interacting with local populations.[16] He calls the global flow of the world's peoples "ethnoscapes." The global movement of people includes those relocating to other nations, tourists, and workers, particularly those working for multinational corporations. Obviously, this flow of people involves a global flow of cultures that interact and change. While migrants who settle in other nations have the greatest impact on global cultural exchanges, there is also an impact from tourism. Local cultures also respond to global flow of popular cultures through movies, television, magazines, and other media. Appadurai calls this movement of images and ideas in popular culture "mediascapes." He refers to the global movement of trade and capital as "financescapes."

Of particular importance for education is the flow of ideas and practices regarding government and other institutional policies which Appadurai calls "ideoscapes." This global flow of ideas interacts with national and local ideas about government and institutional practices. This interaction results in changing the ideas in the global flow and ideas at the local level. Nothing is static in this image: global ideas change at the same time as they affect local school practices.

Global flows are speeded up by advances in transportation, and communication and information technology. Advances in new technology in Appadurai's image are also part of the global flow which he calls "technoscapes." It is new transportation technology that makes possible the quicker movement of global migrants, workers, and tourists and makes it possible for educational and government leaders to easily meet almost any place on the globe. Communication and information technologies allow for the global exchange of ideas about educational practices and create a world library of information. Of course, new educational technologies have an impact on local pedagogies. Therefore, using Appadurai's imagery, the educational superstructure consists of global flows of ideas, institutions, and people with dynamic interactions with local organizations and people.

Another image is that of global networks. These networks are composed of people, intergovernmental and nongovernmental organizations, and multinational organizations. Communications and information technology enhances the possibility of building and sustaining global networks. In education, there are global networks linking educational institutions, educational policymakers, professional educational organizations, and intergovernmental organizations. Because of the Internet, networks can compress time and space so that communication becomes almost instantaneous. Also, networks continue to expand and attract members. Being in a network increases the possibilities of success in most endeavors. Larger networks can encompass smaller networks. For instance, there might exist a global network of educational scholars whose members participate in other networks that link intergovernmental agencies and multinational educational corporations.[17]

In studying the global transformation of political economy, Held, McGrew, Goldblatt, and Perraton utilized the concepts of flows and networks to categorize six areas of globalization: military, governance, trade and finance, environment, migration, popular media, and communications and transportation. In their conceptualization of globalization, these areas stretch across the boundaries of nations and continents with the local and the global becoming enmeshed.[18]

Flow and network images of globalization have been criticized for portraying individuals as being passive participants or subjects.[19] In the imagery of flows and networks, there is a danger of thinking that a teacher's educational practices are simply a product of the influences of global ideoscapes, technoscapes, and ethnoscapes, and global networks linking education policymakers and intergovernmental and nongovernmental institutions. In reality, local school officials and teachers do not simply dance to the tune of global flows and networks. First, they might give meaning to the influence of global educational policies and practices through the lens of their own cultural perspectives. Second, they might adapt global educational practices to local conditions. And lastly, they might reject or resist global influences.

In summary, the globalization of educational institutions and practices can be envisioned as resulting from a superstructure composed of global flows and networks within which their influence is determined by the interpretation, adaptation, or rejection by local educators. This imagery encompasses the following elements of educational globalization.

## Key Points: Global Flows and Networks in Education

1. The global flow of ideas or ideoscapes contribute to global similarity in national education policies.
2. Networks of educational policymakers working for intergovernmental organizations, such as UNESCO, OECD, and the World Bank engage in global educational discourses and contribute to the global glow of educational practices.
3. Networks of educational policymakers and scholars who through e-mail and other forms of communication, scholarly publications, and international meetings contribute to a global flow of educational ideas and discourses.
4. Global flow of capital and trade or financescapes include multinational corporations marketing educational products and services.
5. Global networks includes those belonging to other global networks of educational policymakers and scholars, members of intergovernmental organizations, and multinational corporations who contribute to the flow of educational discourses and practices.
6. Global networks linking global educational networks with local educational policymakers, administrators, and teachers which contribute to the flow of educational discourses and practices.
7. Global migration or ethnoscapes contribute to the formation of global communities that extend beyond the boundaries of a nation state.

## World Educational Culture: The Work of World Culture Theorists

An important contribution of world culture theorists is research demonstrating the existence of common global educational practices. A premise of world culture scholars is that all cultures are slowly integrating into a single global culture. Often called "neo-institutionalist," proponents of this school of thought believe that national policymakers draw on this world culture in planning their school systems.[20]

Before considering the general theory of world culture theorists, I would like to consider some of their findings on common educational practices. Two of the most important works in this respect are John Meyer, David Kamens, and Aaron Benavot's *School Knowledge for the Masses: World Models and National Primary Curricular Catego-*

*ries in the Twentieth Century,* and David Baker and Gerald Letendre's *National Differences, Global Similarities: World Culture and the Future of Schooling.*[21]

The authors of *School Knowledge for the Masses* contend that local education policymakers rely on a world education culture to make their policy decisions. As a result the "general outlines of mass education and its curriculum often show surprising degrees of homogeneity around the world."[22] For instance, most of the world's government school systems are structured around an educational ladder leading from primary grades to some form of middle school to secondary education to higher education or some form of post-secondary school. This educational structure is so common that global educational reports can combine national statistics under common headings such as primary or secondary. As an example, the statistical table on education in the 2006 UNICEF report *The State of the World's Children: Excluded and Invisible* simply reports enrollment and attendance figures for the world's nations under columns labeled "primary school" and "secondary school."[23] Most readers of this and similar reports probably don't consider it unusual that the world's nations utilize the same educational ladder.

Regarding curricula, the authors of *School Knowledge for the Masses* found a significant worldwide similarity in organization and course labels for primary education. They concluded from an examination of national curricular outlines that there was "more homogeneity and standardization among the curricula prescribed by nation-states, than might have been expected ... The labels, at least, of mass curricula are so closely tied to great and standardized worldwide visions of social and educational progress, they tend to be patterned in quite consistent ways around the world."[24]

There is an amazing uniformity to the findings. However, it should be kept in mind that their global survey examined course titles but not the content of courses. For example, they collected data on the average percentage of total instructional time in world regions identified as sub-Saharan Africa, MidEast North Africa, Asia, Latin America, Caribbean, Eastern Europe, and the West. In the subject labeled "language" the researchers found that the average percentage of total instructional time for world regions other than Latin America ranged from 34.1 to 38.2 percent. For Latin America the figure was 24.4 percent. For "mathematics" the range for all world regions was 16.6 to 20.7 percent, for "natural science" it was 6.7 to 11.3 percent, for "social sciences" it was 6.3 to 13.1 percent, and for aesthetic education it was 7.7 to 13.5 percent.[25]

As stated previously, authors of *School Knowledge for the Masses* argue that the continuing development of global homogeneity of the curriculum is the result of national policy elites, particularly in developing countries, selecting from a world educational culture of education. In other words, local school people select from a global best educational practices agenda. While the authors do not use the language of global flows, the image they create is of a global flow of best educational practices that national policymakers rely upon. These national policymakers modify global practices to align them with local needs and practices.

How was the world educational culture created? According to the authors of *School Knowledge for the Masses* it was a result of worldwide spread of the Western concept of the nation-state which included a belief in educating the citizenry to ensure political stability and economic growth. By the late nineteenth century, the authors argue, "the gradual rationalization of the Western polity, the modern curricular structure became a taken-for-granted 'model' by the turn of the twentieth century."[26] As the Western concept of the nation-state spread, "the standard model of the curriculum has also diffused throughout the world, creating a worldwide homogeneity in the over-all categorical [curriculum categories] system."[27]

They identify other reasons for the development of a world educational culture:

- Years of educational research have yielded results identifying the best educational practices.
- Local policymakers can select curricular materials and educational practices from a worldwide pool of research.
- Internationalization of educational practices has been aided by foreign language instruction in national school systems.
- While the authors do not directly mention the teaching and spread of English, this phenomenon would support their argument.
- The spread from Western nations of liberal concepts of children, knowledge, and the social world.[28]

Similarly, David Baker and Gerald LeTendre declare in *National Differences, Global Similarities: World Culture and the Future of Schooling*: "In spite of the fact that nations ... have immediate political and fiduciary control over schooling, education as an institution has become a global enterprise."[29] This conclusion was reached after analysis of data from the Third International Mathematics and Science Study (TIMSS). As I will discuss in later chapters, international testing like TIMSS is a factor in the globalization of educational practices. Adding to the list of reasons for the worldwide adoption of mass schooling and a standard educational ladder, they point to the growing importance of educational credentials for employment in the global marketplace. For educational credentials to be of value in the global economy some standardization of the educational ladder and curricula is necessary. University degrees from institutions in India and China should be similar to degrees from universities in the European Union and the United States so that the degree can be used as a credential for global employment.

Baker and LeTendre believe that a world culture of schooling has developed which will lead to homogeneity between global school systems. They argue, "Mass schooling is the predominant model of education in the world today. It pervades every part of people's lives in modern society and creates a cultural [sic] education unparalleled in human existence."[30]

From their analysis of TIMSS, they conclude that the following trends reflect the growth of a world culture of schooling.

1. Global reduction of gender differences in mathematics and science achievement
2. A decline in the global importance of family resources in determining achievement in schools
3. The global demand for educational credentials has resulted in the worldwide growth of "shadow" education systems which include for-profit companies offering tutoring services and preparation for high-stakes testing (exams for entering and exiting institutions, such as university and secondary entrance exams and secondary exit exams).
4. An increasing global similarity in teacher's work, such as methods of instruction and class organization
5. Globally, teachers give similar types of homework (textbook assignments and worksheets)
6. A growing similarity in how nations organize their school systems.

There are several important points about the above list of global trends. Reducing gender differences in math and science (#1 above) is strongly supported by global intergovernmental organizations like the World Bank and UNESCO (later in the book I discuss the work of these two organizations). A contributing factor to the growth of gender equality in school achievement is a belief that the education of women is important, among other things, for national competition in the global economy: as caretakers of children, women are preparing the future generation of workers and women are needed as workers in the knowledge economy. The increase equality of educational opportunities (#2 above) in national school systems reflects the global flow of educational ideas emphasizing that a nation's economic future depends on the education of workers. The importance of the educational credentials for employment is reflected in the growth of shadow education systems (#3 above) with parents believing that school achievement is the key to their children's future economic success. As I discuss later, these parental pressures have contributed to the growth of for-profit educational services.

The growing global uniformity of teachers' work and homework (#4 and 5) reflects the influence of the global flow of educational ideas, and of intergovernmental and of multinational publishers. Global intergovernmental organizations are promoting a particular type of organization for school systems (#6).

In response to critics of the idea that there is an evolving single global model of schooling, Francisco Ramirez explained the origins of the concept of a world education culture. As a participant in a group of sociologists at Stanford University in the 1970s and 1980s whose work focused on the evolution of world culture theory, Ramirez wrote, "The [world] culture at work, we later asserted, was articulated and transmitted through nation–states, organizations, and experts who themselves embodied the triumph of a schooled world 'credential society'."[31] A "credential society" is one where an educational credential is necessary for acquiring employment. He claims that a world culture of education developed as part of an increasing emphasizes on global identities and goals. Schooling provides entrance to the global economy. In Ramirez's words, "schooling arises as a favored technology for identity affirmation and goal attainment; its intense pursuit by individuals and by states makes sense only in a world that strongly privileges schooling."[32]

Ramirez locates the origins of world educational culture in the work of world cultural theorists, particularly that of John Boli, Frank Lechner, Gerald Thomas, and Immanuel Wallerstein.[33] These theorists argue that a world culture began with the spread of Western Christian ideas in the late nineteenth century and escalated after the end of World War II. John Boli and George Thomas claim that,

> Arising out Western Christendom and propagated via the processes and mechanisms analyzed so well in world-system ... research, this transcendent level of social reality began to crystallize organizationally in the second half of the nineteenth century. After the vicissitudes of the two world wars, it has played an astonishing authoritative role in shaping global development for the last fifty years.[34]

According to this perspective, world education culture is nested in a more general world culture. It is argued that a global flow of ideas and the existence of intergovernmental and international nongovernment organizations result in similar world-wide government organizations. One group of world cultural theorists concludes, "A considerable body of evidence supports our proposition that world–society models shape nation-state identities, structures, and behavior via worldwide cultural and associational processes."[35] From this perspective, as stated above, world education culture developed alongside the worldwide spread of Western models of government and nation.

In summary, world education culture theorists believe that the striking similarity between the world's school systems, particularly regarding educational ladders (primary, middle, secondary schools leading higher education) and similar curricula, is a result of:

- The worldwide spread of Western concepts of government and nation in which a component is mass schooling
- National elites and others drawing on world models of schooling when planning school systems
- The spread of credential societies where educational credentials are necessary for employment
- The existence of globally available educational research indicating the best educational practices.

## World System and Postcolonial/Critical Theories

While world culture theorists present an image of national leaders freely selecting from a global flow of educational ideas, world system theorists see these ideas as being imposed by the economic power of a network of global institutions, such as the World Bank and other aid donors.[36] The world system theorists consider the globe to be integrated but with two major unequal zones. The core zone is the United States, the European Union, and Japan, which dominates periphery nations. The goal of the core is to legitimize its power by inculcating its values into periphery nations through national school systems that teach capitalist modes of thought and analysis.[37] German political scientist Hans Weiler identifies this relationship between global knowledge and power as involving a hierarchy of knowledge where one form of knowledge is privileged over another. A dominant form of knowledge is legitimated by a transnational system of power working through global organizations, such as publishing corporations, research organizations, higher education institutions, professional organizations, and testing services, which legitimate one form of knowledge.[38]

From this perspective, globalization of education is part of an effort to impose particular economic and political agendas that benefit wealthy and rich nations at the expense of the world's poor.[39] Supporting the arguments of world system theorists is postcolonial/critical analysis which stresses that Western schooling dominates the world scene as the result of its imposition by European imperialism and their Christian missionary allies. Simply stated, Western-style schools spread around the globe as a result of European cultural imperialism.[40]

I am using the term "postcolonial/critical theorists" to include those who identify themselves as critical theorist. These theorists argue that colonial power continued in new forms after the breakup of colonial empires following World War II. Postcolonial/critical theorists argue that after the dissolving of colonial empires, the power of previous colonizers was reemerged in new forms through the work of intergovernmental organizations, multinational corporations, and trade agreements. In its current manifestation, postcolonial powers promote market economies, human capital education, and neoliberal school reforms to promote the interests of rich nations and powerful multinational corporations. In the framework of postcolonial/critical theory, education is viewed as an economic investment designed to produce better workers to serve multinational corporations.[41]

In describing what they consider to be the negative effects of global intergovernmental organizations and trade agreements on Latin American education, Schugurensky and Davidson-Harden wrote, "we take a postcolonial perspective in considering the historical inequalities ... mark the region's relations with the world's richer countries ... [World Trade Organization/General Agreement on Trade in Services] has the potential to continue the cycles of imperialism which have subdued Latin American countries' development since the time of colonisation."[42]

In general, postcolonial/critical analysis "includes issues of slavery, migration and diaspora formation; the effects of race, culture, class and gender in postcolonial settings; histories of resistance and struggle against colonial and neo–colonial domination; the complexities of identity formation and hybridity; language and language rights; the ongoing struggles of Indigenous peoples for recognition of their rights."[43]

## Culturalist: Educational Borrowing and Lending

Culturalists stress the existence of different "knowledges" or different ways of seeing and knowing the world and the lending and borrowing of educational ideas.[44] Their position differs from those arguing that there exists a single form of knowledge and those believing that the postcolonial period continues the economic and political power of wealthy nations. Culturalists question the idea that models of schooling are simply imposed on local cultures. This group of theorists believes that local actors borrow and adapt multiple models from the global flow of educational ideas. I will discuss the arguments of culturalists in more detail in chapter 5.

An example of educational borrowing can be seen in U.S. policymakers in the 1980s becoming enthralled with the Japanese and other educational systems because of a belief that the U.S. economy was declining in world markets as a result of its school system. The 1983 federal government report *Nation at Risk*, blamed the allegedly poor academic quality of American public schools for causing lower rates of productivity than those of Japan and West Germany along with reducing the lead of the United States in technological development. The report states, "If only to keep and improve on the slim competitive edge we still retain in world markets, we must rededicate ourselves to the reform of the educational system for the benefit of all."[45] Not only was this argument almost impossible to prove, but some have claimed it was based on false data and assumptions as captured in the title of David Berliner and Bruce Biddle's *The Manufactured Crisis: Myths, Fraud and the Attack on America's Public Schools*.[46]

While the analysis may have been wrong, U.S. educators rushed to study Japanese schools as a means of improving U.S. schools. This represented an interesting example of borrowing and lending of educational ideas because the current organization of Japanese schools was imposed on Japan by the U.S. after conquest during World War II. Against the backdrop of Japan's highly test-oriented school system, the Nation at Risk report recommended that the American school system be tightly governed by "standardized tests of achievement."[47] The result was a push by U.S. policymakers to mimic the Japanese schools.[48]

In developing a theory of policy attraction, David Phillips has suggested a study of transnational movement of education reforms which include the borrowing and lending of ideas.

> Analysis of the attraction of aspects of educational provision in Japan to American observers over a long period, for example would be of considerable interest. So too would detailed examination of the foreign models used in the policy discussions in the countries of Eastern Europe following the dramatic changes of 1989, or of the influence of child-centered primary education in Britain on policy and practice in other parts of Europe.[49]

Besides the perspective of the transnational borrowing and lending, culturalists argue that global educational ideas are often adapted to local conditions. Kathryn Anderson-Levitt contends that the colonial imposition of Western education "into new areas ... for example, [by] England versus France, have looked different from the beginning."[50] She argues that while there is an appearance of homogenization of global schooling in reality teachers and other local school officials resist and transform global models of schooling.

Also, culturalists reject the idea that all global organizations are working in unison to promote the same educational agenda. The World Bank and UNESCO, it is argued, sometimes offer different advice to local schools. For instance, the U.S. Agency for International Development (USAID) and France's international development agency offered different advice to school people in Guinea.[51] In Brazil, the religious education model supported by the Catholic Church differed from the model offered by the World Bank and USAID. As described by Lesley Bartlett, nonpublic educational institutions in Brazil supported an education model that emphasized progressive themes of human development and social justice. Within the South American Catholic Church, as I describe in a later section, this humanitarian education model was influenced by liberation theology. On the other hand, Brazilian public schools under the influence of the World Bank and USAID adopted a human capital model. The result was a striking difference in the teaching of literacy. Many Catholic schools, those influenced by liberation theology, taught literacy in a social and political context. In contrast, Bartlett wrote, the human capital model used in the public schools "studiously avoided the political aspects of schooling, utilize[d] phonics-based instruction, and aver[ed] that education can and should contribute to economic development."[52]

Culturalists also argue that there is not one world education model but that there are competing models. In her criticism of world education culture theorists, Kathryn Anderson-Levitt argues that there are two competing world models for education. World culture theorists, she argues, consider the goal of the world education model is preparing students to be workers in the global economy. She identifies two competing world education models which I will label "Human Capital World Model" and "Progressive Education World Model." I propose the existence of two other competing global models which I label "Religious Education World Models" and "Indigenous Education World Models." These last two global models openly reject world models of schooling based on Western education.

## Human Capital World Model

The Human Capital World Model is discussed in more detail in chapters 2 and 3. In general, it is supported by many national leaders because it promises economic growth and development. According to world educational culture theorists, it is the one relied upon by national elites. The primary goal of this model is educating workers for competition for jobs in the global economy. This model, using Anderson-Levitt's schematic divisions contains the following components.

### Human Capital World Model

- National standardization of the curriculum
- Standardized testing for promotion, entrance, and exiting from different levels of schooling

**Key Points: Interpretations by Theorists:
World Educational Culture, World System
and Postcolonial/Critical, and Culturalists**

*World Education Culture*

1. Development of a uniform global education culture sharing similar goals, educational practices, and organizations
2. Similarity of national school systems a result of adoption of Western model of the nation-state which requires mass education
3. Most national schools systems share a common educational ladder and curriculum organization
4. Global uniformity of schooling provides entrance into the global economy

*World System and Postcolonial/Critical*

1. Educational ideas and practices imposed on other nations that favor the economic advantages of rich nations
2. The creation of global educational uniformity will be used to legitimize the power of rich nations
3. Global organizations supporting policies that will benefit rich nations and people such as educating students as workers for the global economy and privatization of schooling

*Culturalist*

1. Rejects the claim of growing uniformity of global policies and goals
2. Emphasizes how local communities change ideas borrowed from the global flow of educational ideas and practices
3. Recognizes the existence of different knowledges and global education models
4. Does not believe that global organizations are working in unison to create global educational uniformity

- Performance evaluation of teaching based on standardized testing of students
- Mandated textbooks
- Scripted lessons
- Teaching of world languages, particularly English.[53]

I would add to Anderson-Levitt's model:

- The goal of education is educating workers to compete in the global economy
- The value of education is measured by economic growth and development.

The human capital model can be criticized for educating citizens that passively accept existing political and economic structures even when they are operating against their interests. There is little attempt to educate active citizens who act to bring about political, economic and social improvements.

## Progressive Education World Model

The progressive education world model will be discussed in more detail in chapter 5. According to Anderson-Levitt this model provides more teacher and student control of curriculum and instruction. And, in contrast to the human capital model, the goal of the progressive model is to educate citizens who are conscious of social injustices and actively work to correct them. Anderson-Levitt includes in this model:

### Progressive Education World Model

- Teacher professionalism and autonomy
- Learning based on students' interests and participation
- Active learning
- Protection of local languages[54]

I would add to this model the following elements:

- Education for ensuring social justice
- Education for active participation in determining social and political change

One problem with Anderson-Levitt's model of what I call the Progressive Education World Model is her inclusion of "school choice, market, or 'liberal' reforms."[55] These reforms are most often referred to as "neoliberalism" and can be linked to the Human Capital World Model. Commentators on global education consider neoliberal school reforms to be designed to privatize traditional government school services and return them to the marketplace in the form of school choice and for-profit schooling.[56] Neoliberalism is most often associated with human capital education. Illustrating the link between neoliberalism and human capital education, Michael Apple concludes, "neoliberals are the most powerful element within the alliance supporting conservative modernization ... Underpinning this position is a vision of students as human capital ... as future workers."[57]

In summary, there is a major difference between the human capital and progressive education models. In schools, the human capital model assumes control of teachers' behaviors through a prescribed national curriculum and reliance on standardized testing with goal of educating workers for the global economy. The progressive model assumes that instruction will involve active learning based on students' interests and participation with high degree of teacher autonomy in lesson planning with the goal of educating citizens who will actively address issues of social justice.

## Religious Education World Models

Both the human capital and progressive education models are part of the Western educational tradition which became part of the global flow of educational ideas. A criticism of both models is that they support a secular society whose goals are either economic development or economic equity. Missing, for some, are spiritual and religious goals and values. I will discuss religious models of education in more detail in chapter 6. Globally, there are large numbers of religious schools serving Christian, Buddhist, Islamic, Hindu, and other religious communities. Some provide religious instruction after school hours or on religious days while others operate full time schools. Religious schools offer instruction that emphasizes spirituality in contrast to the economic and secular emphasis of human capital and progressive education world models. Therefore, I will call these religious world educational models.

### Religious Education World Models

- Study of traditional religious texts
- Study and practice of religious rites
- Emphasis on spirituality
- Emphasis on instilling moral and ethical standards
- Rejection of secularism

## Indigenous Education World Models

In its September 13, 2007, news release announcing ratification of the Declaration on Rights of Indigenous Peoples, the United Nations estimated that there are 370 million indigenous peoples existing around the globe in areas of the South Pacific, Asia, Europe and, of course, including the numerous indigenous nations of Africa and North and South America.[58] Who are the indigenous peoples of the world? One definition emphasizes long-term occupancy of a particular geographical area.[59] For instance, the indigenous nations of Canada emphasize "long–term occupancy" by choosing the self–identifier "First Nations." However, some groups that today identify themselves as indigenous were previously imperialistic powers with empires that dominated other peoples and lands, such as the Aztecs, Mayans, and Incas of the Americas. Are these nations or the peoples they dominated the long–term occupiers? One resolution of who is indigenous can be through self-identification. The World Bank includes in its definition of indigenous "self-identification" and "subsistence-oriented production." The World Bank's definition is:

> The term "indigenous peoples" (also often referred to as "indigenous ethnic minorities," "tribal groups" and "scheduled tribes") describes social groups with a social and cultural identity distinct from the dominant society which makes them vulnerable to being disadvantaged in the development process.

### Characteristics of Indigenous Peoples

- Close attachment to ancestral territories and their natural resources;
- Self-identification and identification by others as members of a distinct cultural group;
- An indigenous language, often different from the national language;
- Presence of customary social and political institutions;
- Primarily subsistence-oriented production.[60]

However, "subsistence-oriented production" does not realistically describe the work of some self-identified indigenous peoples who hold jobs in modern factories, corporate agriculture, or in other professional and business occupations.

Over the last century, indigenous peoples struggled to restore traditional education methods after attempts by some colonialists to use Western forms schooling to eradicate their cultures. In some cases, indigenous peoples were denied schooling as a method for excluding them from entrance into dominant economic and political organizations. Consequently, many indigenous nations are trying to restore their control over education and ensure recognition of traditional educational methods.

I will discuss indigenous models of education in more detail in chapter 6. Indigenous Education World Models include the following:

### Indigenous Education World Models

- Indigenous nations control their own educational institutions.
- Traditional indigenous education serves as a guide for the curriculum and instructional methods.
- Education is provided in the language of the indigenous nation.
- Education reflects the culture of the indigenous nation.

## Examples of the Diffusion of Global Educational Models

World culture theorists present a benign image of national elites and local groups choosing from a world educational culture while world system theorists and postcolonial/critical theorists stress the use of power to impose educational models. Culturalists stress the importance of the borrowing and lending of educational ideas and their local adaptation. However, the story of the global spread of education is much more complicated and involves choice and imposition. Initially, as postcolonial/critical theorists argue, Western forms of schooling were spread around the globe as the result of European imperialism. Besides a quest for wealth, European colonialists were also motivated by a belief in the superiority of Western civilization and a desire to convert the world's peoples to Christianity. I have called this process "white love."[61] Convinced of the inferiority of other civilizations and that Christianity was the only true religion, colonialists believed they were helping others by trying to change local religions and cultures.

The early diffusion of Western schooling did not include, though the process laid the groundwork for its later adoption, the current human capital world model. The global diffusion of the human capital model occurred after World War II. The work of Christian missionaries does represent one global religious model. In the Americas, the Spanish established an extensive network of churches and schools to convert Native Americans. In North America, the British encouraged Protestant missionaries and school people to convert and educate indigenous peoples. In both South and North America, physical force was sometimes used to save souls for a Christian God. In Africa, Europeans established schools and sent church people to win the hearts and minds of those being subjugated. In India, the British made English and education in English-style schools the path for locals into the colonial administration. While the French did not encourage the expansion of European-style schooling for colonized peoples in Cambodia and Indochina, they did establish schools for the education of the children of their colonial administrators and supported the efforts of religious groups to convert and educate the local population. The Dutch followed a similar pattern in Indonesia.[62]

On the other hand, some countries chose Western-style schooling for defensive reasons while trying to protect local ethical systems. In the nineteenth century, Japanese leaders urged the establishment of Western-style schools to learn Western technology and science to build a war machine that could resist European expansionism in Asia. The Charter Oath issued by the newly created Japanese Education Department in 1868 reflected a global view in organizing a new educational system: "Knowledge shall be sought from throughout the world."[63] Adopting a Western-style school structure, Japan's 1872 Fundamental Code of Education mandated the building of 54,760 primary schools, middle school districts, and university districts.[64] A similar development pattern occurred in Arab countries when Napoleon's army marched into Egypt in 1798 and occupied the country for three years. Egyptian leaders decided that their citizens needed to study European technology, science, and military organization. In *Putting Islam to Work: Politics and Religious Transformation in Egypt,* Gregory Starrett summarizes these efforts: to "gain military parity with Europe that motivated the initial importation of the European-style school to Egypt."[65]

China's educational history supports the claim by world education culture theorists that the spread of mass schooling accompanied the adoption of the Western model of the nation-state. In 1912, the Chinese emperor was supplanted by a Western-style republic supported by the followers of revolutionary leader Sun Yat-sen. The future leader of the Chinese Communist Party, Mao Zedong, recalled that after the 1912 abdication of the Emperor, "Modern schools sprang up like bamboo shoots after a summer rain."[66] Modern or Western-style schools were considered essential for maintaining a republican form of government. The new minister of education, Cai Yuanpei, issued an edict eliminating Chinese classic texts from the primary school curriculum and banned all textbooks not in agreement with republican ideals.[67] It is important to note that both China and Japan adopted Western school models while attempting to retain traditional values as exemplified by the educational slogans: *Japanese Spirit, Western Skills* and *Western Science, Eastern Morals,* and in China as *Western Function, Chinese Essence.*[68]

The progressive education model was part of this global flow of educational practices and ideas.[69] It has often been associated with movements for social justice and political and economic change. In 1919, the icon of progressivism education, John Dewey, made a two-year lecture tour of China. In China, he was hailed as the "Second Confucius."[70] The Chinese who invited him were part of the growing transnational movement of students. In 1908, the U.S. Congress agreed to return funds owed to the United States by China which were then to be used to support Chinese students to study in the United States. Between 1921 and 1924, it was estimated that the United States was hosting the largest number of Chinese students studying abroad.[71]

After 1917 Bolshevik revolution, Soviet educators were attracted to American progressive education as part of the action of the People's Commissariat of Education to create an experimental educational system. The People's Commissariat of Education encouraged active learning through class discussion and aesthetic education along with an integrated curriculum in which reading, writing, arithmetic, history, geography, literature, chemistry and other subjects were studied together. The Commissariat recommended the use of the Dalton plan developed by U.S. progressive educator Helen Parkhurst in 1918. In the Dalton plan, students signed monthly contracts in which all subjects were to be studied in the context of a single theme. Students fulfilled their contracts working at their on pace.[72] American progressive educational ideas received further support in 1929 when the People's Commissariat of Education ordered all schools to adopt the project method as the system of instruction.[73] The project method was first proposed in 1918 by American progressive educator William Heard Kilpatrick, a friend and colleague of John Dewey at Teachers College, Columbia University.[74] All of this changed when Stalin rose to power. In 1931, the Commissar of Education Andrei Bubnov condemned the project method at the meeting of the All-Russian Conference of Heads of Regional Departments of Education. He asserted that teachers were inadequately prepared to use the project method and activity-based instruction. He demanded that schools provide systematic instruction in mathematics, chemistry, and physics. The Central Committee of the Communist Party declared, "It is necessary to wage a decisive struggle against thoughtless scheming with methods ... especially against the so-called project method."[75] In 1932, the Central Committee condemned the Dalton plan.

The global spread of educational ideas and institutions is not a one way road from Europe and the United States to the rest of the world. The next section of educational borrowing and lending demonstrates how global ideas are changed and then influence global education discourses.

## Examples of Educational Borrowing and Lending: The Case of South America

South America exemplifies the borrowing and lending of global educational ideas and their adaptation to local conditions. South American countries have been influenced by Spanish colonialism and U.S. human capital education models.[76] The most important contemporary progressive education model developed by Brazilian educator Paulo Freire emerged from concerns about the impact of these other global education models. The South American example demonstrates that the global flow of educational ideas and institutions is not one way. It involves, as captured in the title of a book edited by comparative educationist Gita Steiner-Khamsi, *The Global Politics of Educational Borrowing and Lending.*[77]

A pioneer in progressive educational thought in South American was the Peruvian Jose Mariátegui. His writings influenced the educational philosopher Paulo Freire, the literacy crusade following the Cuban revolution, and the literacy campaigns led by liberation theologists. Mariátegui called for mass political education of peasants and indigenous peoples as a necessary condition for economic justice in South America. He became a Marxist when, after receiving an eighth-grade education, he took a job at the Peruvian newspaper *La Prensa* and began writing political articles. The radicalism of his articles caused the Peruvian government to exile him to Europe in 1919. In Europe he moved in Communist circles in France and Italy and became acquainted with progressive ideas about the importance of freeing human thought from ideological subjugation by the state and economic elites.[78]

Mass political education, Mariátegui believed, was necessary for achieving economic justice in the context of South America, particularly for the recruitment of peasants and indigenous peoples. Mariátegui argued, "The problem of Indian illiteracy goes beyond the pedagogical sphere. It becomes increasingly evident that *to teach a man to read and write is not to educate him* [my emphasis]."[79]

It was the global flow of educational ideas and institutions that Mariátegui partially blamed for the destruction of indigenous cultures and for creating a life of abject poverty for the majority of the Peruvian population. Regarding the effect of Spanish colonialism, he stated:

> The Spanish heritage was not only psychological and intellectual but above all economic and social. Education continued to be a privilege because the privileges of wealth and class continued. The aristocratic and literary concept of education was typical of a feudal system and economy. Not having abolished feudalism in Peru, independence would not abolish its ideas about education.[80]

A human capital educational model borrowed from the United States, he argued, perpetuated Peru's economic divisions. In the early twentieth century, Peruvian education leaders called for the adoption of the U.S. model of education to aid in industrial development or, in other words, to more closely tie education to economic planning. The leading advocate of the U.S. model was Manuel Villarán, who argued, "education in Peru ... suffers from its failure to meet the needs of the developing national economy and from its indifference to the Indigenous element."[81] He argued that the economic future of Peru depended on its educational system preparing workers rather than scribes to enter government bureaucracies and the legal profession. Villarán claimed, "the great nations of Europe today are remodeling their educational programs, largely along North American lines, because they understand that this century requires men of enterprise rather than men of letters ... we should also correct our mistakes and educate practical, industrious, and energetic men, the ones the country needs in order to become wealthy and by the same token powerful."[82]

The 1920 Organic Law of Education converted Peruvian schools to the U.S. model with primary and secondary schooling preparing students for jobs needed for economic development. However, Mariátegui argued that adoption of the U.S. model did not undercut the economic and political power of the descendants of colonial rule. He wrote, "the educational movement was sabotaged by the continued and widespread existence of a feudal regime. It is not possible to democratize the education of a country without democratizing its economy and its political superstructure."[83] The school reforms based on the American model failed to undercut the power of the established upper class of Peru, Mariátegui argued, which therefore proved that countries must develop their own educational reforms based on national needs with foreigners acting as consultants. Similar to other progressive and Marxist educators, Mariátegui advocated the abandonment of idealist forms of education in which knowledge was never linked to its origins in economic and social conditions. He called for education to be linked to the real world of work. He quoted Mexican educational reformer Pedro Ureña, "To learn is not only to learn to know but also to learn to do."[84]

Countering the influence of the human capital educational model, a progressive model of education in Latin American evolved that encompassed concerns about the power of indigenous peoples and cultural differences, breaking the hegemonic control of the ruling class, and helping cultural groups articulate their own needs and desires. In summarizing these traditions, Sheldon Liss wrote, "Latin American radicals believe that genuine education—the process of critical evaluation and questioning, not merely the dissemination of information—is a marvelous instrument of progress that will eventually help negate the 'truths' of the prevailing system."[85] Liss concludes, "Almost all the *pensadores* [Latin American progressive intellectuals] agree that the power of the oppressors exists only as long as the masses obey them."[86]

One of the people influenced by Mariátegui's writings was Che Guevara. Following the completion of the Cuban revolution in 1959, Cuba engaged in a mass literacy program. Che Guevara declared that society must become a "gigantic" school. Referring to the literacy crusade, Che wrote in 1965 that the state should give direct political instruction to the people: "Education takes hold among the masses and the foreseen new attitude tends to become a habit. The masses continue to make it their own and to influence those who have not yet educated themselves. This is the indirect form of educating the masses, as powerful, as the other, structured, one."[87] "What is needed," he stated, "is the development of an ideological-cultural mechanism that permits both free inquiry and the uprooting of the weeds that multiply so easily in the fertilized soil of state subsidies."[88]

Out of this milieu of South American progressivism emerged the great progressive educator Paulo Freire, who might be considered the successor to John Dewey. Freire's model of progressive education embodied many of the cultural and economic concerns of other progressive South Americans. His work had a major influence on the literacy campaigns led by liberation theologians.

Born in 1921 in Recife, Brazil, Paulo Freire abandoned a law career in 1947 because he stated law served the oppressor while education could serve the oppressed. In 1964, Freire went to Chile after being exiled following a coup d'etat by the Brazilian military elite. During his exile, Freire's socialist philosophy and instructional methods crystallized, and he wrote *Pedagogy of the Oppressed*. In the charged atmosphere of Chilean politics, Freire met socialists from many Latin American countries, including Cuba.[89] During his exile in Chile, Freire made several trips to New York City where he experienced "thematic" lessons conducted by Catholic priests. In one these sessions, which he later reports in *Pedagogy of the Oppressed,* an educator presented to a group of African Americans and Puerto Ricans a photo of the street in front of the building in which they were meeting. The photo showed garbage on the sidewalk. Using a pedagogical method that would become central in Freire's work, the group leader asked the participants what they saw in the photo. The responses ranged from a street in Latin America to Africa. Participants refused to believe it was a street in the United States until one of them commented, "Might as well admit it's our street. Where we live."[90]

*Pedagogy of the Oppressed* answered the central problem facing Latin American progressives about how to include peasants and indigenous peoples in a revolutionary movement. Freire attributed the apparent backwardness and lack of revolutionary ardor of these groups to their living in a culture of silence. Freire's educational methodology promised to educate peasants and indigenous peoples to be revolutionary without destroying their cultures. Freire believed that a Marxist revolution could be conducted by rural people. Freire made it possible to imagine a cultural revolution preceding a political and economic revolution. He also made it possible to think of progressive education as the primary instrument for social improvement.

Another example of the global flow of educational ideas was Paulo Freire's recognition of the influence of the educational ideas of Chinese leader Mao Zedong on Freire's greatest work *Pedagogy of the Oppressed* first published in 1968. He referred to the "fundamental aspect of Mao's Cultural Revolution" to support his assertion that:

> The pedagogy of the oppressed, as a humanist and libertarian pedagogy, has two distinct stages. In the first, the oppressed unveil the world of oppression and through the praxis commit themselves to its transformation. In the second stage, in which the reality of oppression has already been transformed, this pedagogy ceases to belong to the oppressed and becomes a pedagogy of all men in the process of permanent liberation. In both stages, it is always through action in depth that the culture of domination is culturally confronted.[91]

Ivan Illich's Center for Intercultural Documentation (CIDOC) in Cuernavaca, Mexico, helped to spread both liberation theology and Freirian educational ideas.[92] Liberation theologists, such as Gustavo Gutiérrez, and North and South American educators, including Paulo Freire, John Holt, and Clarence Karier, gathered at CIDOC to exchange ideas on radical change and education. Illich, a former priest and supporter of liberation theology, advocated abolishing formal schooling because it had become a method of oppression. Priests and educators provided a variety of descriptions of CIDOC's influence, ranging from "shock treatment" to "jolt[ing] ... foreigners into questioning what they were doing." I first met Paulo Freire at CIDOC in 1970 and for the first time learned about his educational theories. I was one of those who carried his ideas back to North America. At CIDOC, I coedited books with liberation theologist Father Jordan Bishop and American educational historians Clarence Karier and Paul Violas. These books contributed to discussions of radical school reform in the United States.[93] By the end of the 1970s, wars of liberation in Nicaragua and El Salvador sparked literacy crusades that reflected the influence of liberation theology and Paulo Freire's pedagogical methods. These literacy crusades will be discussed in more detail in chapter 6.

Today, both John Dewey and Paulo Freire are considered icons of progressive education. The global influence of their education models exemplifies the global diffusion of educational ideas. Their educational models were created to bring about social justice and change in contrast to the emphasis on economic efficiency and growth of the human capital model, the study of religious texts, and indigenous education models.

## Conclusion: Different Lenses for Interpreting Global Education

The remaining chapters will analyze the intertwined set of global processes affecting education. These analyzes will be in the context world education culture theory, world systems and postcolonial/critical theories, and the work of culturalists. These theories provide different lenses for examining global education discourses, the educational work of intergovernmental and nongovernmental organizations, the influence of multinational learning and testing organizations, and the issue of global migration and languages. And in this global arena there are competing global education models: human capital, progressive, religious, and indigenous.

In the next chapter I will analyze global education discourses, particularly those involving the knowledge economy and human capital. Of course, these discourses flow through global networks of government and nongovernment organizations, policy elites, local communities, and multinational corporations. The story of how these networks operate will be discussed after a consideration of the main global education discourses.

## Chapter 2

# Global Education Networks and Discourses

## The World Bank and the Knowledge Economy

The World Bank is the leading global investor in education and is linked through extensive networks to other worldwide organizations. Through these networks the Bank is a major participant in global discourses about education.[1] World culture theorists consider the World Bank to be a major contributor to the development of a global culture.[2] Critics see the World Bank's agenda as serving wealthy nations and multinational organizations.[3] The Bank's worldwide networks influence local education practices.[4] The educational discourses of other global organizations, which are sometimes in conflict the World Bank, will be discussed in later chapters.

World Bank education policies and influence are embedded in an interrelated network of global and local institutions. These are dynamic relationships with members of the network influencing each other. Educational discourses about the knowledge economy, which I describe in this chapter, and other education issues are discussed within these networks. While all members of the networks might or might not agree with each other they are exposed to similar educational ideas. Education and the knowledge economy is one of those important ideas discussed in the Bank's education networks.

World Bank officials have a particular definition and agenda for the "knowledge economy" and "lifelong learning" that is not shared by other global players. This is important to understand because this chapter might mistakenly give the reader the impression that the World Bank's agenda is the common agenda for all the major players in the global education scene. In chapter 3, I will explore concepts of education of the knowledge economy and lifelong learning from the perspective of other global institutions. Also, the reader should be cautioned that a description of the World Bank's global networks does not provide an indication of the degree of mutual influence or the influential power of any particular member of the network. However, few would disagree with the importance of the World Bank in influencing global education policies.

## The World Bank

"Today," declares the 2007 official guide to the World Bank, "the World Bank Group is the world's largest funder of education."[5] Founded in 1944, the World Bank has provided educational loans to developing nations based on the idea that investment in education is the key to economic development.[6] Educational improvement became a goal of the World Bank in 1968 when the then president Robert McNamara announced, "Our aim here will be to provide assistance where it will contribute most to economic development. This will mean emphasis on educational planning, the starting point for the whole process of educational improvement."[7] McNamara went on explain that it would mean an expansion of the World Bank's educational activities. The World Bank continues to present its educational goals in the framework of economic development: "Education is central to development ... It is one of the most powerful instruments for reducing poverty and inequality and lays a foundation for sustained economic growth."[8]

The World Bank consists of the International Bank for Reconstruction and Development (IBRD), which lends money to governments of middle- and low-income countries and the International Development Association (IDA), which provides interest-free loans and grants to governments of the poorest nations. The World Bank is also part of the World Bank Group, which includes three other organizations that provide technical assistance to developing nations, guarantee against losses for investors in developing nations, and arbitrate investment disputes.[9]

Each division of the World Bank is owned by member countries. In 2007, 185 member countries owned the IBRD and 166 member countries owned the IDA. Voting power in the World Bank is based on the number of shares owned by member countries. The five largest shareholders of the World Bank are the United States, Japan, Germany, France, and the United Kingdom. Money for loans through the IBRD (middle- and low-income countries) is primarily raised through the world's financial markets. In contrast, loan money from the IDA (poorest countries) comes primarily from the richest member countries.[10] The countries contributing the most to the IDA are the United States, Japan, Germany, United Kingdom, and France.[11]

Countries were eligible to receive loans from the IBRD (middle- and low-income countries) in 2006 ranged from the Republic of Korea with annual per capita income of $15,810 to the Philippines with an annual per capita income of $1,250. Those eligible for IDA (poorest countries) ranged from the Maldives with an annual per capita income of $2,390 to Burundi with an annual per capita income of $100.[12]

The World Bank provides loans for:

## Key Points: World Bank Structure and Networks

### The World Bank Group

International Bank for Reconstruction and Development (IBRD)—lends money to *governments* of middle- and low-income countries.

International Development Association (IDA)—provides interest-free loans and grants to *governments* of the poorest nations.

International Finance Corporation—provides loans, equity, and advisory services to *private sector* in developing countries.

Multilateral Investment Guarantee Agency—encourages and aids *foreign direct investment* to developing countries.

International Center for Settlement of Investment Disputes—provides facilities for conciliation and arbitration of international investment disputes.

### Examples of Members of World Bank Education Networks

United Nations and its agencies and members, such as UNESCO and UNICEF

World Economic Forum

World Trade Organization

United States Agency for International Development (USAID)

Discovery Channel Global Education Fund

Global Development Alliance

EdInvest operated by the World Bank Group's International Finance Corporation

Human Development Network

United Nations Development Program

Intergovernmental agencies associated with World Bank

National governments associated with World Bank

Multinational Corporations associated with World Bank education efforts.

Nongovernment organizations associated with World Bank

- investing in people, particularly through basic health and education;
- focusing on social development, inclusion, governance, and institution building as key elements of poverty reduction;

- strengthening governments' ability to deliver quality services efficiently and transparently;
- protecting the environment;
- supporting and encouraging private business development; and
- promoting reforms to create a stable macroeconomic environment that is conducive to investment and long-term planning.[13]

## World Bank and the United Nations' Networks

The World Bank and the United Nations share a common educational network. The World Bank entered into a mutual agreement with the United Nations in 1947 which specified that the Bank would act as an independent specialized agency of the United Nations and as an observer in the United Nations' General Assembly.[14]

The World Bank supports the United Nations' Millennium Goals and Targets which were endorsed by 189 countries at the 2000 United Nations Millennium Assembly. The Millennium Goals directly addressing education issues are:

- Goal 2—Achieve Universal Primary Education: Ensure that by 2015, children everywhere, boys and girls, will be able to complete a full course of primary schooling.
- Goal 3—Promote Gender Equality and Empower Women: Eliminate gender disparity in primary and secondary education, preferably by 2005, and at all levels of education no later than 2015.

These two Millennium Goals were part of the Education for All program of the United Nations Educational, Scientific and Cultural Organization (UNESCO), which had established as two of its global goals the provision of free and compulsory primary education for all and the achieving of gender parity by 2005 and gender equality by 2015.[15] Highlighting the intertwined activities of the World Bank and United Nations agencies is the fact that these two goals were a product of the 1990 World Conference on Education for All convened by the World Bank, UNESCO, United Nations Children's Fund (UNICEF), the United Nations Population Fund (UNFPA), and the United Nations Development Program (UNDP). This World Conference was attended by representatives from 155 governments.[16]

The Education for All program is coordinated with another series of organizations and networks cited by UNESCO as:

- International Bureau of Education (IBE), Geneva, Switzerland
- International Institute for Educational Planning (IIEP), Paris, France and Buenos Aires, Argentina

- UNESCO Institute for Lifelong Learning (UIL), Hamburg, Germany
- Institute for Information Technologies in Education (IITE), Moscow, Russian Federation
- International Institute for Higher Education in Latin America and the Caribbean (IESALC), Caracas, Venezuela
- International Institute for Capacity-Building in Africa (IICBA), Addis Ababa, Ethiopia
- European Centre for Higher Education (CEPES), Bucharest, Romania
- International Centre for Technical and Vocational Education and Training (UNEVOC), Bonn, Germany
- UNESCO Institute for Statistics (UIS), Montreal, Canada[17]

These global networks are linked to nongovernment organizations (NGOS) through what UNESCO calls the Collective Consultation of Non-Governmental Organizations on EFA (CCNGO/EFA). UNESCO describes this Collective:

It connects UNESCO and several hundred NGOs, networks and coalitions around the world through a coordination group composed of eight NGO representatives (five regional focal points, two international focal points and one representative of the UNESCO/NGO Liaison Committee), and a list serve for information sharing.[18]

## Public-Private Partnership Networks and Multinational Corporations

Directly connected to the World Bank and UNESCO networks are multinational corporations. For example, a 2006 Workshop organized by the World Economic Forum on Public-Private Partnerships in Education for All and UNESCO. The Workshop included Intel, BT (British Telecom), Cisco, SAP, and Hewlett-Packard. These participants represent some of the world's largest manufacturers of computers, software, and information technology who have a stake in selling products to educational systems.[19] Cynics might interpret their involvement as purely a business interest in selling products and educating future consumers. Others might interpret their involvement as an expression of corporate goodwill or a combination of business interest and desire to do good.

The sponsor of the World Economic Forum workshop was the United States Agency for International Development (USAID), which is promoting public-private partnerships in education. USAID had previously participated in a UNESCO sponsored 2005 study of "Corporate Sector Involvement in Education for All."[20] This study uncritically accepted the role of multinational corporations: "Closely linked to the fact that corporations consider the value of these programs beyond their short-term returns, their motivations are also clearly economically-oriented."[21] In the context of economic development in low-income countries, the study asserted regarding business interests, "In the new paradigm of development, education is worth investing in the long run to enhance prosperity of their business activities (better economic and social environment), as well as the firm's own competitiveness (better trained employees)."[22] What can corporations do? The UNESCO study suggests corporations can improve national school systems through "financing, managing, and provision of educational services and/or materials."[23]

The study raised the possibility of a global network linking government education leaders, multinational corporations, UNESCO, and the World Bank. It recommended the establishment of partnerships between national government officials and corporate leaders involving "the creation of a 'mixed' executive board composed of private and public stakeholders who are responsible for making decisions concerning partnership objectives."[24]

## Networking with the Discovery Channel Global Education Partnership

The interlinked World Bank and UNESCO networks are also tied to global media through the Discovery Channel Global Education Partnership which is one of the major public-private enterprises discussed in the UNESCO study "Corporate Sector Involvement in Education for All." The Partnership operates in Asia, Africa, and Latin America equipping schools with TV, VCR, satellite and cable technologies. The Partnership also sponsors teacher training and video programming to use these technologies. One of the partners of the Discovery Channel Global Education Fund is USAID Global Development Alliance. The UNESCO study lists under "Motivation of Corporations:"

- DCI [Discovery Channel, Inc.] started the initiative in order to use its resources to help under-developed under-resourced areas.
- For Motorola, the project shows commitment to social responsibility
- For ChevronTexaco, it shows commitment to well-being in host countries, positive contribution to communities where they operate [and] "ultimate business success."[25]

The Discovery Channel Global Education Partnership lists as its major supporters the Coca-Cola Africa Foundation, the Discovery Channel, and Chevron along with over 60 other corporate sponsors.[26] Using financial support from these donors, the Partnership creates learning centers in local schools. These learning centers are described as "locally-managed, television-based media hubs."[27] The centers are equipped with a television and a VCR/DVD, and the learning center teachers receive three years of training. Teachers and school systems might become dependent on the use of these learning centers which, over the long run, would require replacement of equipment and the purchase of videos and DVDs.

The Partnership emphasizes the importance of television as an educator in developing nations:

> People all around the globe—in rural villages and in urban centers—seek education, empowerment and opportunity. Television is a powerful and effective way to facilitate learning by delivering information that people need and desire. Television engages. It enlarges perspectives, enhances understanding and creates possibilities by connecting viewers to new people, places and experiences. Television can also reach large groups of people at one time, and convey information regardless of a viewer's ability to read.[28]

To support this claim, the Partnership reported quotes a student Noelia Benites from Peru: "The videos are having a great impact on my parents, my siblings and me, since we share everything I learn in class."[29]

In 2007 it was announced that the Discovery Channel Global Partnership and The Coca-Cola Africa Foundation had formed a new partnership to increase educational opportunities for children and communities across Africa. The Coca-Cola Africa Foundation granted $10 Million over five years to fund the expansion of the organization's future education projects into underserved African communities.[30]

There are two conflicting ways of interpreting the network which leads from the World Bank and UNESCO to the work of the Discovery Channel Global Education Partnership. The world culture theorists might argue that this is another step in the creation of a global culture through the sharing of common media resources. In contrast, postcolonial/critical theorists might argue that the content of media sources is another form of cultural imperialism through its influence on the minds of local students and by making local education systems dependent on the media technology and supporting products manufactured by multinational corporations. Or maybe both interpretations are true.

Regarding the possible charge of cultural imperialism, the Partnership claims that its educational process includes: "Soliciting community input to determine potential program topics—Developing original culturally-relevant programs drawing on the resources of Discovery Channel." Can Discovery Channel resources reflect the cultures of all local communities in which the partnership works? An answer to this question would require cultural anthropologists to examine the Discovery Channels programming. On the other hand, students around the world will be exposed to similar media content. Will this contribute to the creation of a world culture?

## The World Bank Group and Public-Private Partnerships Networks

The complexity of global education networks are exemplified by the Discovery Channel Global Education Partnership and its links to UNESCO, Education for All, the World Bank. Adding to this network is the World Bank's direct support of public-private partnerships. The World Bank encourages private investment in education through EdInvest operated by the World Bank Group's International Finance Corporation.[31] The International Finance Corporation describes its work as "supporting the development of private educational activities in our member countries ... we support the start-up or expansion of initiatives in many subsectors of education. These include: post-secondary, primary and secondary schooling with a particular interest in school networks, e-learning initiatives, student financing programs and other ancillary services."[32]

In 2007, the World Bank and the Human Development Network hosted a conference on Public-Private Partnerships in Education that included speakers not only from the World Bank but from universities from around the world, including ones in the United States, Chile, Singapore, and Venezuela. The Human Development Network is a project of the United Nations Development Program involving 144 representatives from national governments, NGOs, and research institutions.[33] The Network is designed to link those interested in a "concept of sustainable human development as an ... approach [that] regards people's well-being as the goal of development."[34] Expansion of educational opportunities is considered an important part of sustainable human development.

The written introduction to the conference justified public-private partnerships both from the standpoint of the existence of private schools and also from the inability of some governments to finance the expansion of educational opportunities. Encompassed under the conference's concept of public-private partnerships were "a wide range of providers, including for-profit schools (that operate as enterprises), religious schools, non-profit schools run by NGOs, public funded schools operated by private boards, and community owned schools."[35] The inclusion of for-profit schools links the network to global learning corporations, a topic that will be discussed later in the book.

An example of International Finance Corporation's investment in for-profit education is the SABIS International School in Lebanon. It was the first education investment by the Corporation in the Middle East and North Africa. The investment was $8 million with the intention of making it the international headquarters and the flagship of the SABIS Group of Schools. Lars Thunell, the Corporation's Executive Vice President and CEO, said on a recent visit to the school, "Education is vital to ensuring sustainable economic growth, particularly with a rapidly growing and relatively young population across the MENA [Middle Eastern and North Africa] region. By providing high-quality services, the SABIS school is a model for further private investment in education throughout the region."[36] In a World Bank publication, *Mobilizing the Private Sector for Public Education: A View from the Trenches,* SABIS President Carl Bistany describes that, "Since the mid-1950s SABIS has viewed "education" as an industry and has subjected it to the rules that govern successful industries and businesses: efficiency, accountability, and optimization of resources."[37] The company started with a school built in a small village in Lebanon in 1986 and is today a network of 31 K–12 schools in 11 countries, with a total enrollment of 28,000 students from more than 120 nations. Seven of the 31 are charter schools in the United States, and the remaining are private schools. Bistany describes the for-profit attitude of the company regarding education:

> In a country where profit-based economics has played a major role in development and advancement, it comes as no surprise that the United States is leading the way to find appropriate public-private partnerships. It seems natural for the United States to turn to the private sector to seek assistance to enhance public education by subjecting the private sector to the rules inherent in business and industry, that of accountability, efficiency, cost reduction, added value, and results-oriented incentive schemes. SABIS shares the same views and has been successful in implementing the approach to the SABIS network of schools for a long time.[38]

## The World Bank and the Discourse About the Knowledge Economy

Discussions about the knowledge economy occur on the networks linking the World Bank to governments, global intergovernmental and nongovernmental organizations, and multinational corporations. In its book *Constructing Knowledge Societies,* the World Bank declares, "The ability of a society to produce, select, adapt, commercialize, and use knowledge is critical for sustained economic growth and improved living standards."[39] The book states, "Knowledge has become the most important factor in economic development."[40] The World Bank states that its assistance for EKE [Education for the Knowledge Economy] is aimed at helping countries adapt their entire education systems to the new challenges of the "learning" economy in "two complementary ways ... Formation of a strong human capital base ... [and] Construction of an effective national innovation system."[41] The creation of a national innovation system for assisting schools to adapt to the knowledge economy creates another global network. The World Bank describes this network: "A national innovation system is a well-articulated network of firms, research centers, universities, and think tanks that work together to take advantage of the growing stock of global knowledge, assimilate and adapt it to local needs, and create new technology."[42]

What is the origin of the idea of the knowledge economy? The concept of the knowledge economy can be traced to the work of economists Theodore Shultz and Gary Becker.[43] In 1961, Theodore Schultz pointed out that "economists have long known that people are an important part of the wealth of nations."[44] Shultz argued that people invested in themselves through education to improve their jobs opportunities. In a similar fashion, nations could invest increase educational opportunities for people as a stimulus for economic growth.

In his original 1964 book on human capital, Gary Becker asserted that economic growth now depended on the knowledge, information, ideas, skills, and health of the workforce. Investments in education, he argued could improve human capital which would contribute to economic growth.[45] Later, he used the word knowledge economy: "An economy like that of the United States is called a capitalist economy, but the more accurate term is human capital or *knowledge* capital economy."[46] Becker claimed that human capital represented three-fourths of the wealth of the United States and that investment in education would be the key to further economic growth.[47] Following a similar line of reasoning, Daniel Bell in 1973 coined the term "post-industrial" and predicted that there would be a shift from blue-collar to white-collar labor requiring a major increase in educated workers.[48] This notion received support in the 1990s from Peter Drucker who asserted that knowledge rather than ownership of capital generates new wealth and that power was shifting from owner and managers of capital to knowledge workers.[49] During the same decade, Robert Reich claimed that inequality between people and nations was a result of differences in knowledge and skills. Invest in education, he urged, these inequalities would be reduced. Growing income inequality between individuals and nations, according to Robert Reich (1991), was a result of differences in knowledge and skills.[50]

The knowledge economy was also linked to new forms of communication and networking. Referring to the new economy of the late twentieth century, Manuel Castells wrote in *The Rise of the Network Society*: "I call it informational, global, and networked to identify its fundamental distinctive features and to emphasize their intertwining."[51]

By informational, he meant the ability of corporations and governments to "generate, process, and apply efficiently knowledge-based information."[52] It was global because capital, labor, raw materials, management, consumption, and markets were linked through global networks. "It is networked," he contended, because "productivity is generated through and competition is played out in a global network of interaction between business networks."[53] Information or knowledge, he claimed, was now a product that increased productivity and economic growth.

By the end of the twentieth century, national and global policymakers, including the leadership of the World Bank, seemed to uncritically accept the idea that in a knowledge economy investment in education was a panacea for most of the world's economic problems including growing the economies of poor countries; reducing inequalities between rich and poor people and nations; and ensuring continuing economic development of all countries. In *Constructing Knowledge Societies,* the World Bank worries that "the capacity to generate and harness knowledge in the pursuit of sustainable development and improved living standards is not shared equally among nations."[54]

The World Bank uses the measurement of total factor productivity (TFP) to emphasize the importance of knowledge in economic growth. The Bank contends that post-secondary education "is one of the most influential of the set of complex factors that determine TFP for a economy."[55] In other words, the application of knowledge increases the level of productivity; more goods can be produced using fewer hours of human labor.

Nothing better expresses the World Bank's commitment to the idea of a knowledge economy and the role of education in developing human capital then its publication *Lifelong Learning in the Global Knowledge Economy.*[56] The book offers a roadmap for developing countries on how to prepare their populations for the knowledge economy in order to bring about economic growth. The role of the World Bank is to loan money to ensure the growth of an educated labor force that can apply knowledge to increase productivity. These loans, according to Bank policies, might provide support to both public and private educational institutions.[57] In the frame work of public-private partnerships, the World Bank supports private education in developing countries when governments cannot afford to support public schools for all:

> However, in many countries there are other providers of education. Private education encompasses a wide range of providers including for-profit schools (that operate as enterprises), religious schools, non-profit schools run by NGOs, publicly funded schools operated by private boards, and community owned schools. In other words, there is a market for education. In low income countries excess

demand for schooling results in private supply when the state cannot afford schooling for all.[58]

The European Union represents one of the many international responses to the idea of education for the knowledge economy. In March 2000 the European Commission issued its so-called Lisbon strategy for becoming "the most competitive and dynamic knowledge-based economy in the world, capable of sustainable economic growth with more and better jobs and greater social cohesion."[59] The title of the strategy report for creating a knowledge economy captures the spirit of those advocating education for the knowledge economy, "Mobilizing the Brainpower of Europe: Enabling Universities to Make their Full Contribution to the Lisbon Strategy."[60] The first strategic objective of the report is "Improving the quality and effectiveness of education training systems in the EU, in the light of the new requirements of the knowledge society and the changing patterns of teaching and learning."[61]

## The World Bank and the Ideal Personality for the Knowledge Economy

The World Bank's concept of the knowledge economy includes a particular idea about individuals' psychological attitudes and dispositions. A section of the World Bank report *Lifelong Learning in the Global Knowledge Economy* contains a section with the descriptive title: "Equipping Learners with the Skills and Competencies They Need to Succeed in a Knowledge Economy." Two of the three competencies that are listed relate to psychological attitudes and disposition. These competencies could require major changes in some of the world's cultures. For instance, the first listed competency is acting autonomously.

*Acting autonomously:* Building and exercising a sense of self, making choices and acting in the context of a larger picture, being oriented toward the future, being aware of the environment, understanding how one fits in, exercising one's rights and responsibilities, determining and executing a life plan, and planning and carrying out personal projects.[62]

The goal of acting autonomously is echoed in the European Commission's 1998 White Paper on the knowledge economy: "The ultimate aim of education is to develop the autonomy of each person and of his/her professional capacity, to make of the person a privileged element of adaptation and evolution."[63]

Cross-cultural psychologists associate the above character traits with individualist societies as contrasted with collectivist societies that emphasize acting in harmony with the group. Acting autonomously are not values of collectivist communities such as many Asian, Islamic, and Indigenous societies. In fact, the values that the World Bank are recommending instilling in children are those of a competitive marketplace that emphasis individual competition.

In other words, the World Bank is advocating changing the cultural values of many groups of peoples. Cross-cultural psychologist Harry C. Triandis identifies these contrasting character traits of individualist and collectivist societies in Table 2.1.[64]

Overall, the United States, headquarters of the World Bank, is ranked as the most individualist nation in the world. Below is a global ranking of the ten most individualist nations (beginning with the most):

United States
Australia
Denmark
Germany
Finland
Norway
Italy
Austria
Hungary
South Africa[65]

Table 2.1  Individualist and Collectivist Personalities

| Individualist | Collectivist |
| --- | --- |
| Hedonism, stimulation, self-direction | Tradition and conformity |
| Good opinion of self (self–enhancing) | Modest |
| Goals fit personal needs | Goals show concern with needs of others |
| Desire for individual distinctiveness | Desire for blending harmoniously with the group |
| Value success and achievement because it makes the individual look good | Value success and achievement because it reflects well on the group |
| More concerned with knowing one's own feelings | Attuned to feelings of others and striving for interpersonal harmony |
| Exhibits "social loafing" or "gold–bricking"—trying to minimize work in group efforts | No social loafing in group efforts |
| Less sensitive to social rejection | More sensitive to social rejection |
| Less modest in social situations | More modest in social situations |
| Less likely to feel embarrassed | More likely to feel embarrassed |

The ten most collectivist nations (beginning with the most collectivist) are:

China
Columbia
Indonesia
Pakistan
Korea
Peru
Ghana
Nepal
Nigeria
Tanzania[66]

The second of the competencies, using tools interactively, includes skills needed for a knowledge economy by stressing the use of technological tools, information, and symbols.

> *Using tools interactively:* Using tools as instruments for an active dialogue; being aware of and responding to the potential of new tools; and being able to use language, text, symbols information and knowledge and technology interactively to accomplish goals.[67]

These competencies would dramatically replace the reliance of indigenous cultures on traditional tools, ways of knowing, and oral traditions. From a culturalist perspective, local communities would probably adapt these tools to their culture. On the other hand, total acceptance of this package of tools and symbol usages combined with a stress on individualism might result in the transformation of many of the world's cultures.

The final competency implies a world of nomads; workers moving around the globe and having to adapt to multicultural workplaces. In this context, the knowledge economy becomes a world of migrant workers including corporate leaders, managers, technical operatives and professionals, skilled and unskilled laborers. The third competency focuses on social interaction.

> *Functioning in socially heterogeneous groups:* Being able to interact effectively with other people, including those from different backgrounds; recognizing the social embeddedness of individuals; creating social capital; and being able to relate well to others, cooperate, and manage and resolve conflict.[68]

Preparation for competencies in multicultural settings is indicated in learning to interact with "those from different backgrounds" and "recognizing the social embeddedness of others." A phrase that at first glance might not be understood is "creating social capital."

Earlier in the World Bank report, social capital is treated as one aspect of human capital:

> By improving people's ability to function as members of their communities, education and training also increases *social capital* (broadly defined as social cohesion or social ties), thereby helping to build human capital, increase economic growth, and stimulate development. *Social capital* also improves education and health outcomes and child welfare, increases tolerance for gender and racial equity, enhances civil liberty and economic and civic equity, and decreases crime and tax evasion [author's emphasis].[69]

As this quote indicates, social capital can be thought of as ethical or moral values that regulate the interactions, "social cohesion or social ties," of community members. A person with social capital will not commit criminal acts, "decreases crime and tax evasion," and will ensure the welfare of children and social justice. Of course, "crime" and "social justice" are relative concepts depending on the laws and customs of a particular nation or culture. For example, for many years it has been illegal for women in Saudi Arabia to drive automobiles.[70] Does this mean that social capital in Saudi Arabia would include supporting this law? On the other hand, increased social capital as stated above is supposed to lead to "tolerance for gender and racial equity." In this context, for better or worse, the World Bank's goal is to change the laws and customs of Saudi Arabia regarding women's driving through the use of education to increase social capital. While I would not dispute the idea that women should be allowed to drive, it cannot be denied that the World Bank's concept of social capital is designed to change the cultures and laws of societies and nations.

If the concept of social capital is integrated into the concept of human capital, then the goals of education broaden to fostering individualism, developing technical and language skills, learning to function in multicultural settings, and learning to be ethical or moral in relationship to others in the context of promoting civil liberty; racial, gender, and economic equity; and obedience to national laws.

In summary, the World Bank's ideal social personality for the knowledge economy is a person who acts autonomously and is focused on a sense of self. This concept of individualism, in contrast to personalities in collectivist societies, is a reflection of the values of nations like the United States. It is a personality ideally suited for individual competition in economic markets. In addition, the Bank's concept includes the ability to migrate between cultures and work in multicultural settings. While focusing on her/his self, this type of personality also learns to be obedient to the laws and customs of a nation. The focus on individualism raises the important question: Is the World Bank practicing a form of cultural imperialism?

## Schooling for the Knowledge Economy

It is important to remind the reader that the World Bank's educational ideas are shared through a vast global network of contacts and are often part of the educational guidelines for loans to support schooling in developing countries. This doesn't mean that the World Bank is responsible for this educational agenda but only that it is shared through global networks that might affect educational officials, planners, administrators, teachers, and citizens in the world's nations. Local people might ignore

---

### Key Points: Schooling for the Knowledge Economy

The World Bank's Concept of Knowledge Economy includes:

1. Economic growth dependent on the knowledge, information, ideas, skills, and health of the workforce
2. Post-industrial shift from blue-collar to white-collar labor
3. Post-secondary education is one of the most influential determining economic productivity

The World Bank's Concept of Education for the Knowledge Economy includes:

1. Literacy for functioning in the day-to-day life of an economically advanced society
2. Literacy for manipulating information
3. Science and math literacy
4. Foreign language instruction, particularly in English
5. Civic education to achieve rule by law and a good government able to achieve economic development
6. Learning to function in multicultural groups
7. Learning to act autonomously (individualism)
8. Learning to use tools for retrieving and applying knowledge
9. Instruction is assessment-driven
10. Preparation for lifelong learning

---

or adapt the World Bank agenda to local conditions or they might add another interpretation to the global network.

The World Bank proposes focusing school instruction on the second competency it listed for the knowledge economy: "using tools inter-actively." This competency requires learning to use language, text, symbols, information, knowledge, and technology. The World Bank advocates a very specific school curriculum for teaching this competency which includes literacy, foreign languages, science and math, and civic participation based on the "rule of law." Some might complain about the neglect of instruction in the arts, philosophy and literature, and, given the emphasis on creating a personality able to function in multicultural workplaces, the neglect of geography, history, and any form of cultural studies.

The World Bank's concept of literacy is purely instrumental for completing work related to tasks in the knowledge economy. The Bank's concept of literacy does not include critical literacy skills which would prepare readers to analyze the ideological background and hidden messages in a written communication. It does not include reading for personal enjoyment such as learning to read and appreciate literature. It does not include any idea of being literate for political empowerment. It is, as indicate below, literacy for functioning in the global labor market.

Literacy for the knowledge economy, the World Bank states, requires adults to perform at Level 3 of the International Adult Literacy Survey. It should be noted that the survey itself represents the creation of a uniform global standard for literacy. It is a joint project of the Organization for Economic Co-operation and Development (OECD), the Educational Testing Service of Princeton, New Jersey, Statistics Canada, and the United States Department of Education.[71]

The International Adult Literacy Survey identifies 5 levels of literacy:

- Level 1 indicates persons with very poor skills, where the individual may, for example, be unable to determine the correct amount of medicine to give a child from information printed on the package.
- Level 2 respondents can deal only with material that is simple, clearly laid out, and in which the tasks involved are not too complex. It denotes a weak level of skill, but more than Level 1. It identifies people who can read, but test poorly. They may have developed coping skills to manage everyday literacy demands, but their low level of proficiency makes it difficult for them to face novel demands, such as learning new job skills.
- Level 3 is considered a suitable minimum for coping with the demands of everyday life and work in a complex, advanced society.

It denotes roughly the skill level required for successful secondary school completion and college entry. Like higher levels, it requires the ability to integrate several sources of information and solve more complex problems.
- Levels 4 and 5 describe respondents who demonstrate command of higher-order information processing skills.[71]

The World Bank's literacy target of Level 3 for the knowledge economy includes the following:

- *Prose literacy:* Learners should be able to locate information that requires low-level inferences or that meets specified conditions.
- *Document literacy:* Learners should be able to make literal or synonymous matches. They should be able to take conditional information into account or match up pieces of information that have multiple features.
- *Quantitative literacy:* Learners should be able to solve some multiplication and division problems.[72]

In summary, the World Bank's plan of global literacy for the knowledge economy focuses strictly on the functional aspects of literacy and not on critical literacy skills and literacy for personal, for enjoyment or political empowerment. Level 3 literacy, as stated above, is for "the demands of everyday life and work in a complex, advanced society." Level 3 encompasses "Prose literacy" and "Document literacy" which involve low-level inferences and manipulation of information. Also included in this level of literacy is the ability to multiply and divide. The lack of political empowerment associated with this type of literacy will become apparent when I discuss the World Bank's concept of education for participation in civil society.

The World Bank's foreign language instructional goals are directly related to English as the global language. The Bank urges, "Policymakers in developing countries ... to ensure that young people acquire a language with more than just local use, preferably one used internationally."[73] What is this international language? First, the World Bank mentions that schools of higher education around the world are offering courses in English. In addition, the Bank states, "People seeking access to international store of knowledge through the internet require, principally, English language skills."[74]

Learning math and science is also considered important for the global economy. The World Bank reports that male achievement in science has "a statistically positive effect on economic growth" and male accomplishments in math "positively correlated with growth, although the effect is not as strong as for science."[75] Female achievement in science and math is not correlated with growth, because, the Bank contends, of gender discrimination in the labor market. The positive effect of achievement in science reflects, according to the Bank, a broad-based science literacy and not just the education of highly trained researchers.

The Bank's report does not detail recommended learning for participation in civil society. Using a study conducted for the International Association for Evaluation of Educational Achievement, an organization that through its global testing programs contributes to global education uniformity and is part of the World Bank's education network, the Bank concludes that civic education is a good thing because it contributes to economic and social development: "it is linked to good governance and the rule of law, which directly affect economic and social development." Therefore, the World Bank's curricular proposals are directed at increasing economic development through the teaching of functional skills.

## The World Bank's Schools of Tomorrow

What type of teaching and school organization will support the World Bank's curriculum for the knowledge economy? First, the World Bank advocates learner-centered instruction. However, they do not mean by this a progressive model of education where learning is based on the interests of the student and designed for political power. Learner-centered for the World Bank planners means that instruction is related to what students already know. This requires teachers to learn what students already know before introducing new material. The new material should be related to the prior knowledge of the student. The World Bank planners reject the idea of rote learning based on drill. They want students to be actively involved in making connections between the knowledge being presented by the teacher and their own accumulated store of wisdom. From the perspective of the World Bank, learning to make these connections is preparation for making similar connections in the global knowledge economy. "Learner-centered learning," the Bank's report states, "allows new knowledge to become available for use in new situations—that is, it allows knowledge transfer to take place."[76]

It is important to remember that the goal of the World Bank is to prepare workers for a knowledge economy where they will be required to manipulate information. This is the goal of literacy instruction. Consequently, the World Bank education planners advocate the use of knowledge—rich learning that involves teaching a few subjects in depth as contrasted with superficial treatment of many subjects. Students are to be asked to apply their newly gained knowledge in these few subjects to real or simulated problems. This mode of instruction they relate to the educational tradition of "learning by doing" which of course was part of the basic tradition of progressive education. However, progressive educators believed that learning by doing would lead the learner to participate in the reconstruction of society to achieve social justice. In this case, learning by doing is to prepare the learner for the knowledge economy. Referring to knowledge-rich instruction, the Bank claims, "This kind of learning provides learners with a variety of strategies and tools for retrieving and applying or transferring knowledge to new situations."[77]

Learner-centered and knowledge-rich instruction is to be controlled through assessment-driven learning. Standards for learning are to be created and student progress in attaining these standards are to be measured. Students are to participate in discussions in these assessments which are supposed to be "powerful motivators and tools for improved and independent learning."[78] While some might think a test-driven system results in a focus on test preparation and related rote learning, the World Bank claims that assessment-driven instruction promotes "higher-order thinking skills and conceptual understanding."[79]

In addition, Bank planners envision an interconnected learning environment where students learn from each other and their learning is connected to the world outside of school. The Bank refers to this as community-connected learning. Consequently, group work on projects is encouraged as preparation for working with others in the sharing and manipulation of information with group projects involving real-life problems.

Given the goal of preparation for the knowledge-economy, the World Bank emphasizes the classroom use of computers and resources from the Internet. Information and communication technology (ICT) allows the adaptation of globally available information to local learning situations. This results in changing the role of the teacher. Based on the experience of teachers in Chile and Costa Rica, Bank officials claim that ICT creates "a more egalitarian relationship between teacher and learner with learners making more decisions about their work, speaking their minds more freely, and receiving consultations rather than lectures from their teachers."[80]

It is important to highlight that a large percentage of the World Bank's education funds are used for the purchase of educational technology. Critics might complain that this channels large sums of money to be used for education to multinational producers of computers and educational software. On the other hand, ICT is vital for education to enter the knowledge economy. According to the Bank's figures, 40 percent of their education budget in 2000 and 27 percent in 2001 was used to purchase technology. It is estimated that between 1997 and 2001 that 75 percent of the World Bank-financed education projects included ICT, education technology, and education management information systems along with courses being taught over the internet as part of distance learning.[81]

How are teachers to be trained for schools that are learner-centered, knowledge-rich, assessment-driven, and community-connected? The World Bank identifies the following teacher characteristics needed for education for the knowledge economy.

- Teachers need an in-depth knowledge of their subject areas including knowledge of facts, concepts, and an understanding of interconnections between knowledge and facts;
- Teachers need to know methods of instruction related to their subject matter and designed for learner-centered instruction using computers and the internet;
- Teacher training related to the conditions of a classroom that is knowledge-rich, assessment driven, and community connected.

## The World Bank and Lifelong Learning

Lifelong learning has become a buzz word in discussions of the knowledge economy. The assumption is that lifelong learning is essential for individuals to keep pace with the constantly changing global job market and technology.[82] It is preparation for a destabilized life of changing jobs, job requirements, and geographical locations. In this vision of the nomadic worker, people must constantly adapt to new living conditions, technology, and work requirements. This requires, advocates of lifelong learning state, learning skills that help the individual to adjust to an ever changing world.

The World Bank's approach to lifelong learning involves a combination of competencies. Reflecting the above discussions of the World Bank's vision of the psychological construction of humanity and schooling, the Bank defines the knowledge and competencies needed for lifelong learning as:

> These include basic academic skills, such as literacy, foreign language, math, and science skills, and the ability to use information and communication technology. Workers must use these skills effectively, act autonomously and reflectively, and join and function in socially heterogeneous groups.[83]

In other words, the lifelong learner should, according to Bank's approach, act autonomously in devising a life plan and being prepared to work in a multicultural workforce. The lifelong learner will have the literacy, math, and science skills to learn new technologies and jobs and will, with a knowledge of English, be able to participate in the global economy.

The emphasis on teaching learning skills is the major focus of most discussions of lifelong learning. The European Union's statement on lifelong learning defined it as "all purposeful learning activity, undertaken on an ongoing basis with the aim of improving knowledge, skills and competence."[84] In discussing the knowledge economy in Hong Kong and Shanghai in a World Bank publication, Cheng and Yip explain the meaning of lifelong learning among Chinese school officials wanting to prepare students for the knowledge economy: "ability to learn new things, to work in teams, to communicate effectively, to manage oneself, to question and to innovate, to assume personal responsibility, etc."[85] In one document issued by the European Union, the skills needed for lifelong learning, skills that are to be taught in primary and secondary schools, are described as: "The general elementary and/or cognitive competencies required for a whole series of jobs, indeed all jobs: mathematics, writing, problem-solving, social communication and interpersonal competencies."[86] In the United States, several business surveys found corporate leaders believing that the knowledge economy required primary and secondary students to learn computation, communication, problem-solving skills, and proper work attitudes.[87] The report on the 2005 summit on U.S. high schools limited the recommended core curriculum to four years of English (communication skills) and four years of math including data analysis and statistics. These were considered the only essential subjects needed for preparation of students for lifelong learning in the knowledge economy.[88]

## Criticisms of Education for the Knowledge Economy

One criticism of focusing schools on preparing students for the needs of the knowledge economy is that there are not enough jobs in the knowledge economy to absorb school graduates into skilled jobs and that the anticipated increased demand for knowledge workers has not occurred. Also, so-called knowledge work has been routinized allowing for the hiring of less skilled workers. "It is, therefore," Phillip Brown and Hugh Lauder conclude, "not just a matter of the oversupply of skills that threatens the equation between high skills and high income, where knowledge is 'routinized' it can be substituted with less-skilled and cheaper workers at home or further afield."[89]

Brown and Lauder argue that multinational corporations are able to keep salaries low by encouraging nations to invest in schools that prepare for the knowledge economy. For instance, there has been an increased demand for higher education in India where computer programmers annually earned in 1997 between US$2,200–2,900 as compared to programmers in the United States who earned in 1997 between US$35,500 to 39,000.[90] The result has been a brain migration from

India to the United States resulting in putting a lid on wage increases in the host country while depleting the human capital resources of India.

Another effect is so-called brain waste where well-educated school graduates are unable to find jobs commensurate with their skills. This results in dampening income growth for college graduates in industrial countries and forcing many into occupations not requiring a high level of education. This phenomenon is called "brain waste." Brain waste can occur in high income countries when there are only a limited number of jobs requiring high levels of education. Brown and Lauder write, "Britain, along with America, is not a high-skilled, high-waged economy but one in which this accurately reflects only a minority of workers, who stand alongside an increasingly large proportion of well-qualified but low-waged workers, who in turn stand beside the low-skilled and low-waged."[91]

As a result of pressure to expand educational opportunities to meet the demand of the global knowledge economy, Brown and Lauder conclude, "vast numbers of highly-skilled are available in developing economies, the global expansion of tertiary education has outstripped the demand for high-skilled workers, creating downward pressure on the incomes of skilled workers in developed countries along with some upward pressure on those in emerging economies."[92]

The result for developing countries has been disastrous with governments being forced to pay back educational loans to the World Bank while experiencing little economic growth from investment in schooling. In addition, educated workers from developing nations have become part of the so-called "brain migration" moving from their countries to wealthier nations where salaries are higher. Thus a developing nation invests in education but does not receive the expected rewards from improving its knowledge economy. Some countries have experienced extraordinary depletion of their skilled and educated workforce. According to statistics provided by the Organization of Economic Cooperation and Development, 89 percent of skilled workers have immigrated from Guyana; 85.1 percent from Jamaica, 63.3 percent from Gambia, 62.2 from Fiji, 46.9 from Ghana, and 38.4 percent from Kenya.[93]

A good percentage of these immigrants are unable to obtain in their host countries employment commensurate with their education. This is referred to as "brain waste." For example, statistics released by the United States Census Bureau show that many immigrants with bachelor's degrees are unable to obtain skilled jobs in the United States. The most successful group of immigrants with college degrees who were able to gain skilled employment were from Ireland (69%), the United Kingdom (65%), Australia (67%), and Canada (64%). Even these percentages suggest some level of brain waste. However, in comparison to other countries, these percentages are high. In contrast, immigrants with college degrees able to gain skilled employment were low for many countries such as Guatemala (21%), former Yugoslavia (31%), Poland (33%), Italy (38%) and Korea (33%).[94]

The oversupply of educated workers, it could be argued, depresses wages to the advantage of employers. Therefore, arguments for the knowledge economy may have a disrupting effect on human lives and may cause national educational expenditures to favor higher education. Seeking high paying jobs, citizens may pressure governments to provide more opportunities for higher education or stimulate the development of private higher education institutions. This demand might redirect government money away from support of needed social programs such as those for health, nutrition, and shelter. The result might be frustrated college graduates who face the prospect of brain waste and seek global employment through brain migration. As needed social programs are neglected, increasing numbers of college graduates become discontented. Another criticism is that the World Bank's advocacy of a knowledge economy can result in changing local cultural practices and can be detrimental to local economies. For instance, the World Bank advocates replacing traditional farming methods with scientific agricultural methods and corporate farming. The World Bank warns, "Lagging countries will miss out on opportunities to improve their economies through, for example, more efficient agricultural production and distribution systems which would increase yields and lower the proportion of food wasted due to poor distribution."[95] In other words, it claims, knowledge applied to agricultural would increase productivity.

What type of knowledge should be applied to agriculture? The World Bank recommends the use of genetically modified crops that would increase yields, enhance nutritional values, and create plants resistant "to drought, pests, salinity, and *herbicides* [my emphasis]."[96] In other words, traditional plants and cultivation would be replaced by products of biotechnology and chemical eradication of unwanted plants that interfere with crop growth. In addition, knowledge could be applied to ensure that local crops can compete in global markets; this means some form of corporate farming. The little family plot yields to the increased efficiency of the large scale scientific farming.

The World Bank recognizes the possible dangers from genetically modified plants and chemical crop sprays to human health and the environment. Their answer to these problems is improving the knowledge base of a country. In other words, knowledge, in this case biotechnology and chemistry, might change agricultural production to the detriment of the local population which can be corrected, the Bank claims, by further growth of the knowledge economy. Referring to biosafety and risk management, the World Bank asserts: "To make informed decisions on how to address these challenges, countries need to call on highly quali-

---

**Key Points: Summary of The World Bank's Global Education Agenda**

1. Support of public-private partnerships and networks in education particularly between national education systems, private school groups, and education corporations.
2. Financial support of for-profit global learning corporations through loans from the World Bank Group's International Finance Corporation
3. Advocacy of education for a knowledge economy as the key to economic growth.
4. Advocacy of education for self autonomy, in contrast to a collectivist personality, for the worker in the global economy.
5. Advocacy of education for working in multicultural workplaces, including the possibility of learners being part of the world's brain migration.
6. Support of a global school curriculum that would focus on literacy, math and science, foreign languages for the global economy (mainly English), and education for civic responsibilities.
7. Support of learner-centered instruction and learning by doing so that global workers will be able to utilize new knowledge in their jobs and lives.
8. Support of lifelong learning so that global workers would be able to adapt new technological advances, job changes, and possible global migration.

---

fied specialist—who will not be available unless investment in advanced human capital are made."[97]

Despite the somewhat convoluted logic that the application of knowledge to agriculture then requires further expansion of the educational system to correct problems caused by the original application of knowledge, world culture theorists might argue that this process represents the local culture utilizing the scientific knowledge available in the global flow of ideas. In the end, world culture theorists could argue that this will result in a creation of a common global culture of agricultural practices, namely, scientific corporate farming. This global agricultural model, it might be argued, will ensure that all people have enough to eat.

On the other hand, postcolonial/critical theorists might consider the Bank's agricultural programs lack an understanding of local agricultural conditions and land ownership. The result has been making the rich richer and the poor poorer. Richard Peet writes regarding the World Bank's policies when applied in Africa, "it turned out little was known about rain-fed tropical agriculture in Africa ... that attitudes and local conditions were more difficult to change than technology ... land tenure reforms were a prerequisite of any agricultural development aimed at the poor."[98] The result was that the loans went mainly to rich farmers, according to Peet, which caused "increasing income inequalities?"[99]

## Conclusion

In summary, the World Bank is able to advance its educational agenda through an extensive global network that includes intergovernmental and nongovernmental organizations, national governments, local officials, and multinational corporations. Global discourses on education for the knowledge economy and lifelong learning are strongly influenced by the World Bank's agenda. However, as I mentioned at the beginning of this chapter, the World Bank's views on the knowledge economy and lifelong learning are not shared by all global education players. In the next chapter, I will explore the global agendas and discourses of some other major global institutions including the United Nations and OECD.

## Chapter 3

# The Cyberschoolbus and *Sesame Street* Meet the Global Knowledge Economy

## OECD and the United Nations

The organizations discussed in this chapter support different types of world education cultures. The Organization for Economic Cooperation and Development (OECD) provides global education data and international assessments comparing nations. The United Nations is interlinked, as described in chapter 2, through common global networks with the OECD and the World Bank. However, it offers a counterpoint to human capital education through its Cyberschoolbus Web site, which emphasizes problems related to human rights, peace, poverty, and global hunger. In addition, the United Nations' Cyberschoolbus is linked to the Sesame Street Workshop through the co-production of an online civic education learning site called Explore Panwapa.[1] The Sesame Street Workshop also markets international children's educational television programs.[2]

There are important questions about the work of the above organizations. Does OECD's global message and data reinforce the World Bank's attempt to structure national school systems to meet the needs of the global knowledge economy? Will the combination of their work contribute to the growth of a world education culture? Does the United Nations' Cyberschoolbus provide an alternative to proposed curricula for the knowledge economy? Will exposure to *Sesame Street*'s international television and online educational programming contribute to the development of a world culture?

## OECD

The OECD has the same global reach as the World Bank. The OECD's 1961 founding document states as its goal: "to achieve the highest sustainable economic growth and employment and a rising standard of living in Member countries, while maintaining financial stability, and thus to contribute to the development of the world economy."[3] From its original membership of twenty nations, it has expanded to thirty of the richest nations of the world. In addition, OECD provides expertise and exchanges ideas with more than 100 other countries including the least developed countries in Africa.[4]

To help achieve economic growth in member nations and other nations, the OECD focuses on the collection and dissemination of data including statistics about education. The organization claims that:

> For more than 40 years, the OECD has been one of the world's largest and most reliable sources of comparable statistics, and economic and social data. As well as collecting data, the OECD monitors trends, analyses and forecasts economic developments and researches social changes or evolving patterns in trade, environment, agriculture, technology, taxation and more.[5]

In keeping with its concerns with economic growth, OECD promotes the role of education in economic development. Along with economic growth, OECD leaders express concern about nations having shared values to ensure against social disintegration and crime. The stated value of education according to OECD is: "Both individuals and countries benefit from education. For individuals, the potential benefits lie in general quality of life and in the economic returns of sustained, satisfying employment. For countries, the potential benefits lie in economic growth and the development of shared values that underpin social cohesion."[6]

To help achieve these education benefits to member nations and cooperating nations, OECD:

- Develops and reviews policies to enhance the efficiency and the effectiveness of education provisions and the equity with which their benefits are shared;
- Collects detailed statistical information on education systems, including measures of the competence levels of individuals;
- Reviews and analyzes policies related to aid provided by OECD members for expansion of education and training in developing nations.[7]

OECD operates four important education programs: Centre for Educational Research and Innovation (CERI), the Programme on Institutional Management in Higher Education (IMHE), the Programme on Educational Building (PEB), and the Programme for International Student Assessment (PISA) (OECD, 2006, 2007d). In recent years, these programs supported educational privatization in the context of free markets. Rizvi and Lingard state, "OECD ... has largely constituted globalization in a performative way ... [including for education] marketization and privatization on the one hand and strong systems of accountability on the other."[8] A defender of OECD, the Deputy Director for Education for OECD, claimed that OECD's acceptance of these policies was "because these tendencies prevail in the world of which its is an extricable part. Yes, it is a think tank but, as with all our thoughts, those of the OECD are embedded in the lifeworlds and cultural settings of its members."[9]

Besides, as stated above, supporting education policies similar to the World Bank, OECD has played a major role in the global standardization of education through its assessment program PISA.[10] By becoming an international standard, PISA has the direct potential for determining the curriculum content in the areas tested which are mathematics, reading, and science. The OECD's CERI offers the world a large collection of publications and statistics including case studies, country surveys, research publications, and reports.[11] OECD's IMHE supports the global marketing of higher education: "Higher education is undergoing far-reaching change ... Among the changes are shifts in the balance between state and market, global and local, public and private, mass education and individualisation, and competition and cooperation."[12]

OECD is contributing to a world culture of schooling through its testing, research, and higher education programs. In fact, one of its programs promotes the international sharing of educational ideas:

> The OECD Programme on Educational Building (PEB) promotes the exchange and analysis of policy, research and experience in all matters related to educational building. The planning and design of educational facilities—schools, colleges and universities—has an impact on educational outcomes which is significant but hard to quantify.[13]

### OECD and Social Capital

The focus on developed nations in contrast to developing nations explains an important difference between the World Bank and OECD regarding education and the knowledge economy. Both organizations share a similar conceptualization of the knowledge economy. At the 2007 UNESCO Ministerial Round Table on Education and Economic Development, the OECD Secretary-General Angel Gurría echoed the dominant global discourse on education and the knowledge economy:

> In a highly competitive globalized economy, knowledge, skills and know-how are key factors for productivity, economic growth and better living conditions ... Our estimates show that adding one extra year to the average years of schooling increases GDP per capita by 4 to 6 per cent. Two main paths of transmission can explain this result: First, education builds human capital and enables workers to

be more productive. Second, education increases countries' capacity to innovate—an indispensable prerequisite for growth and competitiveness in today's global knowledge economy.[14]

While OECD policies do influence developing nations and the organization's data collection reflects concern about poor countries, the major concern is the economies of member nations. In other words, what problems are faced by the world's wealthiest nations in educating their populations for competition in the global knowledge economy. This difference in emphasis on developed as contrasted to developing nations is captured in the definition of the knowledge economy given in a 2007 OECD book *Human Capital*: "In *developed* economies, the value of knowledge and information in all their forms is becoming ever more apparent, a trend that is being facilitated by the rapid spread of high-speed information technology" (author's emphasis).[15]

What is emphasized in discussions about the knowledge economy in developed member nations of OECD? Consider the story told as "By way of introduction" on the opening pages of the OECD's book *Human Capital*.[16] The story is about Linda who lives in a Paris suburb with other immigrants from North Africa. The suburb was the scene of youth riots that resulted in the burning of thousands of cars. Linda is described as being raised in a "traditionally minded North African family."[17] At a local community center, men are described as sitting around listening to rap music while Linda and three other unemployed women from differing ethnic backgrounds meet with an employment counselor. All the women complain that getting a job is difficult due to transportation problems and prejudice and discrimination. Linda regrets that her schooling was cut short even though she was a model student. Her father believed that women shouldn't work and that they should stay home until marriage. Consequently, her father withdrew her from school before she could graduate. Married as a teenager and then separated from her husband she faces a potential life of unemployment. Faced with this situation, the author comments, "To get on, to get a better job and to improve their incomes, the women know they need to have an education."[18]

But in this story education is not just about getting a job. It is also about reducing the potential for more riots in French immigrant communities. Human capital is tied to both job skills and reducing community tensions by teaching shared values in schools. "Indeed," the author writes, "even the relationships and shared values in societies can be seen as a *form of capital* that make it easier for people to work together and achieve economic success."[19]

The above scenario adds a different emphasis to human capital education as compared to the policies of the World Bank. While the World Bank addresses the issue of multicultural workforces, the developed nations of OECD face intense multicultural problems as a result of the growth of immigrant populations. Consequently, OECD members are very concerned about education increasing social cohesion to reduce conflicts between immigrant communities and the existing populations of host countries.

Consequently, OECD policymakers give special emphasize to the social capital aspects human capital. Using the language of networks, OECD defines social capital as "networks together with shared norms, values and understandings that facilitate co-operation within and among groups."[20] The organization divides social capital into three main categories. The first category is the *bonds* that link people to a shared identity through family, close friends, and culture. The second category is the *bridges* that link people to those who do not share a common identity. The last category is the *linkages* that connect people to those up and down the social scale or, in other words, those from different social classes.

The problem with the first category is that *bonds* through a shared identity might be so strong that it hinders making *bridges* to others. This, the OECD claims, is a problem with some immigrant communities in member nations. Consequently, schools need to ensure an education that builds these bridges to others and linkages that reduce conflict between social classes. OECD warns that: "Companies and organizations can also suffer if they have the wrong sort of social capital—relationships between colleagues that are too inward-looking and fail to take account of what's going on in the wider world."

## Birth Rates, Female Workers, and Lifelong Learning

In recent years, OECD nations have turned to foreign workers to compensate for a shortage of workers resulting from declining birth rates. OECD asserts that women must have 2.1 children each to maintain a nation's population. Since the 1970s, the birth rate in OECD countries has fallen below that rate. For example, in Austria, Germany, Italy, and Korea the birth rate has declined to an average of 1.3 children per woman. With the decline in birth rate, OECD nations have had to fill the labor shortage through immigration policies or contracting for foreign workers. The results, as exemplified above, are increasing tensions between the families of immigrant and contracted workers and local populations.

Adding to the problem of declining birth rates is the increase in mortality rates. As people live longer in OECD nations, there is greater dependence of retirees on a shrinking labor force. OECD's response to this situation: "Part of the answer is getting women working."[21] OECD's policymakers hail the fact that more and more women are working in

OECD countries and are helping to expand the workforce. The OECD's *Employment Outlook 2006* celebrated the fact that "Increased female participation has been a major component in labor supply growth during past decades."[22]

How do you balance the need for women to work with having more babies? From the standpoint of educational policy, the answer is better and more preschools to free mothers to enter the workforce. What should these preschools look like? OECD studies show a range of approaches to preschool in member nations ranging from French- and English-speaking countries where the emphasis is getting children ready for school, to schools in Nordic countries where children spend many hours outdoors as a place for learning. In Finland, children attend day-care centers before entering school at the age of seven. There is only a minimum of academic training in these day-care centers.

Using a human capital perspective, OECD policies support preschools that prepare students for elementary school. Calling for more coordination of school policies in OECD nations, the organization calls for "giving thought to both children's care and learning needs and ensuring that there's *continuity between their preschool and school years.*" (author's emphasis).[23]

On the other end of the age scale, OECD advocates keeping people working longer as a means of ensuring an adequate labor supply and to balance the number of workers with retirees. In OECD countries, there is a general fear about the ability of government pension and other retirement plans to support retirees when there is an increased proportion of retired in relationship to the number of people in the workforce. "Not surprisingly," OECD states, "governments in developed countries are encouraging people to work for longer."[24]

Lifelong learning is one answer to keeping people working longer. This adds another dimension to the lifelong learning policies discussed in chapter 2 regarding the World Bank. The reader will recall that lifelong learning was promoted as an antidote to technological change and changes in occupational requirements. The worker in the knowledge economy, according to this reasoning, must be prepared to update and learn new skills. In the scenario for advanced economic countries of OECD, lifelong learning serves the dual purpose of preparing workers for changing job requirements and ensuring that older workers can remain active in the labor force.

Cynics might argue that it is exploitive of workers to use lifelong learning as a means of increasing the retirement age to solve labor shortages and reduce the costs of supporting a retired generation. In the past, early retirement was considered a benefit. Now, OECD claims that early retirement shortens one's life. The organization cites a study by Shell Oil that workers who retire at 55 were twice as likely to die in ten years then those who retire at 60 or 65. Within the framework of this reasoning, OECD concludes: "If we need to go on working for longer, we'll also have to go on upgrading our skills, education and abilities—our human capital—throughout our lives."[25]

In summary, the concerns of the developed nations belonging to OECD gives a different emphasis to the implementation of human capital education policies as compared to the World Bank's focus on developing nations. Both institutions share the same beliefs about the importance of the role of human capital education in the knowledge economy. The following list contains the particular concerns and related education policies of economically advanced OECD countries in the context of the knowledge economy. As a result of a labor shortage, OECD countries, while still emphasizing education for the knowledge economy, are concerned about multicultural education regarding their foreign and immigrant

---

### Key Points: Labor Market and Educational Concerns of OECD Countries

I. Development of human capital for competition in knowledge economy
   a. Same policies advocated by the World Bank as discussed in chapter 2
II. Labor shortage because of declining birth rates and aging of population
   a. Need for immigrants and contract foreign workers for labor shortage
      (1) Problem: tensions between local populations and immigrants and contract foreign workers
      (2) Solution: Education to improve social capital
III. Bring more women into the workforce
   a. Problem: Ensuring a sustained and high birth rate
   b. Solution: Preschool education as preparation for further schooling to free mothers to work
      (3) Problem: Lack of equal educational opportunity for women
      (4) Solution: Policies that ensure educational equity for women and support women's educational efforts
IV. Reduce retirement age and keep people working longer
   a. Problem: Increasing portion of retirees in relation to workforce
   b. Solution: Lifelong learning and policies that prepare older workers to continue working

workforces, preschool education to free women to enter the workforce, and lifelong education to keep people working for more years.

### OECD/PISA and the World Culture of Education

OECD contributes to the creation of a world education culture through the development and implementation of PISA. The importance of PISA in creating a world education culture is its emphasis on measuring skills needed for the global economy as contrasted with the goals of national curricula. In describing the knowledge and skills tested, OECD's *PISA 2003 Assessment Framework* states: "These are defined not primarily in terms of a common denominator of national school curricula but in terms of what skills are deemed to be *essential for future life* ... They [national curricula] focus even less on more general competencies, developed across the curriculum, to solve problems and apply ideas and understanding to situations *encountered in life* [author's emphasis]."[26] In other words, PISA is creating global standards for the knowledge required to function in what OECD defines as the everyday life of a global economy. By shifting the emphasis from national curricula to global needs, PISA is defining educational standards for a global economy.

What is the global influence of international assessment? International assessments like PISA create global standards that are used to compare the achievement of national school systems. A similar international assessment is Trends in International Mathematics and Science Study (TIMSS). Wanting to impress their national leaders, school officials hope their students do well on these tests in comparison to other countries. The consequence is a trend to uniformly national curricula as school leaders attempt to prepare their students to do well on the test. Writing about the effect of PISA and TIMSS on world education culture, David Baker and Gerald LeTendre assert that, "After the first set of TIMSS results became public, the United States went into a kind of soul searching... The release of the more recent international study on OECD nations called PISA led Germany into a national education crisis. Around the world, countries are using the results of international tests as a kind of Academic Olympiad, serving as a referendum on their school system's performance."[27]

The potential global influence of PISA is vast since the participating member nations and partners represent, according to OECD, 90 percent of the world economy.[28] The assessments are on a three year cycle beginning in 2000 with each assessment year devoted to a particular topic. For instance, international assessment of reading is scheduled for 2009, mathematics for 2012, and science for 2015.[29] OECD promotes PISA as an important element in the global knowledge economy: "PISA seeks to measure how well young adults, at age 15 and therefore approaching the end of compulsory schooling, are prepared to meet the challenges of today's knowledge societies—what PISA refers to as 'literacy'."[30]

The definition of literacy is a key component in the potential global educational uniformity created by PISA. It is PISA's definition of literacy that could result in national school leaders stressing particular subjects at the expense of others so that their country's school system will look good in international comparisons. The reader will recall that the World Bank's definition of literacy included reading and the manipulation of information and basic arithmetical skills. In addition, the World Bank's education for the knowledge economy included competency in foreign languages, science and math, and civic participation. PISA's definition of literacy includes "mathematical literacy," "problem solving," "reading literacy," and "scientific literacy."[31] In the context of PISA, OECD defines literacy as the "capacity of students to apply knowledge and skills in key subject areas and to analyze, reason and communicate effectively as they pose, solve and interpret problems in a variety of situations."[32]

The reader will recall from chapter 2, that the World Bank based its definition of literacy on the International Adult Literacy Survey created by OECD in partnership with other organizations. Consequently, there are close parallels between PISA's definition of reading literacy and that used by the World Bank. For the World Bank the literacy standard includes the ability to cope with the demands of everyday life and work in a complex, advanced society with a skill level required for successful secondary school completion and college entry. Similar to the World Bank, the definition of literacy used by PISA is focused on work and living in modern society without any suggestion that literacy should include critical literacy for understanding controversial political and social ideas. In other words, both institutions stress functional literacy. PISA's conceives of the function of literacy as:

> literacy enables the fulfilment of individual aspirations—from defined aspirations such as gaining an educational qualification or obtaining a job, to those less immediate goals which enrich and extend one's personal life. Literacy also provides the reader with a set of linguistic tools that are increasingly important for meeting *the demands of modern societies with their formal institutions, large bureaucracies and complex legal systems.* (author's emphasis)[33]

Again, it is important to emphasize that OECD's definition of literacy ignores differences in national cultures for what it conceives as the literacy skills needed for living in the global economy. In a similar fashion, PISA's math assessment is directed to problems of everyday life and not as an assessment of national curricula:

The OECD/PISA assessment focuses on *real-world problems*, moving beyond the kinds of situations and problems typically encountered in school classrooms. In *real-world settings*, citizens frequently face situations when shopping, traveling, cooking, dealing with personal finances ... in which use of quantitative or spatial reasoning or other mathematical competencies would help clarify, formulate or solve a problem. (author's emphasis)[34]

OECD/PISA's science assessment reflects the interconnecting networks in the discourse about the knowledge economy. OECD/PISA uses the definition provided in the 1993 UNESCO International Forum on Scientific and Technological Literacy for All: "The capability to function with understanding and confidence, and at appropriate levels, in ways that bring about empowerment in the made world and in the world of scientific and technological ideas."[35] In describing the desired outcomes of science education, OECD/PISA states, "It values the ability to apply this understanding to real situations involving science in which claims need to be assessed and decisions made."[36]

In summary, OECD/PISA contributes to world education culture by using common assessments for OECD countries and partners representing 90 percent of the world economy. These assessments ignore specific national curricula and focus on what test designers consider as the basic skills needed to function in a global knowledge economy. Of course, national school leaders might take the comparative scores resulting from PISA as a judgment about the quality of their schools. Consequently, they might be inclined to adjust their curricula to prepare students to do well on the assessments. This could result in a growing similarity in the skills taught in global school systems or, in other words, a global education culture.

Also, PISA contributes to the formulation of the ideal person needed for a global knowledge economy. Table 3.1 summarizes both the World Bank and OECD/PISA's conceptions of the ideal educated person for the knowledge economy.

Both OECD and the World Bank reinforce the idea in global networks that the core global curricula should consist of literacy, math, science, and the skills needed for lifelong learning and the tools to use information and data. Both organizations propagate the message that some form of multicultural education is needed for adjustment to global migration. OECD does not emphasize the teaching of foreign languages or civic education to teach the rule of law. Despite these minor differences, OECD and the World Bank are disseminating similar ideas about the education need for a global knowledge economy.

A major difference between the two organizations is the World Bank's stress on individualism (acting autonomously) versus OECD's concern

*Table 3.1*  The Ideal Person for the Knowledge Economy According to the World Bank and OECD/PISA

| World Bank Social Capital | OECD/PISA Social Capital | World Bank Educational Capital | OECD/PISA Educational Capital |
|---|---|---|---|
| Acts autonomously | Establishes *bonds* linking them to a shared identity through family, close friends, and culture. | Literacy to manipulate information | Literacy to function in modern global society |
| Uses tools interactively | Has knowledge and skills needed to function in a knowledge economy *for future life* | Science and math with an emphasis on all students becoming scientifically literate to function in global economy | Science and math literacy to function in modern global society |
| Can function in socially heterogeneous groups (multicultural workforce and community) | Builds bridges and linkages to those who do not share a common identity or social class (multicultural workforce and community) | Foreign language instruction, particularly in English | |
| | | Lifelong learning | Lifelong learning |
| | | Civic education to achieve rule by law and a good government able to achieve economic development | |

with social bonds. These are conflicting messages being sent over global networks. This could be a result of differences in focus. The World Bank is interested instilling in developing nations a competitive spirit of individualism associated with market economies, while advanced OECD countries are concerned with conflicts between immigrant and resident populations, and crime.

Other organizations in the global networks linked to the World Bank and OECD also present alternative views of the ideal global person and curriculum. In other words, the World Bank and OECD are *not* monolithic forces shaping global education discourses and practices.

---

**Key Points: OECD**

Representation:
1. Member countries and partners represent 90 percent of world economy.

Programs:
1. Centre for Educational Research and Innovation (CERI)
   a. Offers a large collection of publications and statistics including case studies, country surveys, research publications, and reports.
2. Programme on Institutional Management in Higher Education (IMHE)
   a. Supports the global marketing of higher education
3. Programme on Educational Building (PEB)
   a. Promotes the exchange and analysis of policy, research, and experience in all matters related to educational building
4. Programme for International Student Assessment
   *PISA 2003 Assessment Framework* states: "These are defined not primarily in terms of a common denominator of national school curricula but in terms of what skills are deemed to be *essential for future life* ...

Objectives:
1  Human capital education:
   a  Education for the knowledge economy
   b. Educational equity for women
   c. Preschool
   d. Lifelong learning
2. Social Capital:
   a. Bonds linking people to a shared identity
   b. Bridges to people who do not share same identity
   c. Linkages to connect people from different social class

---

UNESCO, which shares global education networks with both OECD and the World Bank, offers an alternative global discourse.

## UNESCO and Lifelong Learning: A Different Vision

UNESCO supports a more humanistic vision of lifelong learning as compared to the starkly economic arguments of the World Bank and OECD. This difference represents competing ideas within global education discourses. In reviewing UNESCO's ideas on lifelong learning, Madhu Singh of the UNESCO-Institute of Education describes the ideas of organizations like the World Bank, OECD and some national government leaders: "the official discourse is narrowly economic and instrumental and often means little more than short-term retraining and adaptation. Most governments are concerned more with national competitiveness and economic growth than individual development."[37]

UNESCO's discourse on lifelong learning has focused on the full development of the individual in its 1972 major report on lifelong learning sponsored by the International Commission on the Development of Education. The report was titled *Learning to Be: The World of Education Today and Tomorrow*.[38] In *Learning to Be*, the primary proposal is the creation of a learning society and the promotion of lifelong learning. The reports lead author, Edgar Faure, Chair of the International Commission on the Development of Education and former Prime Minister of France stated that there were four assumptions underlying the arguments in *Learning to Be*. The first is that the world is progressing to a common unity of cultures and political organizations based on human rights principles. In other words, the report supported the ideas of world culture theorists but placed emphasis on human rights as part of the learning society and a component of lifelong learning.

The second assumption was the universal value of democracy. The Commission defined democracy "as implying each man's right to realize his own potential and to share in the building of his own future. The keystone of democracy ... is education."[39] However, the Commission did not believe that any form of education would promote democracy. After all, education can be used to support despotic governments. Therefore, they wanted a learning society to teach about and support democracy.

The third assumption of the report focused on the development of the individual in contrast to economic development. This concept of development goes far beyond the concerns of the World Bank and OECD. The report states,

> the aim of development is the complete fulfillment of man, in all the richness of his personality, the complexity of his forms of expression and his various commitments—as individual, member of a family and of a community, citizen and producer, inventor of techniques and creative dreamer.[40]

The last assumption presents lifelong learning as a cure for individual and social problems caused by alienation from others and a loss of a sense of community. "Lifelong learning," the report dramatically claims, "can produce the kind of complete man the need for whom is increasing with the continually more stringent constraints tearing the individual asunder."[41] The "complete man" will be educated for political action. Education for political action, the report suggests, is an important part of education for the new age of information. For instance, the report contends that one result of the new information and media age was the obsolescence of representative democracy. Representative democracy, according to the report, "is not capable of providing him [the individual] with an adequate share of the benefits of expansion or with the possibility of influencing his own fate in a world of flux and change; nor does it allow him to develop his own potential to best advantage."[42] In the information and media age, individuals must exert their own control in contrast to turning it over to an elected government representative. The exercise of this individual democratic power requires, according to the report, changes in education. "The new man," the report declares, "must be capable of understanding the global consequences of individual behavior, of conceiving of priorities and shouldering his share of the joint responsibility involved in the destiny of the human race."[43]

What type of education will produce this "new man?" The Commission proposed an education based on scientific humanism that would focus on the use of technological and scientific advances to enhance the welfare of humans and democracy. The statement of the Commission on education for scientific humanism emphasizes individual control and power.

> For these reasons the commission considered that it was essential for science and technology to become fundamental, ever-present elements in any educational enterprises for them to become part of all educational activities designed for children, young people and adults, *so as to help the individual to control not only natural and productive forces, but social forces too, and in so doing to acquire mastery over himself, his choices and actions; and, finally, for them to help man to develop a scientific frame of mind in order to promote the sciences without becoming enslaved by them.* (author's emphasis)[44]

To achieve scientific humanism, the report argued, required changes in motivation and teaching methods. In a fascinating assertion, considering the World Bank and OECD's emphasis lifelong learning for economic growth, the Commission states: "Modern democratic education requires a revival of man's natural drive towards knowledge."[45] The Commission specifically rejected a reliance on future employment as a motivation for learning. Education for employment quickly reduced, according to the Commission, schooling to a joyless and boring activity. Contributing to damping of the spark of joy in learning was an excessive emphasis on theory and memory. Instead, the Commission argued, the emphasis should be on learning to learn. Educational systems should not be concerned with achieving a match between schooling and the needs of the labor market. The emphasis should be on the joy of learning, learning to learn, and development of the whole person. In this regard, the Commission states, "The aim of education is to enable man to be himself ... and the aim of education in relation to employment and economic progress should be not so much to prepare ... for a specific, lifetime vocation, as to 'optimse' mobility among the professions and afford permanent stimulus to the desire to learn and to train oneself.[46]

From the Commission's perspective, the love of learning creates a desire for lifelong learning and maintenance of a learning society. In this context, the goal of lifelong learning was to give people the power to exercise democratic control over economic, scientific, and technological development. Lifelong learning provides the tools to ensure that scientific and technological progress resulted in benefiting all. The learning society is one in which people continually develop the skills and knowledge needed to enhance their well-being and ensure a democratic society.

In the 1990s, UNESCO's humanistic approach to lifelong learning was swept up in the rhetoric of the knowledge economy and human capital development. Despite this UNESCO avoided the purely economic arguments for lifelong learning. This continuing humanistic concern is evident in UNESCO's 1996 report on lifelong learning called *Learning: the Treasure Within*. The report was a product of the work the International Commission on Education for the Twenty-first Century, chaired by Jacques Delors, the former President of the European Commission (1985–95) and former French Minister of Economy and Finance.[47]

An extensive worldwide network was involved in completing the report. This network was propagating a different discourse on lifelong learning than that of the OECD and the World Bank. The International Commission on Education included representatives from fourteen different countries many of whom were or had been government officials. Three members did not, and to the best of my knowledge, have not held government positions.[48] Eight members of the Commission were currently or past Ministers of Departments of Education, Social Development and Family Affairs.[49] One member had been a Prime Minister, another was a member of Parliament, and another was a member of an international governing organization.[50]

The difference in global discourse between the Commission and the World Bank and OECD was captured in the opening lines of Jacques Delors' introduction to the report, aptly titled "Education: The Necessary Utopia." Delors' declared that education was "an indispensable asset in its attempt to attain the ideals of peace, freedom and social justice."[51] The goal of the International Commission on Education for the

Twenty-First Century Delors stated, was to foster "a deeper and more harmonious form of human development and thereby to reduce poverty, exclusion, ignorance, oppression and war."[52]

The Commission suggested that lifelong learning could solve multiple educational ills. The Commission defined lifelong learning as adaptation to changes in technology and as the continuous "process of forming whole human beings—their knowledge and aptitudes, as well as the critical faculty and the ability to act."[53] For the Commission, education for a knowledge economy required the teaching of how to acquire, renew, and use knowledge in the context of an information society. Preparation for the information society, according to the Commission and similar to the World Bank and OECD, required learning to select, arrange, manage, and use data. Consequently, lifelong learning required, the Commission asserted, a basic education that included:

- Learning to know
- Learning to do
- Learning to be.[54]

According to the Commission, these intellectual skills provided the tools for lifelong learning and a learning society. "Learning to know" and "Learning to do" were similar to the human capital definitions of the World Bank and OECD. "Learning to know" according to the Commissions definition, involved a broad general education based on an in-depth study of a selected number of subjects. This would, the Commission contended, provide the foundation for the ability and the desire to continue learning. "Learning to do" involved work skills and the acquisition of "competence that enables people to deal with a variety of situations often unforeseeable ... by becoming involved in work experience schemes or social work while they are still in education."[55] "Learning to be" reflected the more humanistic thrust of UNESCO. "Learning to be" resolved the potential tension between personal independence and common goals. The Commission worried that competitive markets might destroy a sense of unity. The Commission hoped to wed the individual to common goals by developing the untapped "buried treasure in every person."[56] The unleashing of this buried treasure, the Commission asserted, would create a desire to work for common goals. The Commission located the source of social unity in the inherent psychological make-up of the individual. Education releases the inherent drive for cultural unity. What are these inherent psychological characteristics? The Commission's list includes "memory, reasoning power, imagination, physical ability, aesthetic sense, the aptitude to communicate with others and the natural charisma of the group leader."[57]

Creating a world culture was an important part of the Commission's discussion of social unity. The Commission asserted that the world was in "erratic progress towards a certain unity."[58] Commission members believed that education should play a major role in this supposed inevitable progress to world unity. How? Their answer was an "emphasis on the moral and cultural dimensions of education" which would enable each person to grasp the individuality of other people and to understand the world's progression towards cultural unity.[59] An emphasis on the moral and cultural dimensions of education should begin, according to the Commission, with "self-understanding through an inner voyage whose milestones are knowledge, mediation and the practice of self criticism."[60]

In another action that suggested a concerted effort to create a world culture, the United Nations General Assembly in December 2002 adopted a resolution requesting UNESCO to lead the United Nations Decade of Education for Sustainable Development from 2005 to 2014. UNESCO was to use its global network to develop an International Implementation Scheme for the Decade. UNESCO's plan for Education for Sustainable Development would take place "within a perspective of lifelong learning, engaging all possible spaces of learning, formal, non-formal and informal, from early childhood to adult life."[61]

In keeping with the global nature of the project, UNESCO's plan declares that "Networks and alliances will be the crucial element, forging a common agenda in relevant forums."[62] In another document, UNESCO announces its leadership role would be used to: "catalyze new partnerships with the private sector, with youth, and with media groups."[63] Through these consciously created global networks, UNESCO supports an education agenda that encompasses some of the organization's earlier pronouncements on lifelong learning along with environmental education. Present are earlier concerns with education for democratic power and social cohesion. The economic goals of human capital education are replaced with concerns about the impact of economics on the environment. The elements of education for sustainable development are given as:

- Society: an understanding of social institutions and their role in change and development, as well as the democratic and participatory systems which give opportunity for the expression of opinion, the selection of governments, the forging of consensus and the resolution of differences.
- Environment: an awareness of the resources and fragility of the physical environment and the affects on it of human activity and decisions, with a commitment to factoring environmental concerns into social and economic policy development.

- Economy: a sensitivity to the limits and potential of economic growth and their impact on society and on the environment, with a commitment to assess personal and societal levels of consumption out of concern for the environment and for social justice.[64]

As stated above, UNESCO's global educational discourse includes preparing citizens to actively wield political power and to understand environmental problems. Global education for development includes creating an awareness of the potential negative impact of economic growth on the environment and a concern for social justice.

Therefore through its global networks, UNESCO offers an alternative educational discourse to that of the World Bank and OECD. This is most evident alternative in UNESCO's list on high quality instruction. According to UNESCO's plan, education for sustainable development:

- Interdisciplinary and holistic: learning for sustainable development embedded in the whole curriculum, not as a separate subject;
- Values-driven: sharing the values and principles underpinning sustainable development;
- Critical thinking and problem solving: leading to confidence in addressing the dilemmas and challenges of sustainable development;
- Multi-method: word, art, drama, debate, experience,... different pedagogies which model the processes;
- Participatory decision making: learners participate in decisions on how they are to learn;
- Locally relevant: addressing local as well as global issues, and using the language(s) which learners most commonly use.[65]

## Competing Global Discourses

Table 3.2 includes the competing global discourses on education between UNESCO's education for sustainable development and the World Bank's education for the knowledge economy.

An examination of Table 3.2 shows some dramatic differences between the world education culture disseminated by the World Bank and UNESCO. First is the difference in the extent of student control over instructional methods with the World Bank advocating that learner centered instruction using the student's existing knowledge and that learning should involve work on real world problems. In contrast, UNESCO calls for student participation in deciding instructional methods and that there should be a focus on critical thinking and problem solving. One might construe the World Bank's focus on solving real world prob-

*Table 3.2* Competing Global Discourses on Instruction; World Bank and UNESCO

| World Bank | UNESCO |
| --- | --- |
| Learner-centered: instruction is related to what students already know | Participatory decision making: learners participate in decisions on how they are to learn |
| Knowledge-rich learning: involves teaching a few subjects in depth as contrasted with superficial treatment of many subjects | Interdisciplinary and holistic: learning for sustainable development embedded in the whole curriculum, not as a separate subject |
| Learning by doing: students apply newly gained knowledge to real or simulated problems | Critical thinking and problem solving: leading to confidence in addressing the dilemmas and challenges of sustainable development |
| Assessment-driven instruction | Multi-method: word, art, drama, debate, experience.... |
| Group work: preparation for working with others in sharing and manipulation of information with real-life problems | Values-driven: sharing the values and principles underpinning sustainable development |
| Information and communication technology (ICT): allows the adaptation of globally available information to local learning situations | Locally relevant: addressing local as well as global issues, and using the language(s) which learners most commonly use |

lems as being similar to critical thinking and problem solving. However, there is a major difference between saying that instruction will be based on the learner's prior knowledge and giving students a active part in deciding the method of instruction. The approach to curricula is quite different between the two organizations with the World Bank calling for a focus on a few subjects while UNESCO calls for an interdisciplinary and holistic approach with all subjects combined and interrelated with sustainable development issues. While the World Bank calls for group work so that students can share manipulation of information and real-life problems, UNESCO wants students to learn to share the values of sustainable development. Regarding the adjustment of learning to local cultures and conditions, the World Bank advocates doing this with information and communication technology, while UNESCO wants instruction to consider local problems and use the common language of the students.

Is there a concise way of describing these differences? One might say that the World Bank's instructional methods are designed to educate a worker for the global knowledge economy who is able to use the global flow of information to solve real world problems. In contrast,

UNESCO's instructional approach might be described as preparing students to exercise political power and to think about how to solve problems threatening the well-being of the planet and human life. These differences are highlighted on the United Nations' *Cyberschoolbus* Web site.

## A Global Curriculum: Cyberschoolbus

"To create an on-line global education community" is the stated goal of the United Nations' Cyberschoolbus, which is available online in Arabic, Chinese, English, French, Russian, and Spanish.[66] Selected by James Lerner for the International Society for Technology in Education as one of the best Web sites for teachers, the Cyberschoolbus site embodies the attempt to globalize educational practices and ideas.[67] First, the Web site represents the ability of information technology to connect teachers and children from around the world. This fulfills the slogan of the International Society for Technology in Education: "Providing leadership and service to improve teaching and learning by advancing the effective use of technology in education."[68] Second, the Web site offers curricula, lessons, and learning games designed for a global audience. This represents another important contribution to the globalization of educational practices. Finally, the Web site offers a clear alternative global educational discourse to that of the World Bank and OECD.

The Web site was created in 1996 as the online education part of the United Nation's Global Teaching and Learning Project "to provide exceptional educational resources (both online and in print) to students growing up in a world undergoing increased globalization."[69] In addition to creating an online global education community, the other stated global goals of the Cyberschoolbus are:

• To create educational action projects to show students that they have a role in finding solutions to global problems;
• To give students a voice in global issues;
• To provide high-quality teaching resources to a wide range of educators in a cost-effective manner.[70]

The Cyberschoolbus's global reach and commitment to use information and communication technology (ICT) is given in the organization's description: "The UN *Cyberschoolbus* captures the growing potential of the Internet as an educational tool and provides an effective medium with which to disseminate information and resources about international affairs, as well as bring together diverse communities of students and educators from around the world."[71] It is also exemplified by its support of a poster contest for the World Summit on the Information Society and the display on its Web site of 1,600 entries from 38 countries.[72] The contest required posters that represented the following themes related to how ICT can be used to transform global living. The poster themes were:

- ICTs help people learn about the world
- ICTs help people appreciate cultural diversity
- ICTs help improve our quality of life
- ICTs make it easier for people to participate in local government
- The many ways ICTs are used to give and receive information
- ICTs and the digital divide[73]

These poster themes represent different aspects of the actual goals of the Cyberschoolbus. For instance, the Cyberschoolbus demonstrates the ability of ICT to help people learn about the world. One of the major components of the Cyberschoolbus is "Infonation," an interactive database providing current information and statistics on the world's countries.[74] The site allows the user to access information about individual countries by intergovernmental, socioeconomic, and geographical groupings. The intergovernmental groupings are important parts of the global superstructure, such as the African Union, Caribbean Community (CARICOM), the European Union, League of Arab States (Arab League), Organization of Islamic States, OECD, Association of Southeast Asian Nations (ASEAN), Commonwealth of Independent States, Group of 8 (G8), Council Organization of American States (OAS), South Asian Association of Regional Cooperation (SAARC), South African Development Community; and the Organization of Petroleum Exporting Countries (OPEC).[75] Links describe each of these intergovernmental organizations.

In other words, Infonation users are exposed to the globalizing effect of intergovernmental organizations as they search for information about particular countries. Users are also made aware of global economic differences by dividing the world's nations into socioeconomic categories, such as economies in transition; developing economies and least developed countries; high-, medium-, and low-human development countries; and high-, middle-, and low-income nations.[76] Statistics on population, economy, health, technology, and statistics are available for all these categories.

As part of creating a global education community, two of the Cyberschoolbus goals mentioned above are to "create educational action projects to show students that they have a role in finding solutions to global problems" and "give students a voice in global issues." These goals are represented in Cyberschoolbus games such as "Food Force" which is an

Internet game for eight to thirteen year olds that sends players on six different missions to solve world hunger problems and "Stop Disasters" where players learn to respond to different types of disasters. There is a connecting Web site on how people help with the problem of land mines. There is a link to the United Nations Environment Program where students are asked to sign a tree planting pledge and there is a link to World Water Day. Other games and lessons are all designed to prepare students to be activist in solving global problems.[77]

The globalization of educational practices can occur through the Cyberschoolbus's section on curriculum. The curriculum offerings are designed for teachers and include for different subjects a curriculum guide, model lessons, and suggested resources. The curricula represent a social justice agenda in contrast to human capital education. The list of available curricula include peace education, poverty, human rights, world hunger, indigenous people, rights at work, ethnic discrimination, and racial discrimination. The center piece of Cyberschoolbus lessons is human rights. At the site users can download an instructional guide called *ABC: Teaching Human Rights—Practical Activities for Primary and Secondary Schools.*[78]

## Educating Global Citizens: Cyberschoolbus and *Sesame Street*

Social justice as an alternative to the global human capital discourse received further support when two global educators, the United Nations and *Sesame Street*, joined hands with a global financial management company, Merrill Lynch, to create a worldwide online learning game called Panwapa, which is available in Arabic, English, Chinese, Spanish, and Japanese. *Sesame Street*, as I will explain, is a global educator working in 120 countries.[79] It has traditionally used television as the medium of instruction for poor children and children of war. In addition to *Sesame Street*'s links to Merrill Lynch and the United Nations, it was funded by the William J. Clinton Foundation as part of the Clinton Global Initiative to provide civic education to children in Afghanistan.[80]

There is a potential worldwide educational impact resulting from these linkages. Panwapa claims to "Inspire and Empower Young Children to Become Responsible Global Citizens."[81] *Sesame Street* and its educational agendas are broadcast through special adaptations to local cultures and languages in Bangladesh, China, Egypt, Germany, Israel, Jordan, Mexico, the Netherlands, Palestine, Russia, and South Africa along with American programming dubbed into local languages shown around the world.[82] And lastly, the Clinton Foundation's support of

*Sesame Street* programming in Afghanistan raises the issue of whether there is a common global meaning of citizenship.

Panwapa is meant to symbolize globalization. It is the name of an imaginary floating island that drifts between the five oceans of the world. The word "panwapa" is from the Tshiluba language of the Democratic Republic of the Congo in central Africa and means "here on this earth."[83] As it floats around the world, the island's residents are true global citizens. The official description of the program states: "So Panwapa Island is here but also everywhere, and its inhabitants are simply 'of the earth'. They are citizens of the global community."[84] The producers of the program provide this description: "Panwapa, created by the educational experts behind *Sesame Street*, is a multimedia, global initiative that is designed to inspire and empower a new generation of children, ages four to seven, to be responsible global citizens."[85]

As they float around the world, the inhabitants of Panwapa encounter and learn to live with people of differing nationalities, religions, cultures, and language groups. How did humanity symbolically come to live on this island without national borders and moving across global space? The answer given by Panwapa's creators contain the very role the program is playing in globalization: "Media and technology are bringing people closer together. The international economy is more interdependent than ever before. These circumstances place a new set of demands on the youngest generation of the world."[86]

Panwapa's agenda is to create activist global citizens who get along with others of different cultures and language groups. The first goal of the game is to get kids to make the connection between their local and the global communities: "1) Awareness of the Wider World: A recognition of the wider world in which we live; an understanding of the link between local neighborhoods and communities and national and global issues."[87] In other words, children are being educated to think globally.

The second goal is to educate citizens who can function in a multicultural and multilingual global society and who understand the worldwide interconnections between people. Within the context of this goal, Panwapa is suppose to teach the "concept of similarities and differences"; "languages and forms of communication"; "value of diversity"; and "equity of personal rights." The third goal is to teach players the impact of their actions on others and to take responsibility for personal actions. Being an active citizen who participates in solving local and global issues is the fourth goal.

It is the fifth goal that truly makes Panwapa's educational goals distinct from those advocating human capital objectives to educate global workers. This goal focuses on economic inequalities. The education goal is given as:

Understanding of and Responsiveness to Economic Disparity: Promote an understanding that all people share certain basic needs; that disparities in resources affect individuals' abilities to fulfill these needs; and that there is a desire to address these disparities.[88]

In the context of this goal, the game claims to teach what universal needs are for humans and to prepare learners to help others meet their basic needs.

## *Sesame Street*: Global Preschool for Social Justice

Panwapa is a continuation of what the creators of *Sesame Street* envisioned as a preschool television program that would aid in ending poverty and promote peaceful multicultural societies while teaching basic skills related to numbers, letters, and words. Now the program spans the globe carrying a similar message to the world's children. The original *Sesame Street* was broadcast in 1969 as part of the so-called American war on poverty. The idea of creating an educational program for preschool children from low income families was proposed by Lloyd Morrisett who at the time worked as a supervisor of grants for the Carnegie Corporation. Morrisett worried that preschool education, which he considered important for the cognitive development of children, "would slowly, if at all, reach many of the children who needed them, particularly underprivileged children for whom preschool facilities might not be available." The answer to this problem, he felt, was in using television to reach large numbers of children.[89]

Gerald Lesser, Professor of Education and Developmental Psychology at Harvard, was chosen as chief advisor for the program. He believed that television had certain elements that made it superior to schools. Schools, he maintained, depended on control of the student by others, public humiliation, and the continuous threat of failure. Television learning contained none of these elements. In front of the television, Lesser argued, the child learns without fear of a teacher. Consequently, he believed that television was an ideal educator. It was nonpunitive and it provided a shelter from the emotional stresses of society. "We may regret the conditions in our society that make sanctuaries necessary and must guard against a child's permanent retreat into them," Lesser wrote, "but sanctuaries are needed, and television is one of the few shelters children have."[90]

Later *Sesame Street* producers would consider television learning a welcome sanctuary for the world's poor children, particularly those forced to work at a young age. For instance, in the production of the program for Bangladesh, one of the world's poorest nations, it was estimated that while a majority of young children were not in school almost

80 percent watched television.[91] Under these conditions, educational television was considered the best hope for any form of education to reach poor children.

Another vision carried around the world was that *Sesame Street* characters could serve as models for children's future actions. Originally, Lesser believed that a great deal of learning took place through modeling. According to Lesser, children do not need to interact to learn; they can model themselves after television characters. In fact, modeling fit Lesser's concept of a nonpunitive form of education. "The child," Lesser wrote, "imitates the model without being induced or compelled to do so. ... By watching televised models, children learn both socially desirable and undesirable behaviors."[92] Through preschool education on television with the use of appropriate models, Lesser asserted that "Surely it can ... help them [children] toward a more humane vision of life."[93]

*Sesame Street* has taken its philosophy of creating behavioral models for children around the world. Many programs are international co-productions adapted to local cultures and issues. The Sesame Street Workshop Web site provides this description of their efforts:

> Each of Sesame Workshop's international co-productions is carefully crafted to meet the specific needs of the local children. Child-development experts in each country work with local directors, producers, and writers to translate the magic of *Sesame Street* in a way that captures the rich cultural flavors of each region. The engaging live action, animation, and colorful characters create a world of fun for young children and their families.[94]

As stated above, Sesame Workshop is engaged in a global effort to adapt a particular television framework on local cultures. By hiring local experts, the program hopes to escape the charge of cultural imperialism. A basic element of the program is the use of muppets. For example, in the 1996 Russian co-production, local educators and writers planned the curriculum. The result was that the American program's Big Bird was replaced by a muppet named Zeliboba who is described as "a tall furry blue spirit who enjoys nature and lives in the hollow of a gigantic oak tree. He is a very large, somewhat awkward, kind-hearted, warm and trusting character."[95] The Russian show is set in a courtyard filled with shops and homes in contrast to urban neighborhood in the American version. In the courtyard Zeliboba is a "Dvorovoi" or spirit of the courtyard. In the Egyptian co-production, which is broadcast throughout the Middle East, the Big Bird like character is called Nimnim who is described as a "charming character who delights in life and nature ... [and] loves to share his love and enthusiasm for life and nature with his many friends."[96]

Examples of modeling good behavior according to local needs can be found in all programs. For instance, co-producers for the South African program introduced the muppet Kami who is HIV-positive. The South African producers were concerned about the large numbers of South African children who are HIV-positive. The goal was to create toleration of HIV-positive children and disseminate information about the disease.[97] The South African program is described as having a "rich curriculum ... designed especially for preschoolers—presenting messages that encourage children to develop positive self-esteem and self-image, to respect and appreciate others, to celebrate South Africa's diverse culture, to develop basic skills with letters and numbers, and to encourage a lifelong love of learning."[98]

A goal of the Bangladesh production was to promote equality between social classes, genders, castes and religions.[99] Meeting under a Banyan tree, the program's characters are suppose to promote cultural nationalism. In the words of writers for the Sesame Workshop International:

> With a curriculum defined by Bangladeshi educators, the series emphasizes not only literacy, math and science, but also helps foster values such as self-respect, empathy and cooperation. Other key objectives include improving educational opportunities for young girls; promoting good nutrition, hygiene and safety; and encouraging appreciation of the shared cultural heritage of diverse segments of Bangladeshi society.[100]

## Conclusion: Spreading a World Education Culture: Human Capital and Progressive Educational Models

Are the major intergovernmental organizations discussed so far in this book undermining national allegiance through their advocacy of educating global citizens? They all want to create global citizens but differ over the attributes they would give that citizen. The World Bank, OECD, UNESCO, the United Nation's Cyberschoolbus, and the international producers of *Sesame Street* are very explicit in the values they want to embed in global culture. Even though the World Bank and OECD share human capital goals they differ somewhat in their focus. In contrast to these organizations, UNESCO, the United Nations' Cyberschoolbus, and the international producers of *Sesame Street* support a progressive educational model as discussed in chapter 1. Differences in approaches to the education of global citizens are summarized in Table 3.3.

The summary provided in Table 3.3 was elaborated on in the last three chapters. While differences exist in these various approaches to

Table 3.3 World Education Culture: Educating the Global Citizen

*[handwritten annotation: "Human capital" bracketing World Bank and OECD columns]*
*[handwritten annotation: "Social justice" pointing to United Nations and Sesame Street columns]*

| | World Bank | OECD | UNESCO: Sustainable Development | United Nations: Cyberschoolbus | Sesame Street Workshop International |
|---|---|---|---|---|---|
| Goals | Educating workers for the knowledge economy; ability to function in a multicultural society and workforce; gender equality; social cohesion | Educating workers for the knowledge economy; ability to function in a multicultural society and workforce; gender equality; social cohesion | Educating global citizens committed to sustainable development; sustain and protect cultures and languages; gender equality; activist citizen | Social justice: Peace, human rights, anti-poverty; human rights; gender equality; anti-racism; multicultural cooperation; activist citizen | To give young children models for promoting social justice and ability to live in a multicultural world and gender equality; provide poor children the basic tools for further education |
| Instruction | Standardized curriculum; assessment driven; ICT; learner centered; knowledge rich; group work | Standardized curriculum; assessment driven; ICT; learner centered; knowledge rich; group work | Participatory decision-making; interdisciplinary and holistic; critical thinking; locally relevant; values driven–sustainable development | Internet learning games; infonation; curricular materials made available on peace education; human rights and other social justice issues | Television as sanctuary from emotional stress of living; instruction in basic educational concepts; nonpunitive; behavioral models |

world education culture there is one issue that is present in all, namely gender equality. While the reasons for supporting gender equality vary between intergovernmental organizations, they all support this as a goal with full realization of the impact on local cultures and the changes that will be required in cultural values. The World Bank advocates gender equality, particularly in education, to ensure the health of children and expanding global labor markets. OECD advocates gender equality with a special emphasis on the need to expand the labor supply in developed nations. UNESCO, the United Nations Cyberschoolbus, and the Sesame Street Workshop International support gender equality in the context of human rights. Whatever the reasons, if these organizations help to create a world culture, then that world culture most likely will value gender equality.

## Chapter 4

# The Marketing of Knowledge

Multinational Learning Corporations,
Global Assessment, and Higher Education

A free trade zone for educational services! Emblematic of the new global world of educational entrepreneurship, Dubia opened its free trade zone in educational services in 2003 calling it Knowledge Village.[1] Dubia's actions exemplify the worldwide marketing of higher education and the activities of multinational learning corporations that add another dimension to the global superstructure of educational practices and policies. The World Trade Organization (WTO) and its General Agreement on Trade in Services (GATS) and Agreement on Trade-Related Intellectual Property Rights (TRIPs) have smooth the way for educational marketers and vendors and the commodification of higher education and knowledge. As discussed below, the WTO, GATS, and TRIPs are contributors to the growth of a global educational culture. However, as I indicated in chapter 3, this global educational culture is not uniform and contains contradictory ideas and emphasis. Also, as I suggested in chapter 1, there are global religious education models outside this more general trend to a world education culture.

Trade in educational services is not new and dates back centuries when missionaries and colonialists transported education to other countries, students and scholars traveled between nations, and some national schools opened branches in other countries. This early story should not be thought of as just another example of Western cultural imperialism. Certainly, the West played a major role in providing international educational services but also many countries outside of the West traded in educational services, such as Chinese scholars studying in Japan in the nineteenth century and the centuries of international movement of Islamic scholars and students. The past history of international education is important, but my focus is on the present globalized trade in educational services.[2]

What is strikingly new is the conceptualization of trade in educational services as a source of income to be included in the financial planning of nations, educational institutions, and for-profit multinational corporations. The income generating aspects of international education are aided by the free trade policies created by GATS, the worldwide networks of scholars, and information technology which makes possible online learning, the rapid communication of scholarly information, and the transportation revolution which allows for the easy global movement of scholars and students. Today, trade in educational services involves substantial financial transactions. The global market in educational services is estimated by Merrill Lynch to be worth outside of the United States $111 billion a year with a "potential consumer base of 32 million students."[3]

## The WTO, GATS, and TRIPs

The 1995 creation of the WTO opened the door to the prospect of free trade in educational materials and services, and the marketing of higher education. The WTO was an outgrowth of 1948 General Agreement on Tariffs and Trade which was called the "third institution" along with the World Bank and the International Monetary Fund. The general goal was to reduce national tariffs to promote free trade in goods. The Uruguay Round of trade talks from 1986–1994 resulted in the WTO, GATS, and TRIPs. GATS expanded the idea of free trade from just free trade in goods to free trade in services. GATS' Article XXVIII provides the following definition: "'supply of a service' includes the production, distribution, marketing, sale and delivery of a service."[4] Educational services are included under this definition. TRIPs provides protection for the global sale of called knowledge-related products.

What type of educational services are covered by GATS? Writing about the effect of GATS on higher education, Jane Knight used the following classifications of educational services.[5] First, according to Knight's classification, is "cross–border supply," which includes distance learning, e-learning, and virtual universities. "Consumption abroad" is the largest share of the global market in educational services involving students who go to another country to study. "Commercial presence" means the establishment of facilities in another country, such as branch campuses and franchising arrangements in another country. The travel of scholars, researchers, and teachers to another country to work falls under the classification of "presence of natural persons."[6]

The international trade in educational services is aided by TRIPs, which protects intellectual property sold by individuals, universities, corporations, and other institutions. Its protection is broader than traditional concerns with copyrighted printed material. TRIPs also covers software, compilation of data, recorded media, digital online media, and patents on industrial, health, and agricultural technologies. Also included are integrated circuit designs, utility models, industrial designs, trademarks, trade names, and geographical names.[7]

GATS and TRIPs are governed by the three fundamental obligations of WTO members. The first obligation is equal and consistent treatment of all trading partners. For instance, if a foreign university is allowed to establish a branch in another country, then that country must allow other foreign universities to establish branches. The same is true of other educational services. The second obligation is that all foreign providers of educational services will receive equal treatment within the host country. And the third is that each country determines the extent of market access to foreign providers. In other words, a country could decide to not allow any foreign university to establish a branch campus, but if they decide to allow one, then they must allow other foreign universities to establish branch campuses. The same obligations cover the protection of intellectual property under TRIPs.[8]

GATS and TRIPs aids in the transformation of higher education into a business enterprise that sells services and knowledge.[9] As Helen Raduntz explains:

> Universities as idea-generating powerhouses are prime targets for investment, by those knowledge-based industries involved in telecommunications, computers, electronics, and biotechnology. As lucrative sites of investment, their potential has been enhanced by the protection of ideas, as intellectual property generated by research, under copyright and patent laws and global trade agreements.[10]

How many countries are involved in GATS and TRIPs? As of 2007 WTO had 151 member countries and 31 observer countries. The WTO is controlled by member nations with all major decisions requiring agreement by all members. The WTO meets every two years. The trade agreements are enforced by the membership. The WTO explains how trade rules are enforced:

> The rules are enforced by the members themselves under agreed procedures that they negotiated, including the possibility of trade sanctions. But those sanctions are imposed by member countries, and authorized by the membership as a whole. This is quite different from other agencies whose bureaucracies can, for example, influence a country's policy by threatening to withhold credit.[11]

The WTO and GATS are based on the assumption that free trade in goods and services will contribute to the economic growth of all nations. This is a questionable assumption. One could ask: Does free trade primarily benefit developed nations? For instance, free trade applied to higher education might financially help those nations who already have well established higher education systems that can be globally marketed.

## Key Points: World Trade Organization (WTO), General Agreement on Trade in Services (GATS), Agreement on Trade-Related Intellectual Property Rights(TRIPS)

### World Trade Organization (WTO)

1. Origins and Structure
   a. Outgrowth of 1948 General Agreement on Tariffs and Trade
   b. The Uruguay Round of Trade Talks 1986–1994 resulted in the creation of the WTO, GATS, and TRIPS
   c. WTO membership in 2007 151 member nations and 31 observer nations
   d. Rules enforced by members
2. General Trade Obligations
   a. Equal and consistent treatment of all trading partners
   b. All foreign traders and companies will receive equal treatment in host country
   c. Each country determines the extent of market access to foreign companies and traders

### General Agreement on Trade in Services (GATS)

1. Trade in services governed by the general trade obligations of the WTO
2. Agreement includes the production, distribution, marketing, sale, and delivery of a service
3. Classification of educational services under GATS
   a. Cross–border supply such as distance learning, e-learning, and virtual universities
   b. Consumption abroad involves students who go to another country to study
   c. Commercial presence of facilities in another country such as branch campuses and franchising arrangements in another country
   d. Presence of natural persons includes the travel of scholars, researchers and teachers to another country to work

---

**Agreement on Trade-Related Intellectual
Property Rights (TRIPS)**

1. Protects intellectual property sold by individuals, corporations, universities
2. Intellectual property includes copyrighted printed material, software, compilation of data, recorded media, digital on-line media, patents on industrial, health, and agricultural technologies, integrated circuit designs, utility models, industrial designs, trademarks, trade names, and geographical names

---

The WTO bases its free trade arguments on the theory of "comparative advantage" articulated by nineteenth-century English classical economist David Ricardo. According to the official pronouncement of the WTO: "Simply put, the principle of "comparative advantage" says that countries prosper first by taking advantage of their assets in order to concentrate on what they can produce best, and then by trading these products for products that other countries produce best."[12] What happens if one country is better than another at making everything? The WTO asserts:

> The answer, according to Ricardo, is no. The reason is the principle of comparative advantage. It says, countries A and B still stand to benefit from trading with each other even if A is better than B at making everything. If A is much more superior at making automobiles and only slightly superior at making bread, then A should still invest resources in what it does best—producing automobiles—and export the product to B. B should still invest in what it does best— making bread—and export that product to A, even if it is not as efficient as A. Both would still benefit from the trade. A country does not have to be best at anything to gain from trade. That is comparative advantage.[13]

It is not within the scope of this book to defend or criticize Ricardo's theory. What is important for the reader to understand is that the free trade arguments of the WTO are based on a particular theory and that it is a theory. It is this theory that underpins GATS.

Ricardo probably never thought of his theory as being the basis for creating a world culture. Trade often results in the exchange of cultural artifacts and knowledge. Global free trade would maximize this exchange. Free trade might change local cultures and contribute to the making of world culture. Legal scholar Christopher Arup wrote about the global impact of GATS, "Services, particularly those with intellectual content, carry far deeper messages than goods."[14] Arup worries that "Not only do services comprise a growing proportion of international trade overall, but the ways in which services are supplied provide potential to undermine the economic sufficiency, political sovereignty and cultural identity of the locality."[15]

## Global Marketing of For-Profit Education and Knowledge Industries

"Thank You For Your Interest in the Premier Brands in the Education Industry!" is emblazoned on the Web site of Educate, Inc.[16] The company embodies the entanglement of politics, universities, and private financiers in the new world of global for-profit education and knowledge industries, such as publishing and information services. What are the consequences of the growth of these multinational corporations? While the actual impact is difficult to measure, there are certain hypotheses that can be made. First is that global knowledge industries might be creating a level of uniformity in global education culture as the result of the marketing of for-profit schools, the international use of testing products, global databases, and, most importantly, the publishing of textbooks for global markets. Second, global knowledge industries might try to exert corporate control of the ideologies disseminated through schools around the world. While it is always possible that textbooks might reflect differing ideologies, it seems unlikely that global publishers would be distributing textbooks that contained ideas that threatened their control of global markets. Third, globally marketed schools and worldwide information and publishing corporations might transform and displace local cultures. Again, these are only speculative hypothesizes without any concrete proof.

There is a burgeoning global market for corporately controlled for-profit schools. But I must warn the reader that after publication of this book the rapid buying and selling of educational enterprises may change some of the following examples. However, these examples do provide an understanding of the workings of the educational marketplace. In 2006, the *Chronicle of Higher Education* reported that for-profit colleges were the fastest-growing sector in higher education with the eight largest corporations having a combined market value of about $26 billion.[17] Some economists criticize for-profit higher education institutions for spending more money on recruitment than other nonprofit and private schools. Stanford economist Samuel Wood, according a report in the *Chronicle of Higher Education,* suggests that "for-profits have a lot more in common with a chain of Bally's health clubs than they do with, say, Arizona State or Emory Universities."[18] According to his calculations nonprofits spend from 1 to 2 percent of their revenue on recruiting students, while for-profits spend 23 percent. However, as Wood suggests, this may change as nonprofit colleges spend more money on advertising and public relations to attract foreign students and to establish branch campuses in other countries; I discuss these aspects of marketing of higher education in a later section.

Linked to a complex network of business and financial institutions, the corporate structure of Educate, Inc. is similar to that of other for-profit schools and knowledge industries. After the 2007 purchase of Sylvan Learning Centers from Laureate Education Inc., Educate, Inc. could boast about its ownership of Hooked on Phonics, Catapult Learning, Educate Online, and Progressus Therapy. Educate, Inc. markets its products in Europe under the Schülerhilfe brand.[19] Exemplifying the complex financial arrangements of education companies, Educate, Inc. is owned by Edge Acquisition, LLC with Citigroup Capital Partners and Sterling Capital Partners as investors.[20] The chairman of Edge Acquisition, R. Christopher Hoehn-Saric, is also a trustee of Johns Hopkins University.[21] The interplay of politics and education is evident on the Board of Directors of Educate, Inc. One director, Raul Yzaguirre, is a professor at Arizona State University, the director of the Mexican American advocacy group LaRaza, and was co-chair of the 2008 Hillary Rodham Clinton presidential campaign.[22] Another director, Douglas Becker, is Chairman and CEO of Laureate Education Inc. along with being director of Baltimore Gas and Electric Company and director of For Inspiration and Recognition of Science and Technology.[23] Director Cheryl Gordon Krongard is a regent of the University System of Maryland and director of US Airways Group Inc.[24] Other directors of Educate, Inc. have similar ties to industry, investment companies, and higher education.

For-profits are undergoing a period of global expansion. For instance, Laureate Education Inc. has a presence in 15 countries serving 240,000 students with ownership in the United States of Walden University and 23 other universities in Asia, Europe, and the Americas.[25] Laureate Education Inc. claims to potential investors that the global market for for-profit higher education is increasing because of the worldwide expansion of the middle class, expanding youth populations in Latin America and Asia, the need for educated human capital and, most importantly, the difficulties faced by governments in financing public higher education.[26] In 2007, the company announced: "Laureate International Universities, one of the world's largest networks of private higher education institutions, and the University of Liverpool today announced the expansion of a unique partnership to leverage programs and expertise to create the next generation of international programs for students worldwide."[27]

In September of 2007, Laureate made a dramatic move to capture the Asian market when Douglas L. Becker its Chairman and Chief Executive Officer announced that he and his family were moving to Hong Kong to ensure the expansion of the company and to establish Asian headquarters. In an example of the international financing of for-profit education, Becker and an investor group engineered a $3.8-billion private-equity buyout of the company in June of 2007. The international investor group included Harvard University, Citigroup, Microsoft co-founder Paul Allen, global philanthropist George Soros, Kohlberg Kravis Roberts & Co. (KKR); S.A.C. Capital Management, LLC; SPG Partners; Bregal Investments; Caisse de depot et placement du Quebec; Sterling Capital; Makena Capital; Torreal S.A.; and Brenthurst Funds. In reporting the move, a *Chronicle of Higher Education* article commented, "Mr. Becker devised the transformation of Laureate into an internationally focused higher-education company from its roots as a tutoring business called Sylvan Learning Systems."[28]

While the above represent examples of for-profit schools, there is also the important arena of for-profit knowledge companies. Some public librarians fear that GATS will result in a reduction of government support of public libraries in favor of for-profit knowledge companies.[29] The International Federation of Library Associations and Institutions warned in 2001 that GATS "has the potential to open up all aspects of a national economy to foreign competition including public sector services such as libraries."[30]

In *Constraining Public Libraries: The World Trade Organization's General Agreement on Trade in Services*, Samuel Trosow and Kirsti Nilsen detail the library services that can be done by for-profit corporations. One area is the selection of books which is increasingly being handled by private-sector international vendors. One major example of private vendors is the Ingram Book Group which boasts of being "the world's largest wholesale distributor of book product."[31] Ingram Library Services, one member of the Ingram Book Group, "provides an array of programs and services tailored to meet the specific needs of public, school, and college libraries."[32] Another member of the Ingram Book Group, Coutts Information Services, provides a full array of services including supplying books, "collection management and shelf-ready services."[33] "We understand libraries," asserts the Coutts Web site, "We understand the challenges facing today's libraries. Through continued investment in people and by staying ahead in technology we help libraries meet those challenges."[34] Through a system called OASIS, Coutts offers "a complete online interface for bibliographic information and searching, book and eBook acquisition, collection development and workflow management."[35]

There are other information and publishing services that are supplanting libraries. There are many so-called global knowledge companies including publishers who benefit from a global free market such as Bertelsmann, HCIRN, Holtzbrinck Publishers, Informa, Pearson Education, Reed Elsevier, The McGraw-Hill Companies, and Thomson.[36] All of these companies include publishing and vast information systems. For instance, Bertelsmann, which identifies itself as "media worldwide," is composed of six corporate divisions including media groups RTL, Aravato, DirectGroup, and BMG. It also owns Random House book publishers and a magazine and newspaper conglomerate called G+J.[37] HCRIN stands for Human-Computer Interaction Resource Network and it is comprised of, among other products, Kluwer Academic Publishers.[38]

The global publishing and information conglomerates are vast. With home offices in Stuttgart, Germany, Holtzbrinck Publishers describes its company as: "active in more than 80 countries and publishes works in both print and electronic media, providing information, disseminating knowledge, and serving the needs of educational, professional, and general readership markets."[39] In the United States alone, the company owns Audio Renaissance, Bedford/St. Martin's, Farrar, Straus & Giroux, Henry Holt and Company, Palgrave Macmillan, Picador, St. Martin's Press, Tor Books, W.H. Freeman, Bedford, Freeman and Worth Publishing Group, and Worth Publishers.[40] Informa, which advertises that it provides "Specialist Information for Global Markets," owns an array of publications including Taylor & Francis Group comprised of Routledge, Garland Science, and Psychology Press.[41]

Pearson, headquartered in England, boasts that it "is an international media company with world-leading publishing and data services for education, business information and consumer publishing."[42] With 29,000 employees working in 60 countries, Pearson lists its valuable assets as the Financial Times, Penguin, Dorling Kindersley, Scott Foresman, Prentice Hall, Addison Wesley, and Longman. The company's Web site declares: "From our roots as the world's largest book publisher, we've grown to provide a range of related services: testing and learning software for students of all ages; data for financial institutions; public information systems for government departments."[43] Pearson Education North Asia has offices in China, Korea, Japan, and Taiwan and offers pre-K to adult English Language Teaching (ELT) resources, including Longman dictionaries, companion Web sites, and teaching tools. Pearson Education Indochina, which includes Cambodia, Laos, Myanmar, Thailand, and Vietnam and Pearson Education India, offers pre-K–12 ELT, materials for higher education, and professional/technical print and online resources. In India, the company sells sixty locally produced books for school and college.

McGraw-Hill boldly displays the companies' global economic philosophy on its Web site:

McGraw-Hill aligns with three enduring global needs
- the need for Capital
- the need for Knowledge
- the need for Transparency

"These are the foundations necessary to foster economic growth and to allow individuals, markets and societies to reach their full potential."[44]

In the 1990s, McGraw-Hill began focusing on three global markets—education, financial services, and media. With headquarters in New York City and offices in ten Asia-Pacific, eleven Latin American, and eight European countries, McGraw-Hill is a major player in global publishing and information services. Like other global conglomerates, McGraw-Hill is involved in a range of activities including magazines, broadcasting, television, investor education, research services, network information solutions, databases, geospatial tools, and, of course, education publishing.[45] Education publishing is broken down into a number of divisions including McGraw-Hill Education International with education offices and individual Web sites for Asia, Australia, Europe, Spain, Latin America, Canada, the United Kingdom and India. The company is also involved in testing programs through CTB/McGraw-Hill division.[46]

Many of these global information and publishing corporations target developing countries such as Springer Science+Business Media corporation, which states in its Developing Countries Initiatives: "As a global scientific, technical and medical publisher, we are aware of the role we play in the distribution of scientific information and access to knowledge and research. We make a concerted effort to ensure that the knowledge we manage is also accessible in those parts of the world that are still developing."[47]

## Global Testing Services: Standardization of Subjects and Global Intercultural English

What is the cultural effect on students preparing for the same examinations? Does the global marketing of tests and testing programs of international organizations contribute to a uniformity of world education culture and promotion of English as the global language? Is worldwide testing leading to a global standardization of knowledge in professional fields? At this time any answer would have to be speculative since there is no concrete evidence about the effect of global testing programs. However, one could argue that if students worldwide are preparing for similar tests than they are being exposed to a uniform educational and professional culture which might contribute to creating a world culture.

The International Association for the Evaluation of Educational (IEA) first demonstrated the possibility of making comparisons between test scores of different nations. Founded in 1967 with origins dating back to a UNESCO gathering in 1958, the IEA initially attempted to identify through testing effective educational methods that could be shared between nations. According to the organization's official history, the original group of psychometricians, educational psychologists, and sociologists thought of education as global enterprise to be evaluated by national comparisons of test scores. They "viewed the world as a natural educational laboratory, where different school systems experiment in different ways to obtain optimal results in the education of their youth."[48] They assumed that educational goals were similar between nations but that the methods of achieving those goals were different. International testing, it was believed, would reveal to the world community the best educational practices. The organization tried to prove that large-scale cross-cultural testing was possible when between 1959–1962 they tested thirteen-year-olds in twelve countries in mathematics, reading comprehension, geography, science, and non-verbal ability. The results of this project showed, according to an IEA statement, that "it is possible to construct common tests and questionnaires that 'work' cross-culturally. Furthermore, the study revealed that the effects of language differences can be minimized through the careful translation of instruments."[49]

Besides demonstrating the possibility of global testing programs, IEA claimed to have an effect on the curriculum of participating nations. After a 1970 seminar on Curriculum Development and Evaluation involving twenty-three countries, IEA officials claimed that "this seminar had a major influence on curriculum development in at least two-thirds of the countries that attended."[50] Through the years IEA has conducted a number of international testing programs and studies, including First International Mathematics Study (FIMS), International Mathematics Study (SIMS), International Science Study (ISS), Preprimary Education (PPP), Computers in Education Study (COMPED), Information Technology in Education (ITE), Civic Education Study (CIVED), and Languages in Education Study (LES).

In 1995 IEA worked with OECD to collect data for the Third International Mathematics and Science Study (TIMSS). In chapter 3, I mentioned OECD's global testing products, the Programme for International Student Assessment (PISA) and the Trends in International Mathematics and Science Study (TIMSS). As I suggested, these tests are creating global standards for the knowledge required to function in what OECD defines as the everyday life of a global economy. Also, the tests are serving as an "Academic Olympiad" with nations comparing the scores of their students with those of other nations. The result is national education policy leaders trying to plan their curriculum to meet the challenge of OECD testing particularly preparation for TIMSS. IEA officials called 1995 TIMSS "the largest and most ambitious study of comparative education undertaken."[51] And they claimed that: "It was made possible by virtue of IEA experience and expertise, developed through the years of consecutive studies, which saw research vision combining with practical needs as defined by educational policy-makers."[52]

Today, IEA remains a possible source for creating uniform worldwide educational practices. The organization's stated goal is to create global educational benchmarks by which educational systems can be judged. In fact, the mission statement given below includes the creation of a global network of educational evaluators.

### IEA Mission Statement

Through its comparative research and assessment projects, IEA aims to:

- provide international benchmarks that may assist policy-makers in identifying the comparative strength and weaknesses of their educational systems
- provide high-quality data that will increase policy-makers' understanding of key school- and non-school-based factors that influence teaching and learning
- provide high-quality data which will serve as a resource for identifying areas of concern and action, and for preparing and evaluating educational reforms
- develop and improve educational systems' capacity to engage in national strategies for educational monitoring and improvement
- contribute to development of the world-wide community of researchers in educational evaluation[53]

The worldwide standardization of professional knowledge might be a result of the marketing prowess of Pearson, the global corporation discussed in the last section. Pearson markets its international computer-based tests through its Pearson VUE division. According to the company's official history, the Virtual University Enterprises (VUE) was established in 1994 by three pioneers in the field of electronic tests, including the developer of the first electronic system, E. Clarke Porter. Pearson purchased VUE in 2000. In 2006, Pearson acquired Promissor, a provider of knowledge measurement services, which certifies professionals in a variety of fields. Focusing on the certification of professionals, Pearson VUE serves 162 countries with 4,400 Pearson VUE Testing

Centers. "Today," according to its company description, "Pearson VUE, Pearson's computer-based testing business unit, serves the Information Technology industry and the professional certification, licensor, and regulatory markets. From operational centers in the United States, the United Kingdom, India, Japan, and China, the business provides a variety of services to the electronic testing market."[54]

The range of computer-based tests offered by Pearson is astonishing, and it is beyond the scope of this book to list all the tests. However, Pearson VUE provides the following categories of online tests: academic/admissions; driving tests; employment, human resources & safety; financial services, health, medicine; Information Technology (IT), insurance; legal services: real estate, appraisers and inspectors; and state regulated.[55] On December 17, 2007, Pearson VUE announced that it had signed a contract with the Association for Financial Professions to provide test development to be delivered globally in over 230 Pearson Professional Centers by its Pearson VUE Authorized Test Centers."[56] On the same date it announced renewal of its contracts with Kaplan Test Prep for delivery of the "Ultimate Practice Test" for another Pearson VUE test—the Graduate Management Admission Test.[57]

As I was writing this book, the Technology Training Center of my school, Queens College of the City University of New York, sent an e-mail to faculty announcing that "Queens College is now part of the Pearson VUE Test Center family."[58] The e-mail claimed, "Our Technology Training Center has partnered with Pearson VUE to offer the best service in delivering exams for technology, business, and other professional industry certifications. We also provide advanced, reliable technology access to many exclusive promotions and exam vouchers."[59] It was planned that the Queens College VUE test center would offer testing for admission, licensing, and employment for about forty-eight organizations and companies.

While Pearson VUE may be aiding the global standardization of professions and government licensing, worldwide language testing is possibly resulting in the standardization of a global English language as contrasted with forms of English associated with particular cultures or nations. As I discuss below, global standardization of English, which in part involves the global reach of the U.S.-based Educational Testing Services (ETS), seems to be in the form of a global business English, which allows communication across cultures in the world's workplaces. Focused primarily on work situations, it may result in teaching a limited vocabulary. This form of English may, and again I want to stress the word "may," limit the ability of workers to express in English their discontent and demands for change regarding economic, political, and social conditions. The trend to a global business English was reflected on a sign I saw in Shanghai: "Learn the English words your bosses want to hear!"

Until 2000, ETS primarily focused on the U.S. testing market. In 2000, businessman Kurt Landgraf became president and CEO turning a non-profit organization into one that looks like a for-profit with earnings of more than $800 million a year. As part of Landgraf's planning, the company expanded into 180 countries. "Our mission is not just a U.S.-oriented mission but a global mission," Landgraf is quoted in a magazine article. "We can offer educational systems to the world, but to do that, you have to take a *lesson from the commercial world* [author's emphasis]."[60] The official corporate description of ETS's global marketing is:

> ETS's Global Division and its subsidiaries fulfill ETS's mission in markets around the world. We assist businesses, educational institutions, governments, ministries of education, professional organizations, and test takers by designing, developing and delivering ETS's standard and customized measurement products and services which include assessments, preparation materials and technical assistance.[61]

An important role of the Global Division is standardizing English as a global language. Almost all of its products are for English language learners. The Division markets the widely used Test of English as a Foreign Language (TOEFL), Test of English for International Communication (TOEIC), and Test of Spoken English (TSE). TOEFL has long served as an assessment tool for determining the English language ability of foreign students seeking admission into U.S. universities. In 2002, ETS opened a Beijing, China office and began marketing TOEIC along with TOEFL. In addition, the Global Division offers TOEFL Practice Online which indirectly serves as a teaching tool for English instruction. In March, 2007 ETS proudly announced that the service had been extended to its Chinese market. The Test of English for Distance Education (TEDE) is used worldwide to determine if a student has enough skills in English to participate in online courses conducted in English. Criterion is a Web-based Online Writing Evaluation which promises to evaluate student writing skills in seconds. ETS's Criterion won highest honors from the Global Learning Consortium in 2007. In addition to all these tests associated with global English, ETS offers ProofWriter an online tool that provides immediate feedback on grammar and editing issues for English language essays.[62]

In another major step in the global standardization of English, ETS and G2nd Systems signed an agreement in 2007 for G2nd Systems to join ETS's Preferred Vendor Network and to use TOEIC. G2nd Systems is promoting an intercultural form of English for use in the global workplace. "G2nd Systems defines the way people use non-culture-specific

English in workplace environments as intercultural English, which is not the same as any national version of English that naturally includes cultural presumptions, idioms and local ways of communicating ideas," explains Lorelei Carobolante, CEO of G2nd Systems in a news release from ETS. "TOEIC test scores indicate how well people can communicate in English with others in today's globally diverse workplace. G2nd Systems recognizes that measuring proficiency in English speaking and writing capabilities allows business professionals, teams and organizations to implement focused language strategies that will improve organizational effectiveness, customer satisfaction and employee productivity."[63]

A for-profit corporation, G2nd advertises itself as "Global Collaborative Business Environments across multiple cultures at the same time!" and "Global SecondLanguage Approach." The corporate announcement of its affiliation with ETS states: "Today, over 5,000 corporations in more than 60 countries use the TOEIC test, and 4.5 million people take the test every year."[64] G2nd Systems offers instruction in an intercultural form of English as opposed to the Englishes of particular countries, such as India, Britain or the United States. Referring to "Intercultural English—A New Global Tool," the company explains, "Intercultural English developed in response to the new dynamics emerging in today's global business environment, characterized by multiple cultures operating in a collaborative structure to execute projects that are often geographically dispersed."[65] Highlighting the supposedly culturally neutral form of English taught by the organization it claims: "Intercultural English is a communication tool rather than a national version of any language, and *this tool is as vital as mathematics or computer literacy in facilitating normal business processes*" (author's emphasis).[66]

In summary, the expansion of international testing might be resulting in global standardization of school subjects, professional knowledge requirements, and English. It would be interesting to analysis the content of all the various tests offered by Pearson on the standardization of professional knowledge. By using online tests, Pearson is able to engage in global marketing. It would seem hard to deny that between ETS's range of English tests, its online services in English composition, and its connection with G2nd Systems that it is having a global impact on how English is spoken and written. Can English as a global language be standardized so that it is not identified with a particular culture or nation?

## The Apollo Group and the University of Phoenix: A New Model for a Global University?

Are the University of Phoenix and Phoenix University Online the new models for consumer-oriented universities selling pre-packaged knowledge? Both for-profit university systems are part of a conglomerate owned

by the Apollo Group, owner of the Institute for Professional Development, the College for Financial Planning, Western International University and Insight Schools, based in Portland, Oregon, and offer K–12
online education.[67] The University of Phoenix operates campus locations
for face-to-face instruction in twenty-six states and Puerto Rico in the
United States, and in Canada and the Netherlands. Phoenix University
Online enrolls students from forty different countries.[68]

The University of Phoenix is based on a consumer model of adult education. Founded in 1973 before the advent of online learning, its founder
John Sperling believed "that lifelong employment with a single employer
would be replaced by lifelong learning and employment with a variety
of employers. Lifelong learning requires an institution dedicated solely
to the education of working adults."[69] At the time, Sperling found that
there was a gradual shift in higher education demographics from a student population dominated by youth to one in which approximately half
the students were adults of whom 80 percent worked. Sperling believed
that lifelong employment with a single employer would be replaced by
lifelong learning and employment with a variety of employers. According to Sperling, working adult students were invisible on the traditional
campus and were treated as second-class citizens.[70]

In the end, Sperling turned higher education into a consumer-oriented
enterprise and significantly changed faculty work. Like a factory, the
University of Phoenix and Phoenix University Online sell prepackaged
courses. The focus on working adults, the company claims, "informs
the University's teaching and learning model, approach to designing and
providing student services, and academic and administrative structure.
It also guides the institution as it plans and prepares to meet the needs of
working adult students."[71]

Craig Swenson, Provost and Senior Vice-President for Academic
Affairs at the University of Phoenix, describes what it means to provide
consumers with a standardized educational experience. Like shopping
malls, "campuses and learning centers are located at strategic locations
near major freeways and thoroughfares that permit convenient access."[72]
Classes are scheduled after the usual working hours and on weekends.
This model was significantly changed with the introduction of online
courses which allows students to select learning at their own conve-
nience. According to Swenson, students expect the same level of service
as any all-night store which means "24 × 7 access to student services"
including the online purchase of textbooks and class materials, and
access to learning programs.

How does the University of Phoenix standardize its courses? The most
important step in this process is changing the role of faculty members.
Swenson refers to this as the unbundling and disaggregation of the tra-

ditional faculty model. What this means in practice is taking traditional faculty roles and turning them over to specialists; the factory model. For instance, traditionally individual faculty members make decisions about the readings, class assignments, topics and assessments in a particular course. The only requirement is that the content of the course be related to its description in the college catalogue.

At the University of Phoenix, a contracted faculty team, meaning they receive compensation for their activities, works under the supervision of a "curriculum development manager" and an "instructional designer" to create syllabi and instructional modules for each course. The contracted team is composed of core full-time faculty and part-time "practitioner" faculty; the University prefers *not* to use the word adjuncts for these part-timers. The curriculum development manager oversees the document process in course planning while the instructional designer ensures that the syllabi and instructional module fit program objectives and the University's learning goals.[73]

The content of instruction is tightly controlled through a combination of the design process for the syllabi and modules and an assessment system. The University has instituted assessment systems which it claims to "have brought significant public recognition to University of Phoenix."[74] These assessment systems are reminiscent of those advocated by human capital educators for public school systems. There are two systems. The Academic Quality Management System, which evaluates the performance of faculty, curriculum, and student services, while the Adult Learning Outcomes Assessment measures students learning.

In 2008, the Apollo Group was found guilty of fraud by a U.S. federal court for hiding from its investors a U.S. Department of Education complaint that the University of Phoenix violated federal regulations by paying enrollment counselors solely on the bases of their ability to recruit students.[75] At first glance this would seem to be a reasonable way for a corporation to reward employees. However, the University of Phoenix seemed to have confused methods that might be appropriate for most corporations with the ethical requirements and governing laws for educational institutions. Rewarding recruiters for the number of students they enroll could encourage charlatanism and hucksterism; an almost inevitable problem for for-profit education institutions.

The University of Phoenix and Phoenix University Online's model of control over the content of instruction reflects, one could argue, the corporate composition of the Apollo Group, Inc. The executives and directors of the Apollo Group, Inc. represent the intersection of education and financial institutions. Sperling, a former college professor, remains Acting Executive Chairman of the Board of Directors. The Executive Vice President of Global Strategy, Gregory W. Cappelli, spent ten years as a research analyst for Credit Suisse, where he was Managing Director and Senior Research Analyst and founded the Credit Suisse Global Services Teams. Dino J. DeConcini, the Lead Independent Director, was a Vice President and Senior Associate of Project International, Inc., an international business consulting firm. Director K. Sue Redman was a Vice President and Corporate Controller at AdvancePCS. From 1980 to 1999, she was an Assurance/Business Advisory Services partner with PricewaterhouseCoopers LLP where she provided accounting and consulting services to both public and private companies in a variety of industries. Director James R. Reis is also Executive Vice President of GAINSCO, INC. and was involved in merchant banking and management consulting services through First Western Capital, LLC. He also served as vice chairman of ING Pilgrim Capital Corporation, an asset management company. And the director, who on the surface seems less qualified than others for managing educational services, is George Zimmer the founder, CEO and Chairman of Men's Wearhouse, Inc.[76]

## The Globalization of Higher Education

Similar to other educational services, higher education is engaging in marketing and selling of its training and knowledge-creating functions. Higher education has become a globalized enterprise. Similar to the events discussed in chapter 1 that led to the worldwide spread of Western models of mass schooling, Western models of higher education have been globalized. Nothing better symbolizes the assumption that higher education is globally similar in its structure and educational practices than the 1998 issuance by UNESCO of the World Declaration on Higher Education for the Twenty-First Century.[77] Similar to other United Nations educational documents that assume that all national school systems are divided into primary and secondary schools, this declaration was issued without any members raising the question about whether or not something called higher education existed worldwide and that it had a similar organization across nations.

In the twenty-first century higher education is a global business engaging in marketing strategies to sell their knowledge-based products, attract foreign students, and establish international branches. This means that university leaders now spend time trying to sell their products to others in a global market. Higher education is a knowledge producing enterprise which through research can help corporations in the areas of product development, business management, production technology, information technology, corporate training, public relations, human relations, sales, and marketing. Its other contribution is improvement of human capital through the education of white-collar workers, scientist and engineers, and professionals.

There are critics of this trend. Schugurensky has provided a useful summary of these criticisms against the background of the history of Western higher education.[78] He has identified three historical periods in the history of higher education. First is the early liberal tradition that saw the role of the university as protecting the moral and cultural values. The second is the human capital role of the university as a service station attending to the needs of corporations and public institutions through research and education. A third is the role of the university in promoting social justice and social transformation. This role fits the progressive education model discussed in chapter 1. Recently the human capital model combined with the concept of the service university to create institutions interested in expanding markets and making money with academics becoming entrepreneurs and knowledge treated as a commodity. Critics bemoan the loss of the liberal and social justice traditions in higher education.[79]

### Global Concepts of Higher Education

Global policy statements on higher education have captured some of the historical elements discussed by Schugurensky. There are variations in these statements. For instance, UNESCO's 1998 World Declaration on Higher Education for the Twenty-First Century provides more emphasis on social justice issues than the pronouncements of OECD.[80] However, as I will discuss later in this section, it appears that higher education systems in the twenty-first century are primarily serving corporate enterprises while operating like business enterprises.

The 1998 UNESCO World Conference on Education in the Twenty-first Century was certainly a global affair with representatives from over 180 countries in attendance along with teachers and students. UNESCO convened the World Conference to establish the principles for reforming higher education in the twenty-first century. Reflecting an acceptance of a globalized form of higher education and the participation of all nations in higher education, UNESCO referred in its World Conference goals to a generalized "mankind" when declaring as its intention to forge and confirm "the values and principles laid down in the constitution of UNESCO for the intellectual and moral solidarity of mankind."[81]

What does "intellectual and moral solidarity" mean in the World Declaration on Higher Education for the Twenty-First Century? Let us consider Article 1 of the Declaration:

Mission to Educate, to Train, and to undertake Research
We affirm that the core missions and values of higher education, in particular the mission to contribute to the sustainable development and improvement of society as a whole, should be preserved, reinforced, and further expanded, namely, to:

- educate highly qualified graduates and responsible citizens able to meet the needs of all sectors of human activity, by offering relevant qualifications, including professional training, which combine high-level knowledge and skills, using courses and content continually tailored to the present and future needs of society;
- provide opportunities for higher learning and for learning through-out life, giving to learners an optimal range of choice and a flexibility of entry and exit points within the system, as well as an opportunity for individual development and social mobility in order to educate for citizenship and for active participation in society, with a world-wide vision, for endogenous capacity-building, and for the consoli-dation of human rights, sustainable development, democracy and peace, in a context of justice;
- advance, create and disseminate knowledge through research and provide, as part of its service to the community, relevant expertise to assist societies in cultural, social and economic development, pro-moting and developing scientific and technological research as well as research in the social sciences, the humanities and the creative arts;
- help understand, interpret, preserve, enhance, promote and dissemi-nate national and regional, international and historic cultures, in a context of cultural pluralism and diversity;
- help protect and enhance societal values by training young people in the values which form the basis of democratic citizenship and by providing critical and detached perspectives to assist in the dis-cussion of strategic options and the reinforcement of humanistic perspectives;
- contribute to the development and improvement of education at all levels, including through the training of teachers.[82]

First, I would like to reiterate that the missions and goals of the Declaration are addressed to all systems of higher education with the assumption that globally they are similar in structure and practices. The first three goals of the Declaration place higher education in the catego-ries that Schugurensky called the human capital and service functions of the university. The first and second goals of Article 1 identify the main goals of higher education to be human capital and lifelong learn-ing which places higher education in role of preparing students for the knowledge economy. However, the second goal contains values of social justice when it includes in lifelong learning a goal of "consolidation of human rights, sustainable development, democracy and peace, in a con-text of justice." The third goal identifies the role of higher education as a knowledge-creator in which research serves "cultural, social and economic development."

Goals four and five can be linked to OECD's concerns with social cohesion discussed in chapter 3. Fears of strife between cultures as a result of global migration and the breakdown of a sense of national solidarity are in concerns with preserving historic cultures in the context of "cultural pluralism and diversity." The fifth goal could be considered as trying to maintain civic order by teaching what Schugurensky's referred to as the liberal and social transformative traditions in higher education. And the final goal seems to suggest that higher education should train students to be dedicated to the improvement of the current globalized form of primary and secondary education including the training of teachers.

In general, UNESCO's World Declaration on Higher Education for the Twenty-First Century is hardly a revolutionary document. The answer to the previously posed question about the meaning of "intellectual and moral solidarity" is that globalized forms of higher education will teach similar values to all students. For instance in the third goal, higher education is given the job of protecting "societal values." This goal does not suggest the teaching of different social values but implies that all nations operate by the same "societal values."

Neglecting some of the progressive qualities of the UNESCO Declaration, OECD links the goals of higher education to the workings of a knowledge economy. These goals are clearly expressed in *Higher Education and Regions: Globally Competitive, Locally Engaged*.[83] The opening statement of the Executive Summary of this 2007 book presents a clear statement of the role of higher education in a global knowledge economy:

> In order to be competitive in the globalizing knowledge economy, the OECD countries need to invest in their innovation systems at the national and regional levels. As countries are turning their production towards value-added segments and knowledge-intensive products and services, there is greater dependency on access to new technologies, knowledge and skills ... HEIs [higher education institutions] must do more than simply educate and research—they must engage with others in their regions, provide opportunities for lifelong learning and contribute to the development of knowledge-intensive jobs.[84]

Regarding human capital, OECD asserts: "Higher education can contribute to human capital development ... through educating a wider range of individuals in the local area, ensuring that they are employable when they leave education, helping local employers by responding to new skills requirements, ensuring that employees go on learning by supporting continuous professional development, and helping attract talent from outside."[85]

OECD contends that there has been a neglect of social service by higher education: "Regional development is not only about helping business thrive: wider forms of development both serve economic goals and are ends in themselves. HEIs have long seen service to the community as part of their role, yet this function is often underdeveloped."[86] This statement should not be interpreted as OECD supporting the role of higher education in social transformation. From the examples of how some university systems can render social service, their goals are very limited. They provide four examples. The first is mandatory social service for Mexican university students. The second is the engagement of higher education in public health issues. The third is the role of European universities in creating a sense of unity to the European Union and supporting diversity and multiculturalism. And lastly, without mentioning any specific university or higher education system, they suggest that higher education can play an important role in environmentalism.[87] While public health, multiculturalism, and environmentalist are important there is little emphasis on the liberal tradition that promised a level of humaneness to society or the transformative tradition that hoped that graduates would work for social justice including the elimination of poverty and closing the gap between the rich and poor. Both OECD and UNESCO members assume that national higher education systems are similar in structure and curricula. This global uniformity is highlighted by the ability of universities to globally market their products.

## The Global Marketing of Higher Education

"China is looking to Africa for students. Malaysia aims to become a regional education hub. Britain just made it easier for foreign students to stay on and work after graduation. The competition for foreign students has become heated and complex," reports the *Chronicle of Higher Education*.[88] Operated as businesses, higher education administrators are interested in marketing their products to attract foreign students, establish branches in other countries, and sell the products of campus research. Spending on tuition and living expenses by foreign students provide an important source of income. Higher education systems and countries work hard to attract students including, as discussed below, engaging in advertising and public relations campaigns. Most foreign students attend colleges in English-speaking countries; Singapore is becoming a student destination because it can offer Western-style education in English at a low cost. On the other hand, China has increased its foreign enrollments from 45,000 in 1999 to more than 141,000 in 2005, largely, according to the *Chronicle of Higher Education*, "by increasing the quality of its research institutions."[89]

Ravinder Sidhu's *Universities and Globalization: To Market, To Market* captures the commodification of higher education by examining marketing strategies.[90] Branding is an important aspect of this marketing. The concept of branding dates back to the early twentieth century when manufacturers used advertising to create brand loyalty and confidence among consumers that they could trust a particular brand name.[91] University administrators attempt to accomplish the same thing by creating symbols and slogans to attract students and to open branches in other countries. Sidhu investigates this branding and marketing phenomenon in universities in the three major English-speaking countries engaged in global marketing—the United States, the United Kingdom, and Australia.

Sidhu's first examples are Stanford University and Stony Brook State University of New York. Stanford's approach to marketing is low-key reflecting, according to Sidhu, the elite status of the school. It is already an established brand name among global universities. The marketing emphasis at Stanford is on interdisciplinary inquiry and a culture of innovation as captured in its motto "the wind of freedom blows" and Web site examples like "Stanford ideas that changed the world."[92] Stony Brook issued a generic promotional brochure filled with images highlighting a diverse faculty and student body. Designed to attract foreign students, the pamphlet presents the University as a showcase, according to Sidhu, for "multidisciplinary and multicultural talents."[93]

In the 1990s, the United Kingdom developed a new image for global markets. This was the goal of the 1998 Brand Report of the British Council's Education Counseling Services which involved the hiring of companies involved in market research, public relations, and advertising. The British education brand stresses terms, such as elite, investment, ambition, ownership, and movers and shakers. Foreign students are presented as "ambitious ... movers and shakers when they return to their countries ... They know that an education in an English-speaking country is a passport to intellectual citizenship in the world."[94] Using a combination of historical images of UK institutions and promises of economic success, British higher education promises the foreign student, "A chance to be the best."[95] One British Council ad that Sidhu includes in her book shows a generic dark-skinned male staring supposedly with an overlay of the words "Postgraduate courses" intersected at 90 degrees with the words "Be the best you can be." Inside the commonly used "o" is the "UK" logo.[96] Another ad shows a Japanese student with the logo "UK" superimposed on her statement: "I was a bit nervous to begin with, but I'm settling in now and making friends from so many different countries."[97]

Australian universities have expanded their markets by taking advantage of their close proximity to Asian nations and by being English-speaking. Jan Currie, the Vice Chancellor of Murdoch University, issued his vision of higher education in a 1996 report titled *Preparing the University for the Twenty-first Century*. Based on this vision, the University developed what it called its "Four Pillars," which could be used by any corporation:

- develop market attractiveness
- diversify income streams
- build on management efficiency and effectiveness
- create an entrepreneurial culture.[98]

Developing "market attractiveness" and diversifying "income streams," reflected efforts by Australian schools to attract foreign students and establish branches in other countries. This led to major advertising efforts. For instance one ad for QUT, an amalgamation of the Queensland Institute of Technology and Kelvin Grove College of Advanced Education, shows a runner wearing a tee shirt emblazoned with the name Accenture, which is described as one the world's leading consultants on management and technology. Across the picture are splashed the words: "QUT business graduate," "Real global giant," and "Runner."[99] QUT positioned itself a global university to attract foreign students with the ad "Our campuses are cosmopolitan ... a significant proportion of our students speak at least one other language than English."[100]

Establishing branch campuses is another means of reaching foreign students. The previously mentioned Dubai's Knowledge Village exemplifies the trade in higher education services. The Village claims to be "the world's only Free Zone totally focused on professional training and learning support services."[101] Dubai, one of seven emirates in the federation of United Arab Emirates, founded Dubai Knowledge Village, according to its official Web site, "as part of a long-term economic strategy to develop the region's talent pool and accelerate its move into a knowledge-based economy."[102] Inviting educational services from other nations to participate, the government promised protection of their income: "Benefits for Dubai Knowledge Village partners include 100% foreign ownership, 100% freedom from taxes, 100% repatriation of assets and profits and effortless visa issuance procedures."[103] Knowledge Village consists of branches of universities located in India, Russia, Pakistan, Iran, England, and Australia. One member of the Village is SAE Institute, the largest global provider of training in educational media services with branches throughout Asia, Europe, North America, and the Middle East. SAE's mission statement expresses its goals:

As the world's largest network of media Institutes, SAE Institute will continue to set the pace for a new level of Higher Education &

Vocational Technology training on its existing individual, corporate and government platform by an ongoing process of updating its worldwide campuses.... SAE will also maintain its focus capitalizing on its existing internationally recognized quality profile & accreditation.[104]

Nearby another member of the United Arab Emirates, Abu Dhabi, contracted with Singapore's National Institute of Education to help establish the Emirates College for Advanced Education (ECEA), which has the stated mission: "To become the premier center for teacher education and develop the UAE and the Gulf."[105] Reflecting the commercial nature of selling educational services in an international market, Singapore's National Institute of Education (NIE) reported its contract with Abu Dhabi under "Corporate Developments" in its quarterly publication *News*.[106] The publication explained the financial relationship: "NIE was pivotal in the founding of ECEA after signing a contract with Abu Dhabi Education Council in October 2006 on the provision of related services culminating in the setup of the college."[107]

There are several important things to note about Singapore's sale of educational services to Abu Dhabi and its contribution to the growth of a world education culture. Singapore's NIE relies on global educational research and its own research to guide educational practices and services. For instance, in the same issue of *News* announcing the contract with Abu Dhabi there was an article announcing the founding of a worldwide alliance of dean's of education at the NIE in August 2007. The Institute hosted deans from Denmark's University of Aarhus, Beijing Normal University, University of London, University of Melbourne, Seoul National University, Ontario Institute for Studies in Education, and the University of Wisconsin-Madison. The goal of this new international network is described as: "The alliance acts as a think tank to influence the sector globally, drawing together existing expertise and research ... In doing so, it aims to influence governments, international agencies, funding bodies and the public at large to enhance the profile and quality of education internationally."[108]

Abu Dhabi has also recruited New York University (NYU) to open a branch campus which will be called "NYU Abu Dhabi." A 2007 NYU press release proudly carried the following subtitles: "Important Step in Transforming NYU into a 'Global Network University'" and "First Comprehensive Liberal Arts Campus Abroad Developed by a Major U.S. Research University."[109] The Abu Dhabi government agreed to provide the land, funding, construction, equipment and maintenance of the branch campus. The President of NYU, John Sexton, used the term "idea capitals" when referring to research universities. One can imagine a world map dotted with indicators of the "idea capitals." Regarding the global spread of research universities, Sexton stated, "the evolving global dynamic will bring about the emergence of a set of world centers of intellectual, cultural, and educational strength; and a recognition that research universities will be key to these 'idea capitals'."[110]

In summary, higher education is rushing to market its products by engaging in public relations campaigns, branding, recruiting foreign students and establishing branch campuses. Both government-operated and for-profit schools are tending to operate along the lines of corporations with entrepreneurial faculty and administrators. Will the new global map, as President Sexton of NYU suggests, indicate the location of the new corporate-like idea capitals?

## Higher Education and English

Along with the previously discussed testing and writing programs of ETS and G2nd Systems, the domination of English-speaking institutions in the global trade in educational services contributes to the growth of English as the global language. For instance, while Singapore officially recognizes and supports the use of the languages of their multicultural population, the official language of its higher education institutions is English. English is the language used in NIE's publications, classes, and hosted conferences. The program the Institute helped establish in Abu Dhabi includes preparing future teachers to teach English. The Emirates College for Advanced Education describes its Bachelor of Education program as preparing "trainee educators to teach in grades K-5, specializing in English, Math, and Science."[111]

The Director of the Center for International Higher Education, Philip Altbach, describes the dominant role of English in the global trade in educational services in an article with the descriptive title, "The Imperial Tongue: English as the Dominating Academic Language."[112] Besides being the language of global commerce, Altbach states, "English now serves as the main international academic language."[113] The reasons for the dominant role of English in academic circles is clear. The United States spends half of the world's R&D funds and English-speaking nations (U.S., Canada, Great Britain, and Australia) accommodate more than half of the world's international students. In addition, according to Altbach, the editors of the major scientific and scholarly journals primarily work at English-speaking universities and the journals are published in English. Also, English is the world's most widely studied second language at all levels of the education ladder. The majority of academic Web sites are in English. Universities throughout the world are offering degree programs in English.[114]

As a result, English-speaking countries are in the forefront of establishing branch campuses in other countries. As Altbach states, "The worldwide branch campus movement for the most part uses English as the medium of instruction. The United States, Australia, and the United Kingdom have been most active in establishing branch campuses, and it is not surprising that English is the medium of instruction."[115] Even branches of universities from non-English speaking countries often use English as the medium of instruction. In addition, Altbach claims that curricular developments in higher education are reported in English and often come from English-speaking countries. This aids the development of a global educational culture. Altbach predicts the continued domination of English and, as a result, the domination of trade in educational services from English-speaking countries. Altbach concludes, "If globalization determines the direction of the world economy, science, and other factors, then the growth of English as the global language of science and scholarship is inevitable for the foreseeable future."[116] In the context of GATS, Altbach argues that it will force nations to be receptive to foreign educational services. He asserts, "Should GATS be widely implemented, this will inevitably mean the English-language institutions and programs will further entrench themselves worldwide."[117] In summary, English is the main language in the global trade in educational services resulting in English-speaking nations being in the forefront of the worldwide marketing of higher education and other educational services.

## Higher Education Networks

Underlying the marketing of higher education is a vast global network of university administrators, government education officials, research associations, and international scholarly organizations. The list of international scholarly organizations is too vast to discuss in this book, but they range across academic disciplines including, but not limited to, history, literature, languages, science, mathematics, economics, education, sociology, philosophy, political science, geography, and anthropology. Each of these disciplines has sub-disciplines that hold international meetings. The existence of these global scholarly organizations and meetings is made possible, as Altbach suggests, by the common academic use of English and modern transportation systems.

What is the effect of the increasing international network of academic scholars? It would be interesting to investigate each discipline to determine the consequences of these global academic contacts; a project that would take specialists from each discipline. However, it can be easily imagined what might be the results. First, there is the possibility of worldwide scholarly interactions resulting in common intellectual paradigms within each discipline. Second, there could result a common global academic culture. Third, as part of the process of global academic sharing, there can be mutual influences that fundamentally change the thinking of an academic culture. This has certainly happened in the field of cross-cultural psychology where researchers consistently note cultural differences in thought and as a result scholars in the discipline tend to think biculturally.[118] Since it is impossible in this book to explore all the academic networks, I will focus on university networks which seem to be creating a global university organization and culture.

One organization that has as a specific goal the globalization of higher education culture and structures is the International Association of Universities (IAU) which was founded in 1950 as a UNESCO-based organization. The membership is drawn from 150 countries and collaborates with other international, regional, and national organizations. The organization's mission statement encourages the globalization of practices in higher education. "By encouraging members to work together," the organization's mission statement asserts, the IAU:

- Facilitates the exchange of experience and learning and fosters cooperation;
- Restates and defends the academic values and principles that underlie and determine the proper functioning of universities and other higher education institutions;
- Upholds and contributes to the development of a long-term vision of universities' role and responsibilities in society;
- Voices the concerns for higher education with regard to policies of international bodies such as UNESCO, the World Bank and others;
- Contributes to a better understanding of current trends and policy developments through analysis, research and debate;
- Provides comprehensive and authoritative information on higher education systems, institutions and qualifications worldwide.[119]

In the context of building a world culture of higher education, the mission statement promotes common global academic values. For instance, the globalization of these academic values is captured in the goal of defending "the academic values and principles that underlie and determine the proper functioning of universities and other higher education institutions." The assumption in this statement is that there is general standard among the 180 member nations as to the "proper functioning of universities and other higher education institutions." Also, the organization promotes global cooperation in higher education and the sharing of policy developments and information.

As part of this global networking, IAU "openly" cooperates with international for-profit publishing and information services. I use the term "openly" because some might question these associations as being unethical since the IAU's mission statement calls for the defense of "academic values and principles." Of course, I might be called naive suggesting this is unethical as I often hear colleagues referring to academics as servants of power. In the case of IAU, they promote and sponsor an essay competition on higher education research called the "Palgrave Macmillan Ltd. Prize in Higher Education Policy Research." As discussed earlier in this book, Palgrave Macmillan Ltd. is one division of the huge multinational corporation Holtzbrinck Publishers. Obviously, this prize provides free advertising and functions as a public relations ploy for a publisher of books for higher education courses and scholarly research. This advertising is very cheap since the IAU/Palgrave Prize is only 1,000 British pounds awarded every two years.[120]

One wonders if there was any discussion within the IAU about providing cheap advertising for a multinational for-profit corporation. Or did the members just unquestioningly accept the intertwining of multinational corporations and higher education in the global world of education. The global climate in higher education of marketing, entrepreneurship, and the commodification of knowledge certainly lends itself to acceptance of close ties with for-profit corporations. Maybe, these are the "academic values" of the twenty-first century.

The Center for International Higher Education located at Boston College (Massachusetts) is a major higher education network. The Center's stated mission is "advancing knowledge about the complex realities of higher education in the contemporary world. The colleagues at the Center believe an international and comparative perspective is central to understanding global realities and national circumstances."[121] As part of this endeavor, the Center publishes a quarterly *International Higher Education* and operates an International Higher Education Clearinghouse. The Clearinghouse provides another network linked to other higher education networks or in the words of the Center: "The Clearinghouse create[d] a website that will provide researchers and practitioners with the perfect starting point for searching available resources-web-based 'one-stop shopping'."[122] Often neglected in educational research is the plight of Africa. The Center corrects this problem by offering an extensive International Network for Higher Education in Africa.[123]

What do the Center's networks mean for the globalization of higher education? In an article in the Center's publication, *International Higher Education,* titled "Globalization and Forces for Change in Higher Education," Altbach suggests that massification of higher education (mass access to higher education) will reflect global inequalities. Developing nations, he argues, are at a disadvantage in global competition within higher education. Altbach argues, "Academic systems and institutions that at one time could grow within national boundaries now find themselves competing internationally. National languages compete with English even within national borders. Domestic academic journals, for example, often compete with international publications within national academic systems, and scholars are pressured to publish internationally."[124] The Center's African network in part is designed to overcome these inequalities. Altbach recognizes that global networks in higher education are having a profound effect on the internationalization of higher education:

> The growth of information technology (IT) has created a virtual global community of scholarship and science. The increasing dominance of English as the key language of communicating academic knowledge is enhanced by IT. Global science provides everyone immediate access to the latest knowledge.[125]

However, Altbach believes that inequalities between nations and academic systems work against the creation of "a worldwide academic community based on cooperation and a shared vision of academic development."[126] From his perspective, as long as these inequalities exist there will be no globalized system of higher education.

## A Global University Through Higher Education Networks?

What is the global university? This was the question addressed at a 2007 London conference on Realizing the Global University.[127] Participants in the conference were members of the global network in higher education. One sponsor of the meeting had the slogan: "The Observatory: Crossing tomorrow's higher education borders today." This is the motto for The Observatory on Borderless Higher Education. The kind of global pressure on higher education administrators and their use of global networks is captured in the following testimonial for the Observatory by Vice-Chancellor of Britain's Open University Brenda Gourley that it "provides a really important service to the busy and increasingly pressurized leaders in higher education. It targets the kind of information necessary to decision-making about the strategies fundamental to survival in a complex and fast changing HE landscape. Highly recommended."[128] The Observatory provides information to higher education administrators in fifty countries and is partnered with a vast network of other international organizations including the Association of Commonwealth Universities, Universities UK, UNESCO, the World Bank, the Commonwealth of Learning, the United States Distance Learning Association, the European Distance Educational Network, and the Western Co-operative for Educational Telecommunication.

Other sponsors of the Realizing the Global University conference included the Worldwide Universities Network, Universities UK, Inter-

national Association of Universities, and the Association of Commonwealth Universities. Speakers, mostly higher education officials, were
from the United Kingdom, the World Bank, the United States, China,
Australia, Mexico, and Italy.[129] Searching for a definition of a global
university, the Conference's announcement declared: "Universities are
universal and increasingly international, but they are not yet 'global'. In
a world that is globalizing rapidly, in which the central role of universities in the knowledge economy and in civil society is articulated more
strongly and more widely than ever, we do not have a clear sense of what
it takes or what it means to be a global university."[130] In order to be
global, a university must, according to the announcement, do more than
attract international students and establish branch campuses overseas: it
"requires 'international' to pervade everything a university does and for
it to be embedded in a strategic and operational framework."[131]

What does it mean to internationalize a university beyond having
foreign students and branch campuses? Being part of international networks was one answer given Graham Spanier, President of Pennsylvania
State University: "The call to internationalize the university has gained
traction in recent years. Organizations like the Worldwide Universities
Network [Spanier was a founder of this organization] provide transcon-
tinental opportunities and bring together leaders in education to focus
attention on international education."[132] In addition, he argued, the curriculum should be "internationalized" and students should be taught a
global perspective. Also, part of being a global university, Spanier contends, is for the university to participate in cooperative global research.

"Global brand penetration," is another feature of a global university
suggested at the Conference by Eric Thomas, Vice Chancellor of the
University of Bristol and former chair of Worldwide Universities Network.[133] Most of the world's peoples, he laments, have never heard of his
own university or even the location of Bristol, England. In contrast, most
people have heard of England's most famous brand schools—Cambridge
and Oxford. Of course, he argues, this doesn't mean that every ordinary
person recognizes your school as a global brand but, he states, "I would
argue that if you wish to be considered to be a global university it is
almost a *sine qua non* that your peers and national policy makers should
see you as that."[134] Another qualification, Thomas asserts in agreement
with Spanier: "The pursuit of innovative global research is the absolutely prime characteristic and without it, a university cannot claim to
be global."[135]

Will the global university be a virtual university? In articulating their
views on the nature of a global university, Thomas and Spanier were
reflecting their efforts working with Worldwide Universities Network.
The Network is devoted to integrating its members into a "global university" using modern information and communications technology to

promote, among other things, e-learning, distance learning, cooperative research efforts, and global virtual seminars. Sixteen universities compose the membership of the Network. These schools are located in the United States, Great Britain, Australia, Canada, China, Norway, and the Netherlands. The Network's mission statement emphasizes its global goals:

> The WUN [Worldwide Universities Network] alliance exists to make significant advances in knowledge and understanding in areas of current global concern. By fostering and encouraging collaboration between members, WUN brings together the experience, equipment and expertise necessary to tackle the big issues currently facing societies, governments, corporations and education.[136]

The Network is attempting to achieve this mission by creating global research communities through its networks of contacts and using communication devices such as Web sites, video conferencing, and access grid technology. Also, faculty and students are encouraged to spend time at institutions within the network. There is also an attempt to internationalize the curricula through the "development of e-learning theory, practice and programs."[137] And finally, the Network organizes online seminars between member institutions. An example of these online seminars are those held through the Networks' Contemporary China Center for the 2007–2008 academic year. These "Virtual Seminars" covered topics involving governance and society, media and security, and environment and sustainability. Advertisements indicated start times for seminar at different locations around the globe.[138]

Competing with the Worldwide Universities Network is Universitas 21: The International Network of Higher Education. This is a network of 21 universities in thirteen countries including Australia, Canada, China, Hong Kong, India, Ireland, Japan, Mexico, New Zealand, Singapore, South Korea, Sweden, the United Kingdom, and the United States.[139] This organization claims to be the "leading global network of research universities."[140] As part of the globalization plan, the organization issued in 2003 the "Shanghai Declaration on Universitas 21 Student Mobility" which called for more global student mobility in undergraduate and graduate programs.[141] In its strategic plan it discusses four methods to guarantee that it is "the leading international higher education network." These methods include ensuring that the organization is recognized as the leading higher education network by national higher education commentators; maintaining links to "decision-makers and opinion-formers of global national or regional significance"; and debating issues of "global significance to higher education."[142]

What is the significance of these global higher education networks for the concept of the global university? Based on the work of higher educa-

---

## Key Points: Global Education Industries and Marketing

### Examples of For-Profit School Corporations

1. Educate, Inc.
2. Laureate Education Inc.
3. Apollo Group

### Examples of Information and Publishing Corporations

1. Ingram Book Group
2. Holtzbrinck Publishers
3. Informa
4. Pearson
5. McGraw-Hill Companies
6. Bertelsmann
7. HCIRN
8. Reed Elsevier
9. Thomson

### Examples of Testing Organizations and Corporations

1. International Association for the Evaluation of Education (IEA)
2. Pearson VUE
3. Educational Testing Services (ETS)
4. OECD

### Methods of Marketing Higher Education to Attract Foreign Students, Establish Foreign Branches, and Sell Research Products

1. Branding
2. Slogans
3. Advertising
4. Public relations

---

tion networks something called a global university would probably consist of an organization of universities from around the world that share students and faculties, engage in cooperative research, internationalize and share curricula, use e-learning, and hold virtual seminars. Most importantly, and this hasn't to my knowledge occurred, grant a diploma from the network organization rather than from a member university. One can imagine that in this global university local schools would retain their identities while surrendering their degree granting powers to the global organization. Students at all the national localities would be studying common curricula while utilizing faculty from throughout the network either through elearning, virtual classes and seminars, or moving from campus to campus. A global university might result from the work of organizations like the Observatory on Borderless Higher Education, the Worldwide Universities Network, the International Association of Universities, and Universitas 21.

## Conclusion: Name Brands and a Global University

Helped by GATS and TRIPS, the world trade in education and knowledge-related products could be contributing to a uniformity of institutions and practices. Global for-profit school corporations are presently selling worldwide similar products. International testing organizations such as OECD, Pearson, and Educational Testing Services may be ushering in an era when professionals and students will be preparing for the same examinations in their particular fields. The testing products and online language services of Educational Testing Services and G2nd Systems is standardizing a form of English to be used in global workplaces. Higher education has become a global business both in its internal operations and in its marketing systems and establishment of branch campuses. Are we entering a time when universities with world recognized brand names will franchise like fast food chains? All of these activities are occurring across global networks composed of scholars, university administrations, for-profit publishing and knowledge companies, intergovernmental organizations, and higher education organizations. However, Philip Altbach may be correct in suggesting that these trends will favor English-speaking nations, established publishing corporations and testing, and name-brand universities. Is there a global university in the world's future?

# Chapter 5

# From the Global to the Local
## Global Progressive Education
## Models and INGOs

Seldom do local schools adopt an exact copy of the policy agendas of global organizations and networks, such as the World Bank, OECD, UNESCO, higher education and scholarly networks, media, and multinational corporations. That these global structures and networks exist is a reality. However, their actual effect is determined by local conditions and people. Also, as I indicated in chapter 1, there are other global educational models in competition with those so far discussed in this book. These two factors add more complicated dimensions to the globalization of educational practices with local actors changing and adapting policies while also possibly considering progressive, indigenous, and religious educational models.

In this chapter, I will discuss the work of "culturalists" who have examined the way global policies are interpreted, adapted, and changed at the local level. These theorists focus on how local actors borrow and adapt concepts and practices from the global flow of educational ideas. Culturalists reject what they consider to be a simplistic view of world cultural theorists that national elites select the best model of schooling from global models. In addition, culturalists argue that in the global flow there are other educational ideas besides human capital education, such as multiple forms of progressive and religious education.

In addition, I examine the culturalists' assertions that global models often undergo change when adapted to local conditions. Also, they argue that there exist different global models of education rather than a single best model as maintained by world culture theorists. One is the "Progressive Education World Model" as described in chapter 1. In addition, progressive education exists in a variety of forms. The progressive model exists in a revolutionary form and as one utilized by international nongovernment organizations (INGOs), such as human rights and environmental organizations.

## Global Uniformity or Diversity of Educational Practices and Policies?

In chapter 1, I presented the basic ideas of world culture theorists that the spread of mass schooling and a uniform curriculum accompanied the spread of the Western concept of the nation state and that national policy leaders select from a global flow of best educational practices. Also, in the last three chapters, I have detailed the contribution of global organizations to a global education culture. Is this global education culture uniformly adapted to local school systems? The answer by culturalists is "no."

But saying "no" to cultural uniformity at the local level does not negate the existence of what I have called a global education superstructure interacting with local actors. The global education superstructure, as I have so far described it, is composed of intergovernmental and nongovernmental organizations; multinational publishing, information, learning and testing corporations; global media projects; global networks of educators and policymakers; and globalized forms of higher education.

It is not surprising that the influence of this global education superstructure varies with local conditions. Of course, these variations complicate the description of the globalization of educational policies and practices. Also, these variations raise the question asked by culturalists: Will global education culture result in global uniformity of educational policies and practices? It is difficult to predict the future particularly in a world of violent conflict. All that can be said at this point in time is that there does exist a growing global educational superstructure that influences local actors. Whether this will mean eventual global education uniformity or continued local diversity cannot be determined.

## Culturalists: The Anthropologists

In the next three sections, I focus my discussion on two collections of essays that were specifically organized to question the arguments of world cultural theorists.[1] One collection is edited by anthropologist Kathryn Anderson-Leavitt and the other by comparative educationist Gait Steiner-Khamsi. Anderson-Leavitt describes the differences between anthropologists and world cultural theorists: "anthropologists and many scholars in comparative education emphasize national variation.... From that point of view, the nearly 200 different national school systems in the world today represent some 200 different and diverging school cultures."[2] She goes on to state the opposing perspective of world culture theorists: "According to world culture theory, rather than diverging, schools are converging toward a single global model."[3] Referring to the transfer of educational ideas and practices from one locality to another, Steiner-Khamsi rejects the idea of a convergence toward a single global model:

> Educational transfer from one context to another not only occurs for different reasons, but also plays out differently. For example, despite all the political and economic pressure on low-income countries to comply with 'international standards' in education, imported policies do not have homogenizing effects, that is, they do not lead to a convergence of educational systems.[4]

There are areas of agreement between anthropologists and world culture theorists. There is an acceptance among anthropologists of the existence at an "abstract" level of common global practices, such as an educational ladder leading from primary to post-secondary schooling; the placement of students by age into "egg-carton" classrooms with desks facing forward or desks arranged for group work; similarity of curricula for core subjects; and a steady increase in the education of women. There are global approaches to pedagogy in some subjects such as literacy instruction where reading and writing are taught together. Also, they agree that there is a global expansion of early childhood education.

In contrast to these areas of agreement, anthropologists note variations within the globalization process. For instance, Anderson-Levitt argues that on the issue of decentralization and standardization some countries are implementing decentralization of services, site-based management, and school choice, while others are implementing plans for central governments to standardize the curriculum and control student learning and teacher performance with national standardized testing. These differences are evident regarding teacher autonomy with some national education plans emphasizing teacher professionalism and autonomy. Others are reducing teacher autonomy with standardized curricula and testing and, in some cases, requiring teachers to use scripted lessons. There are pedagogical differences with some governments emphasizing active learning and student interests while others focus on direct instruction of a mandated curriculum. Some want to protect local languages while others stress increasing instruction in world languages, particularly English.[5]

What about these inconsistencies between nations? One answer given by world culture theorists is that global educational culture and practices are still evolving and differences will disappear after full integration of the global culture. In other words, nations may begin at opposing positions but converge on the same educational policies and practices. Anderson-Levitt's example is: "Thus a U.S. system that tightened national standards and a Japanese system that deregulates schools might end up more similar than they began."[6] Another explanation is that there are cultural lags between countries.

Anderson-Levitt feels that these explanations of national differences by world culture theorists do not make sense. Is there a policy line where nations started out at opposite ends and end up converging in the center? Do cultural lags exist? For example, Anderson-Levitt wonders about the recent growth of scripted teaching in the United States and the abandonment of learner-centered pedagogy. If there exists a policy line, then the United States has moved from one end of the pedagogy line to the opposite end. There is no convergence in the middle. If there is a cultural lag, then has the United States moved forward with scripted teaching or backwards? What about reading instruction where there are major differences between pedagogies that stress whole language and meaning and those that stress phonics? Anderson-Levitt argues that rather then seeing a convergence of educational practices: "It seems more likely that we are witnessing a swing of the pendulum back and forth over the decades between phonics and reading for meaning, and between scripted and autonomous teachers."[7] Regarding the major actors contributing to globalization of education practices, Anderson-Levitt argues that they have different policies, such as the World Bank and UNESCO. As I previously stated, the World Bank does focus on human capital theory while UNESCO includes concerns about human rights. Key Points: Educational

---

### Key Points: Educational Globalization from the Perspective of Anthropologists

1. Local actors select from multiple and competing educational models existing in the global flow, such as human capital, progressive, religious and Indigenous models.
2. Global organizations offer differing world models of education.
3. Education models are often imposed by national governments rather than local actors making a free choice from the global flow.
4. Local resistance can result from imposition by national governments of education models borrowed from the global flow.
5. The implementation of education policies in local communities often differ from official policies.
6. Local actors might use the same language as educational policies and practices in the global flow but they often change the global model.

Globalization from the Perspective of Anthropologists summarizes the differences between anthropologists and world culture theorists.

## Culturalists: Comparative Education

Since the nineteenth century, scholars of comparative education have studied the flow of educational ideas and practices between nations. One of their sharpest criticisms of world culture theorists is that there exists an agreed upon global model of education. Comparative educational scholar Gita Steiner-Khamsi states, "globalization is for *real*, but the international community of experts agreeing on a common (international) model of education is *imagined*."[8] What does she mean by imagined? This concept is derived from studies of nationalism where a nation, as opposed to a government, is an imagined entity of people, politically determined boundaries, and a national culture. Nationalism often functions as an emotion of loyalty to an imagined community. Regarding claims of a world education culture, she writes, that decision makers at the national level justify their policies by "resorting to an imagined world culture in education *as if* there exists an international agreement on how reforms in education are supposed to unfold."[9]

In contrast, comparative educators discuss the global flow of education ideas and practices as a process of borrowing and lending. So, an educational policy leader in one country might borrow educational ideas from another country. However, comparative educators make a distinction between borrowing and copying. In other words, educators in one country might borrow an idea from another but local conditions often do not allow it to be copied intact resulting in some form of adaptation.

What is the effect at the local level of the major players in global educational superstructure, such as the OECD, the World Bank, UNESCO, multinational corporations, educational networks and other intergovernmental and nongovernmental organizations? This global superstructure can be described as "lending" educational ideas and practices to governments and local communities. In some cases, such as loans from the World Bank, governments are pressured to adopt their education agendas. Whether lent or through pressure there is no guarantee that a particular educational model will be exactly copied at the local level.

Why are educational models borrowed? One reason, according to Steiner-Khamsi, is their use for certifying or decertifying a local school policy. To validate or criticize a school policy, local actors might refer to an imaginary global community such as "international standards."[10] Or they might refer to the concrete policies of another nation or global organization. In either case, these external authorities are used to justify local actions. This process is called *externalization*. Externalization is particularly applicable during times of political change when local politicians search for justification for their policies which might include adoption of a new educational program or the elimination of another. In other words, during periods of political upheaval, politicians search for outside validation of their actions. But validation does not mean an exact copy of the policies of the outside authority.

Then there is "export for survival."[11] As I discussed in chapter 4, many higher education systems are exporting their schools and programs to increase revenue. What about nonprofit international organizations? They need to justify their existence to their constituencies by exporting or lending their ideas to another country. An international organization, particularly a nonprofit like the World Bank, OECD, and UNESCO, must show member countries that they are actively pursuing worldwide educational change. There is also a need to justify the income of staff and associated expenses. Also, according to Steiner-Khamsi, "prepackaged, modularized, and checklisted programs developed at the headquarters of international organizations and subsequently transferred to their field offices are easier to manage than locally developed programs."[12] Again, this export process does not mean that an educational policy or practice will be exactly copied at the local level.

For example, the results of international examinations, as discussed in chapter 4, can cause policymakers to borrow educational programs from other countries. The global "olympiad" caused by TIMMS and PISA can spur political leaders and educators to criticize or praise their educational systems depending on the test scores. International testing creates a "comparative advantage" or a "comparative disadvantage."[13] If the test results show a comparative disadvantage, then local policymakers often borrow other global or national models in an attempt to rectify test results.

In summary, comparative educators recognize the global borrowing and lending of educational policies and practices but not the existence of the world theorist's common global model of education. David Phillips provides a summary of these ideas in "Toward a Theory of Policy Attraction in Education."[14] His list of reasons nations borrow educational ideas and practices from other nations or global organizations plus my additions to the list are presented in Key Points: Reasons for Nations Borrowing Educational Policies and Practices.[15]

## Culturalists: Examples of Borrowing and Policy Transformations

In summary, the group I have called the culturalists look closely at how policies change after being borrowed and adapted to local conditions and the reasons for borrowing and lending. These arguments create

## Key Points: Reasons for Nations Borrowing Educational Policies and Practices

1. Political change prompts local actors to examine policies in other countries and those of global organizations
2. Failure of existing education policies
3. Local policy leaders borrow educational policies and practices when international examinations report poor results in comparison to other nations (comparative disadvantage)
4. To certify or decertify a local educational policy or practice
5. Dissatisfaction with existing education system
6. New configurations of government alliances such as the forming of the European Union
7. Innovations in knowledge and skills
8 Aftermath of war or natural disaster

a more complex picture of the relationship between the global educational superstructure and local communities. An example is Thailand's attempt to balance indigenous knowledge or "Thai Wisdom" with the borrowing of global educational practices. This example highlights the conditions that create a desire to borrow an educational policy and how it is adapted to local conditions. Thailand's economic collapse in 1997 prompted a search for new educational policies that would support the economy. Human capital school policies were borrowed from global education superstructures. These were incorporated into Thailand's schools with the passage of the National Education Act of 1999.[16]

"Glocalization" is the term used to describe the adaptation of these borrowed policies to Thailand's culture. A major concern of Thai leaders was protecting the indigenous culture. However, the economic crisis did not give school leaders time to develop their own reforms based on local cultural conditions. Consequently, they borrowed from existing global reform ideas. In the words of one Thai educator, Bidhya Bowornwathana, "Adopting a global reform paradigm is a good choice ... because it silences domestic differences, pleases funding agencies, and presents convenient packages of ready-made reform programs."[17]

In translating these global reform packages into the National Education Act of 1999, Thai leaders tried to balance them with preservation of Thai wisdom. The legislation called for a centralized system: "of educational quality assurance to ensure improvement of educational quality and standards at all levels. Such a system shall be comprised of both internal and external policy assurance."[18] The legislation also contained a clause: "The Ministry shall decentralize powers in educational administration regarding academic matters ... directly to the Committees and Offices for Education, Religion, and Culture of the educational service areas and the education institutions in the (local) areas."[19]

The purpose of the second clause was to ensure that local cultures would be protected even though these local cultures might have contradictory ways of life to that of the economic goals of the human capital education model. Regarding the protection of local cultures, it is important to note the reference to a combination of education, religion, and culture in the decentralization of academic matters to "Committees and Offices for Education, Religion, and Culture." In the mind of Thai school reformers, national education cannot be separate from religion and culture. Rung Kaewdang, the secretary-general of Thailand's Office of the National Education Commission, believed decentralization would ensure that school reform included protection of local cultures: "As schools will have more autonomy to decide the local curriculum they deem necessary for local children, there is a possibility that Thai wisdom will enjoy the same status as modern knowledge. Our children and adults will learn to be Thais in parallel with the internationalization [sic]."[20] Supporting the inclusion of Thai wisdom were provisions in the 1997 Thai constitution:

> Section 46: Persons so assembling as to be a traditional community shall have the right to conserve or restore their customs, local knowledge, arts....
>
> Section 81: The state shall promote local knowledge and national arts and culture....
>
> Section 289: A local government organization has the duty to conserve local arts, custom, knowledge and good [sic] culture.[21]

Consequently, global prepackaged-education ideas were borrowed in reaction to an economic crisis but were transformed by the concern for protecting local cultures. Examples of the resulting reform projects reflect this "glocalization." One involved adaptation of the curriculum to local wood craving and basket weaving communities in northern Thailand. Another curriculum was created working with local dairy farms in Central Thailand while another was designed in cooperation with rice and vegetable growing communities.[22]

Another example illustrates how the language of global education practices is used to justify existing practices. In seeking membership in the European Union, Latvia's educational leaders felt it necessary to make references to global educational concepts such as democracy, pluralism, and multiculturalism. In other words, a new political alliance prompted the borrowing of educational concepts. However, in this case the language was used to justify an existing school organization. Under Soviet control, Latvia had two parallel school systems—one using Russian as the language of instruction and the other using Latvian. These two school structures were a result of contradictory Soviet policies. One was indigenization or *korenizatsia* which was implemented prior to the actual annexation of Latvia into the Soviet Union and it supported Latvian as the language of instruction. After annexation, the Soviet government implemented its policy of assimilation or *russification* which resulted in the establishment of schools with Russian as the language of instruction. According to Iveta Silova, this dual school system contributed to Soviet power over Latvia. In Latvian language schools, there was an attempt to curb any sentiments for separation from the Soviet Union and Russian language schools ensured the loyalty of the students to the Soviet Union. In Silova's words, "Thus separate schools for Latvian students allowed for rigid control of any unwanted nationalistic sentiments. Similarly, separate schools for Russian students ensured that all students attending these schools were loyal to their external motherland, that is Russia, rather than the republic they resided in."[23]

With the collapse of the Soviet Union and the desire to enter the European Union, Latvian politicians were compelled to turn to international human rights to prove their readiness to enter the Union. What about the separate school system used to maintain Soviet power? A variety of international human rights protocols stressed protection of linguistic rights and ethnic cultures. The protection of languages is a major issue for the European Union as it brings together countries unwilling to abandon their national languages such as German, French, English, etc. Consequently, Latvian leaders adopted the language of multiculturalism and linguistic rights to justify the existing dual school system. By borrowing the language of human rights and multiculturalism, the justification for the dual school system was transformed from protecting Soviet power to the language of protecting linguistic rights.

Another example is Japan's 2008 borrowing of educational models from India because of public reaction to economic problems and declining international test scores. In the past international test scores placed Japan at the top. "That is no longer true," reported the *New York Times*, "which is why many people here are looking for lessons from India, the country the Japanese see as the world's ascendant education superpower."[24] Japanese political and educational leaders were shocked when OECD reported that Japan had fallen from being first in math skills in 2000 to tenth and from second in science in 2000 to sixth.

Worried about their educational and economic rivalry with India, Japanese bookstores stocked titles such as *Extreme Indian Arithmetic Drills* and *The Unknown Secrets of the Indians*. Japan's Indian international schools reported a surge of applications. "Japan's interest in learning from Indian education is a lot like America's interest in learning from Japanese education," asserted Kaoru Okamoto, a professor specializing in education policy at the National Graduate Institute for Policy Studies in Tokyo.[25] Okamoto recognized that internal problems and the international testing Olympiad caused national leaders to borrow educational models and practices from other countries.

Among the Japanese private schools experiencing increased applications was the Little Angels English Academy & International Kindergarten, which attracted the attention of Japanese and international newspapers and media broadcasts. Located in a Tokyo suburb with mostly Japanese students, the school uses textbooks from India and classroom posters showing animals from Indian stories. Most of the teachers are South Asian. Also, the Global Indian International school announced that 20 percent of enrollment was Japanese and that demand was so high from both Indian and Japanese parents that they are building a second campus. The India International School in Japan is also expanding both its campus and Japanese enrollments. The *New York Times* reported parents' enthusiasm: "My son's level is higher than those of other Japanese children the same age," said Eiko Kikutake, whose son Hayato, 5, attends Little Angels. "Indian education is really amazing! This wouldn't have been possible at a Japanese kindergarten."[26]

## Global Forms of Progressive Education

Rejecting the existence of a single world culture of education, culturalists frequently refer to progressive education models as one of many alternatives to human capital education. Even progressive education, as I explain in this chapter, comes in many forms. While differing types of progressive education exist, they all share the characteristics I listed in chapter 1 as the Progressive Education World Model:

Progressive Education World Model
- Teacher professionalism and autonomy
- Learning based on students' interests and participation
- Active learning
- Protection of local languages
- Education for ensuring social justice
- Education for active participation in determining social and political change

These elements take on different meaning depending on the particular educational theorist. For example, the progressivism associated with American educational philosopher John Dewey was borrowed by many Chinese educators after his visit in the early 1920s and by Soviet educators in the 1920s in the form of the Dalton plan.[27] In a different form, Paulo Freire's progressive educational ideas became part of the global educational discourse after the publication of *Pedagogy of the Oppressed* in 1968.[28]

It is not within the scope of this book to review every form of progressive education, but there is one common element in all its forms, namely *education for active participation in determining social and political change*. This common element is easily contrasted with the human capital model of educating for work within the knowledge economy. The type of participation in social change varies with each form of progressive education ranging from working within existing government structures to revolution.

Jürgen Schriewer and Carlos Martinez demonstrated the borrowing of progressive models in their comparative research on the internationalization of educational knowledge.[29] They did a content analysis of education journals in Spain, Russia/Soviet, and China from the 1920s to the mid-1990s. They found that all three nations from the 1920s to the early 1930s displayed an intense interest in global education discourses particularly in what Schriewer and Martinez call "the international progressive education movement."[30]

Their findings are important because they confirm the early existence of a global progressive education model. In their words, "Based on quantitative data … our findings have come to confirm the thesis of the internationality of the progressive education reform movement, a thesis supported thus far mainly … [by] this movement's self interpretations developed by its followers."[31]

This early global flow of progressive education ideas was not inherently revolutionary but the ideas were sometimes supported by revolutionary movements.[32] John Dewey was not a political revolutionary, and his educational ideas were never intended to foment armed rebellion. When Dewey lectured in China, he introduced ideas about basing education on the interest of the child, the social construction of the curriculum, learning by doing, the use of social imagination, and educating students for active participation in the reconstruction of society using the tools of a democratic government. He never told his audiences that they should use his ideas to arm the people to fight against control by wealthy social classes. By the time Dewey left China in 1921, he had given seventy-eight different series of lectures. At the time of his departure, 100,000 copies of his Peking lectures—a 500-hundred page book—were in circulation and three of his lectures were reprinted as classroom texts.[33] Dewey's visit was sponsored by China's Society for the Promotion of New Education, and the organization used his ideas to justify their reform proposals. In part, this organization was responsible for the Chinese government's School Reform Decree of 1922 which adopted the American school model of a six-year elementary school, a three-year junior high school, and a three-year of high school. When Dewey returned from China in 1922, he expressed his doubts on having any meaningful impact on Chinese education:

> The difficulties in the way of a practical extension and regeneration of Chinese education are all but insuperable. Discussion often ends in an impasse: no political reform of China without education; but no development of schools as long as military men and corrupt officials divert funds and oppose schools from motives of self-interest. Here are the materials of a tragedy of the first magnitude.[34]

Mao Zedong was one revolutionary who become acquainted with Dewey's educational ideas while selling Dewey's lectures from his Cultural Bookstore. Mao opened the bookstore after being trained as a teacher in a Western-style preparatory teaching preparation program at the Hunan Fourth Provincial Normal School. After graduation, Mao tried establishing anarchist-communal villages. In 1920, he founded the Self-Study University of Changsha and the Cultural Bookstore. Indicating the interest being taken in John Dewey's Chinese lecture series, more books were sold through the bookstore by anarchist Prince Kropotkin and John Dewey than by Marx. While Mao was to openly reject Dewey's ideas because they lacked a class analysis, there were parallels in their educational thought. Dewey and Mao Zedong's pedagogies both stressed linking theory and practice, and teaching students the social origins of knowledge.[35]

Another example of the culturalist's framework of borrowing and lending is the work of Paulo Freire, a truly revolutionary progressive educator. He noted the influence of Mao's progressive educational ideas in *Pedagogy of the Oppressed*. Freire wrote: "This appears to be the fundamental aspect of Mao's cultural revolution."[36] Regarding his important proposal for dialogical instruction to help learners understand how their subjective beliefs shape their interpretation of the objective world, Freire noted,

> Mao-Zedong declared, "You know I've proclaimed for a long time: we must teach the masses clearly what we have received from them confusedly" … This affirmation contains an entire dialogical theory of how to construct the program content of education, which cannot be elaborated according to what the *educator* thinks best for his students.[37]

When Paulo Freire referred to the "fundamental aspect of Mao's Cultural Revolution," it was in support of his assertion:

> The pedagogy of the oppressed, as a humanist and libertarian pedagogy, has two distinct stages. In the first, the oppressed unveil the world of oppression and through the praxis commit themselves to its transformation. In the second stage, in which the reality of oppression has already been transformed, this pedagogy ceases to belong to the oppressed and becomes a pedagogy of all men in the process of permanent liberation. In both stages, it is always through action in depth that the culture of domination is culturally confronted.[38]

The new progressive pedagogy of Paulo Freire emerged from the upheaval of South American revolutions which, in part, included the borrowing of Marxist ideas to plan for the liberation of indigenous and peasant populations. Marxist rhetoric was used in the 1952 Bolivian National Revolutionary Movement, the 1953 to 1959 Cuban Revolution, the revolutionary projects of Che Guevara, the 1960 overthrow of the Venezuelan government, the 1963 creation of the Venezuelan Armed Forces of National Liberation (FALN), and the 1961 Nicaraguan insurgency led by the Sandinista National Liberation Front.[39]

An important influence on Freire was the Cuban literacy crusade that took place after Fidel Castro's guerilla forces overthrew the dictatorship of Fulgencio Batista on January 1, 1959. Castro feared without a revolutionary education stressing critical and dialectical thought the Cuban people would never be free of the hegemony of colonial masters. He declared that education should "prevent cultural colonization from surviving economic colonization."[40] Similar to Mao and Latin American Marxists, Castro emphasized the importance of relating theory to practice and schooling to work. He envisioned attaching schools to workplaces. Liss summarized Castro's educational ideas: "people do not learn by indoctrination, by having their heads filled with bits and pieces of theory. They learn by thinking, analyzing, and searching history for lessons and answers. In Castro's ideal revolutionary society, people go to school to learn, dissect, to understand."[41]

Following the Revolution, Che Guevara asserted that society should become a "gigantic" school. Referring to the literacy crusade, Che wrote in 1965 that the state should give direct political instruction to the people: "Education takes hold among the masses and the foreseen new attitude tends to become a habit. The masses continue to make it their own and to influence those who have not yet educated themselves. This is the indirect form of educating the masses, as powerful, as the other, structured, one."[42]

Freire was exposed to the ideas of the Cuban literacy campaign when in 1964 he went to Chile after being exiled following a coup d'etat by the Brazilian military elite. During his exile, Freire's socialist philosophy and instructional methods crystallized, and he wrote *Pedagogy of the Oppressed*. In 1964, Chile was in a political ferment that resulted in the first elected Latin American Marxist government in 1970 under the leadership of Salvador Allende. In the charged atmosphere of Chilean politics, Freire met socialists from many Latin American countries, including Cuba. It was here that he read Che Guevara's statement, "the true revolutionary is guided by great feelings of love." In reference to the Cuban presence and Guevara's statement on love, Freire wrote, "The Cubans showed that changes could be made... Guevara's capacity for love was there."[43] In *Pedagogy of the Oppressed,* he used the quote on love from Guevara to justify the statement, "Dialogue cannot exist, however, in the absence of a profound love for the world and for men. The naming of the world, which is an act of creation and re-creation, is not possible if it is not infused in love."[44] He used Guevara's quote to footnote the following statement: "I am more and more convinced that true revolutionaries must perceive the revolution, because of its creative and liberating nature, as an act of love."

In *Pedagogy of the Oppressed*, Freire emphasized the lessons he learned in Chile. He criticized educators who "approach the peasant or urban masses with projects which may correspond to their own view of the world, but not to that of the people."[45] Interestingly, he supported this conclusion with a lengthy footnote from the writings of Mao Zedong which ended, "There are two principles here: one is the actual needs of the masses rather than what we fancy they need, and the other is the wishes of the masses, who must make up their own minds instead of our making up their minds for them."[46] Freire believed that a dialogical interaction with peasants, indigenous peoples, and urban workers was the key to their involvement in social transformation.

Obviously, there is a lot more to say about the sources Freire borrowed from in developing his educational theory. There is also the question of how many borrowed from Freire. Even today Freire's ideas are influential in the liberation theology movement (which I discuss in more detail in chapter 6). By the end of the 1970s, wars of liberation in Nicaragua and El Salvador sparked literacy crusades that reflected the influence of liberation theology and Paulo Freire's pedagogical methods. Both countries were composed of ruling elites, impoverished peasants, and indigenous peoples. In 1961, the Sandinista National Liberation Front was formed in Nicaragua which overthrew the dictatorship of the Somoza dynasty in 1979. In neighboring El Salvador, the Farabundo Marti National Liberation Front was formed in 1980 resulting in a decade of civil war with major areas of the country captured by the Liberation Front in 1989. In both countries, literacy crusades were considered fundamental parts of the revolutionary movement.[47]

Schriewer and Martinez's previous cited quantitative study of the international progressive education movement includes an example of the spread of Freire's ideas. One of their data analysis used citations from the 1994 *International Encyclopedia of Education*. Paul Freire ranked twenty-third in the number of citations. Not bad considering that UNESCO was second, OECD was fifth, the World Bank was ninth, and John Dewey was thirty-first.[48] Also, Freirian educational methods still operate as a counterpoint to the human capital model. For example, in a detailed study Lesley Bartlett describes two competing literacy projects in Brazil. One funded by the World Bank and the other by liberation theologians in the Brazilian Catholic Church. The World Bank supported human capital forms of education while the Church used Freirian methods.[49]

As I will discuss in the next sections, International Nongovernment Organizations (INGOs) have had a major role in spreading progressive education models.

## International Nongovernment Organizations (INGOs)

World culture theorists consider INGOs an important element in the evolution of a common global culture. However, the two largest groups of INGOs, human rights and environmental organizations, employ the principles of progressive education in their instructional programs. Two important world culture theorists, John Boli and George Thomas highlight the importance of INGOs for world culture theory in the title of their book: *Constructing World Culture: International Nongovernment Organizations Since 1875*.[50] They write, "Our analysis depicts INGOs as embodiments of universalism, individualism, rational voluntaristic authority, progress, and world citizenship."[51] World citizenship, according to John Boli, Thomas Loya, and Teresa Loftin, is the result of the growth of INGOs. They found that Western nations do not dominate the membership of INGOs. While in the nineteenth century international INGOs tended to be concentrated in Western countries by the twenty-first century the researchers found INGOs participation "in all geographical regions of the world, across all levels of development, for old and new countries, for countries of every dominant religion...."[52] With regard to Western influence, the authors conclude, "world culture is increasingly global, decreasingly the provenance of the Europeans and Anglo-Americans, who dominated it in its early stages."[53]

While human rights and environmental organizations might agree with the description that they are an embodiment of "universalism" and "world citizenship," they might disagree about the labels of "individualism" and "progress." Most instructional programs of these organizations stress the progressive education ideal of group work, holistic instruction, cooperation and education for social and activism. Also, the premise of many environmental groups is not the inevitable "progress" of human development but the potential destruction of humanity and the planet as a result of industrial consumerism.

Similar to other worldwide organizations, there are differences between the global rhetoric of INGOs and the actual implementation of policies in local communities. One investigator of this disparity, Dana Burde, agrees with world culture theorists: "Insofar as INGOs' burgeoning presence in the world and increased influence on civil society have allowed, they have been able to promote world-cultural principles."[54] However, in his case study about the introduction of national parent-teachers associations in the former Yugoslavia by an INGO, he found a major difference between the global rhetoric and the results of implementation. The goals of the INGO were to promote high quality early childhood through an alliance of parent-teachers associations. Besides training the parents in early childhood development, the associations were to provide support groups for early childhood education programs. The results of his case study supported the idea of a growth of a world culture of education: "INGO model reforms do seem to be converging on an international level—most INGOs ... share model program interventions and best practices ... even among the local staff ... there is a convergence ... their rhetoric."[55] But when it came to actual implementation: "Program beneficiaries ... seem to either participate in old wars that are familiar to them ... or are left out of the process altogether."[56]

INGOs are part of a global civil society that attempt to educate the public and influence governments. The global civil society exists as a parallel system of power to national governments. Some writers refer to the combination INGOs, intergovernmental organizations, and multinational corporations as the key elements of a *global community*. In *Global Community: The Role of International Organizations in the Making of the Contemporary World*, Akira Iriye contends that traditional histories of international relations primarily focus on national governments and diplomacy.[57] What is missing from this historical perspective, he asserts, is the growth of a global community composed of a tangled web of interrelationships between inter-governmental organizations and INGOs. Since the nineteenth century, the network of INGOs has formed a *global civil society* which sometimes supplants and competes with the actions of nation-states. In his history of the global community, Iriye divides the organizations of global civil society by their functions, such as humanitarian relief, cultural exchange, peace and disarmament, developmental assistance, religious, human rights, and environmentalism.[58] Intertwined with global civil society are inter-governmental organizations such as the World Bank. Together, these form the basic structure of Iriye's *global community*. Iriye uses the International Red Cross as an example of the entanglement of INGOs with national governments. In 1864, the Swiss government convened an international conference of government leaders to write a treaty that would ensure better treatment of those wounded in war. However, prior private efforts had already created the Red Cross headquarters in Geneva. Government representatives attending the conference signed a treaty supporting the Red Cross. The inter-governmental treaty resulted in the Red Cross being caught up in international politics. For instance, Japan insisted that Korea, which it had colonized in the early twentieth century, not be allowed to ratify the original treaty as a separate nation. The International Red Cross acceded to Japan's wishes and the Korean Red Cross was put under the jurisdiction of the Japanese Red Cross. Iriye concludes, "The line between the state apparatus and a nonstate organization was never clear-cut."[59]

It is important to remember this tangled web of relationships when discussing progressive education. An intergovernmental organization like the World Bank might be promoting a human capital form of education while, at the same time, working with INGOs that are espousing different concerns and approaches to education. Cynics might argue that the World Bank's links to human rights and environmental organizations are attempts to co-opt these organizations.[60]

In the global civil society, human rights organizations form the largest group of INGOs. Human rights and other INGOs developed rapidly after World War II. Since 1850, 35,000 not-for-profit INGOs appeared on the world stage. While many of these disappeared overtime, after World War II the rate of dissolutions declined markedly. For instance in 1969 approximately 134 new INGOs were created while only about 20 dissolved.[61] The number of human rights organizations increased from 33 in 1953 to 168 in 1993, and they represent about 26.6 percent of the total global INGOs. The next largest number of INGOs are environmental with ninety groups in 1993 forming 14.3 percent of the global number. Environmental INGOs have been the fastest growing with only two groups having existed in 1953. Following environmentalist groups are women's rights' INGOs whose numbers grew from ten in 1953 to sixty-one in 1993. Other INGOs, in descending order of total number of organizations, are concerned with Peace, Esperanto, World Order, Development, Ethnic Unity/Group rights, and International Law.[62]

## Human Rights INGOs and the Global Progressive Education Model

The orientation of human rights INGOs towards the progressive education model is immediately evident in its attempt to create a global human rights culture. This goal requires educators to develop in students a conscious awareness of human rights protections and abuses, and a desire to defend the human rights of others. In this context, consciousness or awareness of human rights requires all people to think about and interpret events in the context of human rights. This is suppose to create a global culture that shares an interpretative lens that makes sense of social actions by using a common set of human rights values. In other words, in a human rights culture people are to think about how behavior and the behavior of others might or might not violate human rights. Education is to alert students to abuses of human rights and how to take action to correct them. Also, it prepares students to interpret their own actions according to whether or not they support or violate human rights.

Human rights education includes welfare issues such as the right to shelter, nutrition, medical care, and employment at a living wage. Many human rights educators argue that if people share a belief in welfare rights, then people's interpretative lenses would be calibrated to include an evaluation of the welfare of others as part of human rights. This would mean seeing the world through a framework that asks whether or not all people's human rights are protected and if they have adequate shelter, nutrition, medical care, and employment.[63]

The commitment of most human rights education is to promote a form of activism that will lead to the protection of the human rights of others. This represents the social activist part of the progressive model. An example is the Canadian Human Rights Foundation's instructional module for training human rights teachers called *The Global Human Rights Context*. The objectives of this training module are to introduce human rights teachers to the "impact of globalization on human rights" and "issues related to global governance and their impact on civil society."[64] In the instructional module, globalization is presented as a complex phenomenon with both positive and negative effects. In the module's first unit, small groups of teachers are asked to read newspaper headlines with short quotes from the article. Examples of the headlines are, "Amazon Tribe Sues for Survival," "Languages Are in Danger of Extinction," "Information Technology in the 21st Century," "Police say Toronto a World Hub for Child Porn," and "New Front in Aids War."[65] They are then asked to compose lists of what they feel are the positive and negative influences of globalization and present them to the entire class. Two questions are for discussion: "In what ways can globalization create opportunities to better promote and protect human rights?

In what ways do certain dimensions of globalization threaten or pose a danger to human rights?"[66] The second and third activities require human rights teachers to examine the impact of globalization on different world regions. The central question is "How would you try, in this context, to promote respect for human rights in your community and region?"[67]

As illustrated in these training modules, they want to educate students to participate in the regulating the effects of globalization on human rights. In Unit 2 of the *The Global Human Rights Context* module teachers are trained to effect specific organizations by creating a "Spheres of Influence" diagram. At the beginning of the module, human rights educators are told, "An understanding of power relations and structures at all levels of society (i.e., international, national, and local) is an essential tool for the protection of human rights and social change. The aim of this activity is to identify the key actors and their influence on the globalization process in our societies."[68] The class is asked to consider how they might influence groups in the globalization process. These groups include: globalized economic institutions, the World Bank, the International Monetary Fund, regional development banks, multilateral trade organizations (such as the WTO), transnational corporations, national governments, ministries of international trade, ministries of education, ministries of finance, INGOs, and the global communications industry.

Power relations are central to this lesson. After completing the "Spheres of Influence" diagram, the class is given a statement designed to provoke discussion about the role human rights educators in influencing power relations in a global society. The statement is an excerpt from the International Consultation on the Pedagogical Foundations of Human Rights Education declaration "Towards A Pedagogy of Human Rights Education." It begins, "Human rights education should be approached in a fashion that includes the analysis, understanding and reading of power relations and social forces so as to enable a struggle to change those power relations that impede the full realization of human rights."[69]

Another example of promoting human rights activism is the college textbook, *Educating for Human Dignity: Learning About Rights and Responsibilities* written by Betty Reardon, a well-know leader in U.S. human rights and peace education.[70] The book provides instructional guidelines and models of lessons on human rights that can be used in classes ranging from kindergarten to the twelfth grade. An example of activist education is a twelfth-grade lesson titled, "Moral Development—From Awareness to Commitment, the Making of Human Rights Heroes."[71] Accompanying the lesson is a guide to "Phases in the Development of Moral Inclusion." These phases of "moral inclusion" move from "Spectator" to "Solidarity/Victim/Martyr." The guide emphasizes creating a global moral community, "The universal recognition of the full range of human rights for all peoples of the world depends in large part on widening our moral community and extending its boundaries to include all human beings."[72] Supposedly, members of a global human rights community would actively intervene, even to the extent of martyrdom, to protect universal human rights. "Moral inclusion" is defined as "a capacity that can be developed through both experiential and academic learning."[73] According to Reardon, proper instruction could change the mere spectator into a martyr. In her steps of moral inclusion, the first three stages involve progressively greater involvement in human rights issues from "Spectator," "Observer," to "Witness." At the next stage, "Advocate," moral concerns about human rights cause them "to join advocacy groups, write letters to the editor, speak to schools, church groups, etc. Such people *advocate* the cause of the victims." "Advocate" is followed by "Activist" when people are "moved to the acceptance of personal responsibility and risk [in defending human rights]."[74] Activist assume personal responsibility to try and stop human rights' violations. At the final "Solidarity/Victim/Martyr," the person begins to take on personal risk in defending human rights. Reardon provides the following description of the "Solidarity/Victim/Martyr" stage of moral inclusion:

> Activism is most often pursued within one's own group or country, but some activists actually join in *solidarity* with the struggle and suffering of victims to work for human rights as a member of the victimized group. Such an activist risks being victimized herself even to the point of losing her life and thus becoming a *martyr* in the struggle for human rights. Do you know of such martyrs who are now considered heroes of human rights?[75]

Betty Reardon uses the interests of the child and activity-based instruction to have children develop their concepts of human rights. In this case, human rights can be considered human needs. In her model second-grade lesson, "Wishing a World Fit for Children—Understanding Human Needs," Reardon instructs the teacher, "Tell the children that when we make wishes we use our imaginations. When we imagine good things and a better world, we actually begin to make the world better."[76] In the lesson, children write down wishes as gifts for a newborn baby. The gifts are supposed to represent things the baby will actually need, such as a bed, clothes, and food. The wishes are for something that will make the child's life more secure and happy. A class discussion of wishes and needs yields two lists, "Needs of a Child" and "Wishes for a Better World." The lesson concludes with teachers asking the second graders,

"Look at the list of wishes for a better world and think about what we need to learn to make a better world."[77]

Separating needs from wants is a method for students to construct their own human rights list. In this case, a need is a human right, such as food, housing, and freedom from discrimination. This lesson is part of a larger text called *Human Rights Here & Now: Celebrating the Universal Declaration of Human Rights* issued by the Human Rights Educators' Network and Amnesty International USA.[78] An important feature of the book is linking human rights concepts to developmental stages of children's growth. In the context of developmental psychology, learning to differentiate between needs and wants is an activity for upper primary, ages eight to eleven. During these ages there is an emphasis on teaching social responsibility and distinguishing wants from needs. The concept of needs, as opposed to wants, is then related to human rights. All the lessons are geared towards educating an activist citizen. In early childhood, which includes preschool and lower primary grades, it is recommended that human rights education begin with teaching respect for self, parents, teachers, and others. For this age group, the key learning concept is responsibility to the community by practicing in groups situations self-expression and listening to others. Age-appropriate lessons are introduced on racism, sexism, unfairness, and hurting people. Concepts are introduced related to individual and group rights, freedom, equality, justice and rule by law. Students learn to value diversity and to distinguish fact from opinion. Also, they perform school and community service. In lower secondary, ages twelve to fourteen, students are taught about the content of human rights documents. They learn about international law, world peace, world developmental and economic issues, and legal and moral rights. They are taught how to understand another person's point of view, to do research on human rights issues, and to practice sharing information about community activities. And in the final years of high school, students integrate human rights into their personal awareness and behaviors by participating in civic organizations and learning the power of civil disobedience.

## Environmental INGOs and Progressive Education

Environmental INGOs, the second largest group of global nongovernment organizations, also emphasize education for social and political activism. Environmental INGOs are important in promoting the ideas of sustainable environment. For instance a combination of INGOs and the United Nations (the World Conservation Union, the United Nations Environment Programme and the World Wide Fund For Nature) were responsible for the landmark 1991 Second World Conservation Report,

*Caring for the Earth* which declared, "We must act globally... The environment links all nations."[79] INGOs played a role in the demand for global civil action at both of the two major world environmental summits in the 1992 and 2002. In 1992, the Rio Earth Summit issued a declaration defining the basic elements of civic action from local to national levels. Meeting in Rio de Janeiro, the summit attracted representatives from 172 governments including 108 heads of state along with 2,400 representatives from INGOs. "Environmental issues," states the *Rio Declaration on Environment and Development* or as it has been called *Agenda 21,* "are best handled with the participation of all concerned citizens, at the relevant level. At the national level, each individual shall have appropriate access to information concerning the environment that is held by public authorities, including information on hazardous materials and activities in their communities, and the opportunity to participate in decision-making processes."[80] This was a call for direct participation and action by citizens as opposed to a reliance on elected representatives. The Rio Declaration calls on governments to ensure that the public is given information about environmental issues. "States shall facilitate and encourage public awareness," the Declaration demands, "by making information widely available."[81]

Civil society including INGOs spearhead efforts to improve the quality of environmental conditions. Ten years after the Rio summit, another earth summit was held in Johannesburg with the same global participation. Meeting at the Johannesburg summit, the Global People's Forum issued a "Civil Society Declaration." This declaration claims that the Global People's Forum represents those oppressed social groups named in *Agenda 21* of the Rio summit, including "women, youth, labour, indigenous peoples, farmers, NGOs, and others including disabled people, the elderly, faith-based organizations, peoples of African descent, social movements, people under foreign occupation and other underrepresented groups."[82] In other words, the dispossessed and disadvantaged who feel their interests are not represented by nation-states. The declaration asserts that "As the key agents of social change and sustainable development, we are determined to take leadership for our future with utmost seriousness."[83]

Holistic education is supported by the Johannesburg declaration. Holistic education, an important part of progressive education, breaks down the barriers between disciplines. Both John Dewey and Paulo Freire are holistic educators. Holistic education has two important meanings. In the first meaning, all human social issues are considered interrelated to each other and environmental conditions. The second meaning considers all arenas of human knowledge as a whole rather than separated in specific disciplines such as history, economics, physics, and biology. The Johannesburg declaration emphasizes the holistic nature of human and environmental issues in its description of a global civil society and its role in environmental protection.

> The definition of civil society includes, the major groups defined in Agenda 21, formal and informal community-based organizations, INGOs that work with and represent peoples who are victims of racism. Organizations of civil society have a central role to play in the translation of the Rio Principles and Agenda 21 into concrete programs, projects and implementation strategies for sustainable development... We affirm that solidarity and partnerships for sustainable development are those entered into on the basis of clearly defined human needs and related goals, objectives and actions for the elimination of poverty and the enhancement and restoration of the physical, social, and universal spiritual environment.[84]

The social activist aspect of progressive education is embodied in a 1969 definition of environmental education in the United States made by William Stapp of the University of Michigan. Stapp later coauthored important texts on environmental education. His 1969 definition is, "Environmental education is aimed at producing a citizenry that is knowledgeable concerning the biophysical environment and its associated problems, aware of how to help solve these problems, and motivation to work toward their solution."[85]

The WWF (formerly known as the World Wildlife Fund) is a major INGO promoting environmental education. It differentiates between a narrow and broad focus in environmental education based on the degree of social activism. The WWF considers narrowly focused instruction as developing a "caring interest in the environment." This type of education does not attempt to engage the student in direct civic action. Activities are usually limited to picking up trash or planting a tree. In contrast, a broad instructional focus examines the relationship between "human behavior and global eco-systems" and develops "concerned awareness and participatory skills [civic action]."[86] These skills prepare students to engage in a range of activities from simply writing letters to political leaders to the direct action methods against perpetrators of environmental destruction.

Cultivating an awareness of environmental problems without teaching civic activism typifies the educational programs of the WWF. While their educational programs do not instruct in civic activism, the organization's ties to the World Bank, UNESCO, governments, and other international NGOs make it a key player in the global civil society. Officially, the organization states, "WWF ... maintains links with other nongovernmental organizations both national and international. It makes a particular point of responding to local conservation needs, and working with local people. More and more projects involve rural communities in making decisions as to how their environment should be both used and conserved, while providing economic incentives."[87]

There are environmental INGOs that stress what might be considered radical forms of activism. Two examples are Earth First! and People for the Ethical Treatment of Animals (PETA). Earth First! teaches methods of direct action, such as tree sitting and blockading logging trucks to save forests or what it refers to as "monkeywrenching." Officially, Earth First! explains the general educational value of these acts, "You can't hope to change people's minds or put pressure on politicians without calling attention to the damage [to nature]. Civil disobedience or a clever banner-hanging exposes the issue on the front pages of papers ... Arrests, in particular, sway sentiment by impressing on others the depth of our concern and willingness to sacrifice."[88]

"Monkeywrenching" refers to attempts to stop environmental changes using methods described by Edward Abbey in his book, *The Monkey-wrench Gang*.[89] Monkeywrenching involves tree spiking, destruction of billboards, removal of surveying stakes, pouring sugar or sand into the fuel tanks of earthmoving machinery, and other forms of sabotage or as its is called "ecotage." Monkeywrenching, as described by the organization leaders of Earth First!, is a step beyond civil disobedience. It is "nonviolent, aimed only at inanimate objects, and pocketbooks of the industrial despoilers. It is the final defense of the wild ... whereby the wilderness defender becomes the wilderness acting in self-defense."[90] While Earth First! denies any organizational support for monkeywrenching, it does admit that some local groups and individuals participate in this dramatic form public education. Also, Earth First! distributes Dave Foreman and Bill Haywood's book *ECODEFENSE: A Field Guide to Monkeywrenching*.[91]

Acts of civil disobedience to protect the environment are compared to civil rights movements to end human slavery and discrimination among humans. The new civil rights movement is concerned with the rights of all species of animals and plants. A member of Earth First! proclaimed, "Earth First! shares Dr. King's commitment to individual rights. Today ... we publicly extend his vision to include oppressed members of our planetary society."[92] Bill Duvall describes civil disobedience as an important form of public education. Civil disobedience, he asserts, "is aimed at a larger audience, and the action should always be interpreted by the activists. Smart and creative communication of the message is as important as the action itself."[93]

Ecotage as a form of public education is more controversial because it involves potential harm to other humans and the destruction of property. For instance, the spiking of trees could hurt the logger or lumber mill worker. Similar to the arguments supporting civil disobedience, ecotage is compared to the violence used by abolitionists in their efforts to end human slavery. In addition, the intention of an act like spiking trees is to make the cutting of old growth forests unprofitable rather than harm other humans. The destruction of property, such as the burning of suburban construction sites, is justified according to the property rights of all humans as opposed property rights of individuals and corporations. Peg Millett, arrested for knocking down an electrical tower in 1989, defines monkeywrenching as "the dismantling of the present industrial system, but I would define it as dismantling the machinery very carefully."[94]

PETA has used a variety of techniques to educate the public about animal rights from throwing acid on fur coats to passing out literature. One of their more interesting projects involves the distribution of packets of fifty-two cards called *Animal Rights: Weekend Warrior*. Representing each week of the year, the cards carry information and suggestions for civic action. Some of these suggestions are directed at public schools. The card for "Week 4" is titled "Veganize Your Cafeteria" and calls on schools to institute to offer "a healthier, humane lunch program." It is suggested that the card owner meet with school food services and, "Request that a vegan entrée be offered at every meal, and suggest that cruelty-free alternatives, like vegan margarine, tofu sour cream . . . be made available. Be clear—meat flavorings and vegetables cooked in butter are unacceptable."[95] On another card, "Week 11: Cut Out Dissection," students are urged to write their teacher and principal "to express your feelings about dissection."[96] For "Week 2: Make a Library Display," weekend warriors are told to, "Educate others in your community about animal rights issues by creating a display for your local library."[97] Other cards suggest weekend warriors go leather-free, hang banners, leaflet fur stores, and protest animal testing of products.

PETA's activities are having a global effect. For instance, PETA members sued the multinational fast food franchise KFC to improve its treatment of chickens and to stop making false claims about its humane handling of animals. KFC slaughters over 700 million chickens a year. In response to criticism from PETA, KFC created an Animal Welfare Advisory Council to establish standards for farms raising chickens for the franchise. In May, 2003, PETA agreed to stop its boycott of KFC after the franchise required breeders to expand the cage size for chickens by 30 percent and to install cameras to ensure that the animals were killed in the most painless manner possible. However, in July, 2003, PETA filed a legal suit complaining that "the birds raised and killed for the defendants operations suffer great pain and injuries in massive numbers."[98]

What is important about PETA's actions is the resulting establishment of global standards for the ethical treatment of animals. In the case of KFC, the company has officially stated, "As a major purchaser of food products, we have the opportunity, and responsibility, to influence the way animals are treated. We take that responsibility very seriously. We only deal with suppliers who maintain the very highest standards and share our commitment to animal welfare."[99] PETA has also won concessions regarding the treatment of animals from the fast food franchises McDonald's, Wendy's, and Burger King. And, of course, their actions along with those of other environmental groups are an important form of public education.

In summary, most of the educational programs of human rights and environmental INGOs use a framework of progressive education that stresses some form of social activism. Consequently, these INGOs offer

---

### Key Points: Global Civil Society and International Nongovernment Organizations (INGOs)

1. The global civil society consists of voluntary organizations
   a. Formal and informal community-based organizations
   b. Formal and informal nongovernmental organizations within a nation
   c. INGOs
2. Members of the global civil society issue policies and set standards that influence
   a. Local governments
   b. National governments
   c. Global intergovernmental organizations such as the World Bank, the United Nations, OECD, etc.
3. The major global INGOs in rank order of numbers of organizations
   a. Human rights
   b. Environmental
   c. Women's rights
   d. Peace
   e. Esperanto
   f. Ethnic unity/group rights
4. INGOs support the following forms of progressive education
   a. Preparation of students for active participation in solving problems of social justice
   b. Preparation of students to actively change the political and economic system
   c. Cultural liberation using Freirian methods

different global models of education from that of the human capital model. In fact, an INGO like Earth First! rejects the industrial-consumer system on which human capital education is premised. These competing global education models support the contention of culturalists that there is no single uniform global education culture.

## Conclusion: Local Transformation of the Global Education Superstructure

This chapter highlighted the major differences between world culture theorists and culturalists. The chapter stressed the existence of multiple educational models in the global educational superstructure. The findings of culturalists do not negate the existence of this superstructure, but they do bring into question their actual impact on local policies. As culturalists have suggested, economic crises, political upheaval, and even the results of international testing can motivate national policy leaders to borrow from the global superstructure of educational policies and practices. But borrowing does not mean that national and local communities will implement an exact replica of these policies and practices. Changes are made to meet the conditions and desires of local communities.

And, contrary to world culture theorists, there is no single best educational practice from which local policymakers can borrow. As I stressed in this chapter, there exists a multiplicity of policies and practices in the global educational superstructure. This chapter emphasized the availability of different forms of progressive education. And, as I have suggested, INGOs tend to rely on a progressive education model. In the next chapter, I discuss the existence in the global superstructure of various religious and indigenous education models. This adds another dimension to the complicated nature of the global education superstructure.

## Chapter 6

# Religious and Indigenous Education Models

## A Clash of Civilizations?

Many religious organizations and indigenous peoples disagree with the values that world culture theorists believe are part of a growing global uniformity. Consequently, as I will discuss in this chapter, some religious and indigenous groups are major dissenters to the world culture model and the materialism embodied in the human capital and progressive education models. Religious and indigenous groups often resist and change global models when they are used in local level communities. In addition, some argue that religious and cultural differences are resulting in a "clash of civilizations" rather than growing global uniformity.

By religious knowledge I mean those modes of learning, perceptions, beliefs, and forms of reasoning associated with organized religions. Most, if not all, organized religions have some educational program to propagate their particular form of knowledge. Indigenous knowledges have two sources. One is local forms of knowledge that are different from those embedded in world culture and world education culture. The second are knowledges associated with indigenous peoples. In chapter 1, I identified indigenous peoples (sometimes referred to as First Nations, indigenous ethnic minorities, native minorities, and tribes) as those recognized as such by the United Nations and that have as a key characteristic of close attachment to ancestral territories and their natural resources. I will explore the concept of indigenous peoples in more detail later in this chapter.

As I discuss in this chapter, religious and indigenous perspectives add a conflictual dimension to what I have called the global superstructure of education. However a consideration of religious knowledge is vital to understanding globalization. As Eduardo Mendieta asserts, "A theory of globalization that makes no room for religion has major theoretical flaws."[1] Some religious groups reject what they believe are the central values of globalization, namely secularization, individual autonomy, and freedom. In a similar vein, the editors' introduction to *Indigenous Knowledges in Global Contexts* expresses concern that: "For indigenous peoples, the 'crisis of knowledge' can be seen in ... fragmentation of traditional values and beliefs; erosion of spirituality; distortions in local, regional, and national ecosystems and economies; and tensions related in cultural revitalization and reclamation."[2]

## The Existence of Knowledges

The concept of knowledges, in contrast to a single knowledge, assumes the existence of multiple ways of seeing and knowing the world. Many organizations and networks I have so far discussed believe that schools will educate from the perspective of a single world knowledge. However, the adaptation of global ideas to local settings, as I discussed in chapter 5 regarding Thai Wisdom, often involves recognition of other ways of thinking and knowing the world. Paul Wangoola, the founder of Mpambo, the African Multiversity in Uganda, explains the importance of understanding the existence of multiple world knowledges, "A *multi*versity differs from a *uni*versity insofar as it recognizes that the existence of alternative knowledges is important to human knowledge as a whole."[3] Why are indigenous knowledges important? Wangoola argues that the "problems of human kind today cannot be resolved by modern scientific knowledge alone, or by indigenous knowledge alone. More durable solutions will be found in new synthesis between indigenous knowledges and modern scientific knowledge."[4] One group of defenders of the knowledges of indigenous peoples asserts, "Increasingly within [indigenous] communities, refreshing critical voices are emerging to question the processes of knowing and validating knowledge and disseminating it across national and global spaces."[5]

Cross-cultural psychologists have provided a wealth of evidence on differences in ways of knowing and seeing the world. It is certainly beyond the scope of this book to review all of their findings. One cross-cultural psychologist, Richard Nisbett, discusses these findings in *The Geography of Thought: How Asians and Westerners Think Differently ... and Why.*[6] Nisbett's book highlights differences in ways of knowing by comparing results of psychological experiments in the United States and in Confucian-based countries (China, Japan, and the Republic of Korea). The assumption is that there is a difference between the brain (organic) and the mind (organic + experience). Every person has the same basic physical brain which interacts with different environments resulting in a variety ways of thinking and knowing the world. Without going into the details of his complex argument, Nisbett contends that the following differences are a result of historical factors that shaped human minds to know the world differently:

- Regard the self as part of a larger interdependent whole (Confucian)
- Regard the self as a unitary free agent (Western)

- Regard the world as complex, interrelated, and constantly changing (Confucian)—Regard the world as divide into discrete and separate parts (Western)
- Desire for blending harmoniously with the group (Confucian)— Desire for individual distinctiveness (Western)
- Attuned to feelings of others and striving for interpersonal harmony (Confucian)—More concern with knowing one's own feelings (Western)
- Value success and achievement because it reflects well on the group (Confucian)—Value success and achievement because it makes the individual look good (Western)
- Preference for societies governed by social obligations (Confucian)— Preference for societies governed by the rule of law (Western)
- Preference for judging behavior according to the situation (Confucian)—Preference for judging behavior according universal rules (Western)

The importance of Nisbett's arguments and findings cannot be overly stressed. Nisbett's work challenges the assumption that there is only a single way of knowing. At the time of publication, Nisbett's book was a groundbreaking synthesis of work in cross cultural psychology. Famed Yale psychologist Robert Sternberg contends, "Nisbett shows conclusively that laboratory experiments limited to American college students or even individuals from the Western Hemisphere simply cannot provide an adequate understanding of how people, in general, think."[7] Anthropologist and human development expert at the University of Chicago, Richard Shweder contends, "*The Geography of Thought* challenges a fundamental premise of the Western Enlightenment—the idea that modes of thought are, ought to be, or will become the same wherever you go–east or west, north or south—in the world."[8] Multiple intelligence guru Howard Gardner describes Nisbett's work "as a research-based challenge to the assumption, widespread among cognitive scientists, that thinking the world over is the same."[9]

Nisbett's work indirectly confirmed research that found different ways of knowing among indigenous peoples. For example, Marlene Brant Castellano's research among the First Nations of Canada found very distinct differences between indigenous and Western ways of knowing. She divides the distinctive features of First Nations people's way of knowing into "Sources of Knowledge" and "Characteristics of Aboriginal Knowledge." Under sources of knowledge, Catellano identifies three sources of knowledge: traditional knowledge which is handed down from generation to generation; empirical knowledge based on careful observation in contrast to the use of the scientific method; and revealed knowledge "acquired through dreams, visions, and intuition that are understood to be spiritual in nature."[10] Of course, spiritualism, as I discuss later in this chapter, is a central ingredient in religious knowledge and religious education.

What are the "Characteristics of Aboriginal Knowledge?" Catellano states that aboriginal knowledge is based on personal experience and "lays no claim to universality."[11] As Nisbett asserts that Western thought assumes the existence of universal truths that are identified through reason or scientific method. Even though two people might have contradictory experiences of the same event both are accepted as valid. In First Nations, there is no contest to see who is correct. Group discussion and consensus building determine the validity of an interpretation of an event. Or, as Catellano states, "Knowledge is validated through collective analysis and consensus building."[12]

Similar to the Confucian-based societies described by Nesbitt, First Nations people see the world in holistic terms in contrast to seeing it as divided into discrete and separate parts. Catellano quotes a First Nations elder: "There are only two things you have to remember about being Indian. One is that everything is alive, and the second is that we are all related."[13] The first part of the statement about "everything is alive" reflects a spiritual view. Everything is permeated by spirits. In reference to the holistic thought, she writes, "The holistic quality of knowledge implies that isolating pieces of experience and trying to make sense of them apart from the environment that gave rise to them flies in the face of reality and is bound to lead to frustration."[14]

In "Updating Aboriginal Traditions of Knowledge," Marlene Castellano writes about holistic thinking among the First Nations of Canada: "The holistic quality of knowledge implies that isolating pieces of experience and trying to make sense of them apart from the environment that gave rise to them flies in the face of reality and is bound to lead to frustration."[15] For Castellano, the medicine wheel symbolizes holistic knowledge with the circle of the wheel representing the circle of life which "contains all experience, everything in the biosphere—animal, vegetable, mineral, human, spirit—past, present and future."[16] Paul Wangoola, in discussing the African Multiversity, offers a similar image of humans linked to a great chain of being: "At the center of African spirituality was the unshakeable belief that humans were but a weak link in the vast chain of nature, which encompassed the many animals, plants, birds, insects, and worms, and indeed inanimate things such as stones and rocks."[17] Peruvian anthropologist Mahia Maurial uses the term "holisticity" to describe indigenous thought and states, "The holistic basis of indigenous knowledge is produced and reproduced within human relationships as well as in their relationship with nature."[18]

Writing about indigenous peoples in sub-Saharan Africa, George J. Sefa Dei argues that differences in knowledges should not be thought of as being opposites but should be thought of as being at opposite ends of a scale with hybrid knowledges in between: "Different knowledges represent different points on a continuum; they involve ways that people perceive the world and act on it."[19] On this continuum, indigenous knowledges on one end of the scale are oriented towards the metaphysical and physical and at the other end towards science and modernity. The in between points on the continuum represent a blending of traditional knowledge and modernity. Dei states, "Through daily practice, societies 'import' and 'adapt' freely whatever from 'outside' will enrich their accumulated knowledge. In this sense, 'modernity' is embedded in indigenous knowledges."[20]

What are indigenous knowledges in Africa? While claiming there is no "essentialized" Africa because of the variety of indigenous peoples and localities, Dei identifies what he considers to be shared characteristics of sub-Saharan African ways of knowing the world. Shared with Confucian-based societies and First Nations of North America is a holistic view of the world: "the wholeness of relationships in a world that today is fragmented, polarized, and destructive of people and their social aspirations."[21] Embedded in this worldview is an orientation to communal solidarity and community responsibility. Consequently, rather that being driven by a desire to accumulate wealth like Westernized humans, traditional societies were oriented towards sharing wealth. The concept of poverty did not exist in traditional societies because of community sharing. Traditional indigenous peoples, Dei claims, did not share the image with the modern world "of the competitive, isolated individual who lives in fear of others and is protected from them by the state or community."[22] In traditional societies the image was of the cooperative individual who was enriched by his ties to the community.

What about differences in religious knowledges? I will elaborate on some of these differences later in this chapter when exploring religious models of education. It is beyond the scope of this book to review the knowledges of all world religions which can range from the individualistic faith of modern Christian Protestantism to the emphasis on community responsibility in Islamic thought. Given the variety of world religions, it is beyond the scope of this book to describe all of them in detail. A general description of religions might include a knowledge of a spiritual world that cannot be explained by modern science. Therefore, a deeply religious person might view the world and its interactions as a mystery that can only be partially understood through science and the exercise of human reason. Life being a mystery, religious people might seek understanding of existence through a belief in a god or gods and some form of theology. Religions offer a spiritual answer to the meaning of life and the mystery of what happens after death. This way of knowing the world is quite different from one that believes that science can provide all answers to life's questions and that human behavior should be guided by a science of ethics rather than faith. The result is a clash between many religious knowledges and a secularized world where the major goal is economic growth and increasing consumption of the material products.

In summary, religious and indigenous knowledges are often different from the concept of knowledge embodied in the human capital and progressive models of education. In the human capital model, life is considered as knowable through science and that the end goal of human life is the accumulation of wealth and economic growth. Knowledge is considered an aid in achieving an economic goal while most religions see knowledge as a means of following the wishes of a god or gods. Progressive models of education promise that they will educate people to take charge of the reconstruction of society to achieve social justice. Most indigenous cultures and religions would consider this goal as naive and impossible. How can people reconstruct a world that is, from the perspective of many religions and indigenous peoples, unknowable and spiritual? How can social justice be defined outside the context of a religious theology. Does social justice mean providing everyone with an equal chance to accumulate wealth or does it mean the opportunity to enjoy a strong community life that is directed by spiritual ethics?

There are also differences in knowledges between collectivist and individualist societies such as the previously described differences between Western and Confucian-based societies. Cross cultural psychologists suggest that these differences in knowledges involve different values regarding human actions which, as Dei contends, should be considered as opposite ends of a spectrum with blended variations in-between. In *Individualism and Collectivism: Past, Present, and Future*, Harry C. Triandis provides a summary of differing character traits valued in the two types of society I have complied in Table 6.1. Certainly any model of education must consider outcomes related to character traits. Human capital educational models are supportive of individualist character traits while progressive models tend to support collectivist character traits.[23]

Recognizing the various differences in knowledges leads to the question what it means for the phenomenon of globalization particularly the globalization of educational practices. Will these differences continue into the future or will they converge into a common way of knowing the world? Or do these knowledge differences lead to a continuous clash over the goals and content of education?

## The Clash of Civilizations and the Role of Religion

The existence of differing knowledges raises important doubts about globalization leading to a uniform global culture and common educational

*Table 6.1* Basic Character Traits in Individualist and Collectivist Cultures

| Individualist | Collectivist |
| --- | --- |
| Hedonism, stimulation, self-direction | Tradition and conformity |
| Good opinion of self (self-enhancing) | Modest |
| Goals fit personal needs | Goals show concern with needs of others |
| Desire for individual distinctiveness | Desire for blending harmoniously with the group |
| Value success and achievement because it makes the individual look good | Value success and achievement because it reflects well on the group |
| More concerned with knowing one's own feelings | Attuned to feelings of others and striving for interpersonal harmony |
| Exhibits "social loafing" or "gold–bricking"—trying to minimize work in group efforts | No social loafing in group efforts |
| Less sensitive to social rejection | More sensitive to social rejection |
| Less modest in social situations | More modest in social situations |
| Less likely to feel embarrassed | More likely to feel embarrassed |

policies and practices. Also, differences in religious knowledges highlight the importance of religious models of education. Strong objections to growing global uniformity were raised by Samuel P. Huntington's in his 1996 book *The Clash of Civilizations and the Remaking of World Order*.[24] The very title of the book suggests that world cultural uniformity will not occur in the immediate future or may never occur. Huntington's hypothesis is that future world conflicts will not be economic or ideological but they will be cultural. While nation-states will remain important, the main conflicts will be between civilizations. As Huntington uses the term, civilizations exist across nation-states and represent groups of people that share cultural values. Huntington writes, "Civilization and culture both refer to the overall way of life of a people, and a civilization is a culture writ large. They both involve the 'values, norms, institutions, and modes of thinking to which successive generations in a given society have attached primary importance'."[25]

Like Nisbett, Huntington identifies Sinic (Confucian-based) and Western as two of the possibly eight world civilizations. Huntington uses the term "Sinic" to indicate Chinese civilization in which Confucianism is a major element. Regarding other civilizations, he tentatively refers to Africa (sub-Saharan) as a civilization but recognizes problems in identifying a cohesive culture because of the impact of European imperialism and existing divisions between Islamic and Christian groups. However, he does argue that Africa maybe forming a separate civilization. Huntington contends, "Throughout Africa tribal identities are pervasive and intense, but Africans are increasingly developing a sense of African identity, and conceivably sub-Saharan [peoples] could cohere into a distinct civilization with South Africa possibly being its core state."[26] The other four civilizations, according to Huntington, are Japan, Hindu, Islamic, Orthodox, and Latin America. He identifies Japan as a separate civilization even though it was an offshoot of Chinese civilization.

Religion is a defining quality of what Huntington identifies as civilizations. Some of these religions contain elements referred to as "strong religion" or "fundamentalist."[27] The existence of conflicting religious fundamentalisms supports Huntington's vision of a clash of civilizations. For instance, Japan has strong nationalist religious movements associated with Shintoism and new religions such as Soka Gakkai, Agon-shu, and Aum Shinrikyo.[28] In 1995, the Aum Shinrikyo (Supreme Truth) released nerve gas in a Japanese subway killing a dozen people and injuring thousands of others.[29] Hinduism, he identifies, as the core of civilization of the Indian Subcontinent.[30] And within modern Hinduism is an extremely militant and at times violent group of Hindu fundamentalists identified with the nationalist Hindu teachings in V.D. Savakar's 1923 book *Hindutva* which considers Christianity, Buddhism, and Islam major enemies of Hinduism.[31] Islam also has militant factions that believe modernity and particularly the secular state are causing defections from Islamic religions. One of their goals is establishing theocratic states with the Islamic Sharia as the governing law.[32]

What Huntington calls Orthodox civilization is centered in Russia and is distinguished from Western Christianity, which has its roots in the Roman Catholic Church. Russia and others within the Orthodox civilization identify with the Byzantine Church. In this conceptualization, the Russian Orthodox Church developed during the Middle Ages with little contact with the Roman Church. Today, the Russian Orthodox Church is associated with the rise of Russian nationalism which has added another tension to world politics.[33] At the core of Western civilization are forms of Western Christianity including both Roman Catholic and Protestant Churches. Each of these forms contains types of militant fundamentalists who have killed and attacked scores of people.[34]

Huntington considers Latin America to be a separate civilization with roots in Western civilization but also tied to indigenous civilizations. Huntington writes about Latin America: it "has evolved along a very different path from Europe and North America. It has had a corporatist, authoritarian culture, which Europe had to a much lesser degree and North America not at all."[35] There have been many militant indigenous religious movements including the Ecuadorian fundamentalists the Puruha.[36] There are also other militant indigenous movements such as the Zapatista of Mexico and the supporters of the first indigenous president of Bolivia Evo Morales.[37]

Huntington's troubling vision hardly suggests a world moving towards cultural unity. Also, the revolt of indigenous peoples against previous colonialism embodies a rejection of a uniform global society. In contrast to this view of the future are the responses to Huntington's initial argument appearing in an issue of *Foreign Affairs*. "But Huntington is wrong," wrote Fouad Ajami, Professor of Middle Eastern Studies at Johns Hopkins. "He has underestimated the tenacity of modernity and secularism."[38] Robert Bartley, Editor of the *Wall Street Journal*, recognized the possibility that the twenty-first century might demonstrate that Huntington is correct. However, Bartley believes in the triumph of Western values in the global arena: "The dominant flow of historical forces in the 21st century could well be this: economic development leads to demands for democracy and individual (or familial) autonomy; instant worldwide communications reduces power oppressive governments; the spread of democratic states diminishes the potential for conflict."[39] In responding to Huntington's article, the former U.S. Ambassador to the United Nations, Jeane Kirkpatrick argues that Western values will be grafted onto other cultures: "But he [Huntington] ... knows how powerful is the momentum of modern, Western ways of science, technology, democracy and free markets. He knows that the great question for non-Western societies is whether they can be modern without being Western."[40]

The most triumphant support of the West came from Gerard Piel, former Chairman of Scientific American, Inc., in his response titled "The West is Best." Piel writes about the world's people, "They all aspire to the Western model ... As they proceed with their industrialization, they progressively embrace ... 'Western ideas' ... of individualism, liberalism, constitutionalism, liberalism, human rights, equality, liberty, the rule of law, democracy, [and] free markets." And, he claims, "Mass education, which comes with Westernizing industrialization, makes its contribution as well."[41]

An important thing about these responses is that they all assume that the West will continue to be dominant in global cultural change. In this framework, it is Western civilization versus all other civilizations. They also assume that Western civilization will provide the best benefits to the rest of the world. They also assume that the values of Western civilization will triumph over the values of militant and religious groups. But will they?

In assuming the triumph of Western values, they are also assuming the triumph of Western schooling and the continuing development of global educational practices and policies. Militant religious groups see materialistic Western values as antithetical to their beliefs. Even militant Christian groups worry about the secularization of Western nations. Given their historical experiences, many indigenous peoples see the West as the cultural enemy.

In summary, many religious and indigenous education models are in direct conflict with the human capital model of education. Issues of spirituality, the purpose of life, the meaning of wisdom, and traditional knowledge are in conflict with human capital economics that defines the welfare of humans as a function of economic development. I will explore this issue in the next two sections on religious and indigenous educational models.

## Religious Educational Models: A Rejection of Secular Modernity?

First, I want to make clear that I am unable within the limits of this book to cover all forms of religious education. Besides the wide variety of world religions, there are also many splinter groups within each religious tradition. The world's largest religions—Hinduism, Buddhism, Christianity and Islam—contain many different groups claiming to be the authentic voice of their religions. So, my approach will be to highlight common elements of religious education and differences regarding acceptance or rejection of modernity.

In chapter 1, I provided the following generalized model of religious education.

Religious Education World Models
- Study of traditional religious texts
- Study and practice of religious rites
- Emphasis on spirituality
- Emphasis on instilling moral and ethical standards
- Rejection of secularism

Most religious instruction involves learning a religion's rites, studying a religion's core texts, developing ethical or moral standards from religious texts, and learning how god or gods manifest themselves in the world. These elements vary considerably between religions and within religions. Secular public education is sometimes seen as the greatest threat. For example, writing about Protestant (a branch of Christianity) religious education in the United States and Germany, Richard Osmer and Friedrich Schweitzer state, "The advocates of the secularization of public education may not have imagined that this would hinder or diminish religious education in the family or in religious communities;

nevertheless, *the secularization of the school has been accompanied by a gradual weakening of most traditional forms of religious education*" (author's emphasis).[42]

## Religious Content in National School Systems

Some countries have included elements of religious instruction in national school systems in which the overall curriculum is secular in orientation. This has been difficult in the West because of support for a secular state and religious liberty. For instance in the United States, public schools were often called Protestant schools, as contrasted with the privately operated Catholic educational system, because of the Protestant orientation of public school textbooks, the teaching of a secular form of Protestant morality, and religious instruction in the form of school prayer and readings from the Christian Bible. When the U.S. Supreme Court in the 1960s declared school prayer and Bible reading unconstitutional many Christian-oriented parents protested by withdrawing their children from public schools and either home schooled them or sent them to private religious schools.[43]

In some nations, the adoption of Western forms of education have included a continuation of religious instruction through state-operated schools. As previously stated, world culture theorists argue that the spread of the Western concept of the nation-state and constitutional government was accompanied by the spread of mass schooling. However, this does not mean the spread of secular mass schooling. For instance, Article 13 of the Constitution of Saudi Arabia includes the support of religion as a goal of mass schooling: "education will aim at instilling the Islamic faith in the younger generation, providing its members with knowledge and skills and preparing them to become useful members in building of their society, members who love their homeland and are proud of its history."[44] In the Saudi Arabian Constitution, citizens are required to have allegiance to the *Qur'an*. The Saudi Arabian Constitution states:

> Article 6: Citizens are to pay allegiance to the King in accordance with the Holy Koran and the tradition of the Prophet, in submission and obedience, in times of ease and difficulty, fortune and adversity."
>
> Article 26: The state protects human rights in accordance with the Islamic Shari'ah.[45]

The integration of religious instruction into a government-operated school system has been a major goal of Islamic nations after adoption of Western forms of mass schooling including the Western educational ladder of primary, middle, secondary, and higher education. The problem for some Islamic leaders, as I will discuss, is that religious instruction becomes diluted when competing with other subjects. Egypt exemplifies this issue. The Egyptian constitution and educational system is a blend of historic Islamic doctrines, European influences, and Arab nationalism and socialism. In keeping with the tenets of Arab socialism, Article I of the Egyptian constitution declares: "The Arab Republic of Egypt is a democratic, socialist State based on the alliance of the working forces of the people."[46] Article 2 links the Arab language with the Sharia: "Islam is the Religion of the State and Arabic is its official language, Islamic jurisprudence (Sharia) is the principal source of legislation."[47] Islamic political principles require the state to regulate moral values. In the Egyptian constitution this obligation encompasses promotion of nationalism and socialism. Article 12 states: "The society shall be committed to safeguarding and protecting morals, promoting the genuine Egyptian traditions and *abiding by the high standards of religious education*, moral and national values, the historical heritage of the people, scientific facts, socialist conduct and public manners within the limits of the law. The State is committed to abiding by these principles and promoting them" (author's emphasis)."[48]

While adopting a Western-style constitutional government and school system, the Egyptian Constitution identifies religious education as central to public education. In an article that might be envied by those living under other constitutions, such as the United States which lacks an education article in its Constitution, Article 18 of Egyptian Constitution declares education a right of all citizens: "Education is a right guaranteed by the State. It is obligatory in the primary stage. The State shall work to extend obligation to other stages. The State shall supervise all branches of education and guarantee the independence of universities and scientific research centers, with a view to linking all this with the requirements of society and production."[49] Article 20 states that: "Education in the State educational institutions shall be free of charge in its various stages."[50] Article 19 makes religious education a central focus of this educational right. Article 19 states: "Religious education shall be a principal subject in the courses of general education."[51]

The merger of Islamic religious education, Western science and technology, Arab nationalism, and education for economic planning are exemplified by the curriculum for Egyptian primary schools (first to fifth grades). The greatest numbers of class periods in the curriculum are devoted to religious education, Arabic language, and mathematics.

Egyptian Primary Curriculum, 1990–91
  Religious Education
  Arabic Language
  Mathematics
  Social Studies
  Science and Health
  Observation of Nature
  Technical Education (industrial subject, agriculture, or home
    economics)
  Physical Education
  Music and/or Art
  Practical/Technical Training[52]

After adoption of the Constitution, religious study in Egyptian primary schools focused on traditional religious values and students' obligations to society and duties to the government.[53] These religious textbooks contained quotes from the *Qur'an* along with vocabulary lists and summaries. Stories were used to illustrate proper behavior according to Islamic traditions and, of course, to ensure an orderly society. Textbooks contain lists of religious-behavioral rules to be memorized for examinations.[54]

## Education and Religious Nationalism

Some religious leaders object to the limited inclusion of religion in schools and to the secularization of national school systems. These groups want young people to receive traditional forms of religious instruction; the schools established in India by the Vishva Hindu Parishad (V.H.P.) are an example. V.H.P. represents religious nationalism where attempts are made to link a feeling of national spirit to a religion.[55] This effort exists in many other countries, such as in the United States where Christians represented by Pat Robertson's Christian Coalition insist that Christianity is part of the ideal of American nationalism and in Israel where the Gush Emunim associated the destiny of Judaism with Israeli nationalism.[56] Even the U.S. military takes on the trappings of Christianity in a country noted for multi-religious population. In 2008, a controversy developed at the U.S. Naval Academy over the dipping of the American flag in front of a Christian alter in the Academy's chapel. Neela Banerejee reported in the *New York Times* about the controversy:

> Evangelical Christians and their critics alike assert that the academy had to reconsider after an outcry by congregants and alumni. "I think the ceremony is fully representative of the highest traditions of our country," said Bob Morrison, who has attended the 11 a.m. ser-

vice for 12 years and who heads an internship program at the Family Research Council, a conservative Christian group. "It basically says that our country is one nation under God and the nation-state is not the highest authority in the world."[57]

Organized in 1964, V.H.P. was a product of the strong religious-nationalism accompanying the resistance to British colonization of India. An influential book was V.D. Savarkar's *Hindutva*, which linked Hinduism to national unity and rebellion against British colonizers and religiously imposed doctrines of Christianity and Islam. An early section of the book celebrates the "fall of Buddhism" in India and links race, nationalism and religion: "the political consequences of Buddhistic expansion [had] been so disastrous to the national virility and even the national existence of our race."[58] Representative of Savarkar's religious nationalism is the claim that Moslem and Christian Indians should not be considered as Hindus in the context of the "fatherland." He claims they owe their religious allegiance to the lands from which their religions were born.

> That is why in the case of some of our Mohammedan or Christian countrymen who had originally been forcibly converted to a non-Hindu religion and who consequently inherited along with Hindus, a common Fatherland and a greater part of the wealth of a common culture—language, law, customs, folklore and history—are not and cannot be recognized as Hindus ... Their holy land is far off in Arabia or Palestine.[59]

In recent years, the V.H.P. has been associated with violent attacks on Christian Churches and Mosques and the killing of Christians and Moslems. These actions sparked increased religious tensions particularly between Hindus and Moslems.[60]

The V.H.P. has opened a variety of schools to teach its form of Hindu religious nationalism, including a teacher training institute called Peetham. The curriculum of the teacher training institute reflects the V.H.P.'s commitment to religious nationalism. The official description of the institute states, "The Peetham imparts training to schoolteachers and few others who are involved in social services. The Institute not only imparts information to teachers but also creates interest and involvement in value based education."[61] Maintaining a knowledge of Sanskrit is considered important in keeping alive Hindu culture. The following are the advertised courses and diplomas offered by Peetham:

- Diploma in Indian Culture and Moral Values (a full-time course for the duration of nine months)

- Diploma in Sanskrit language
- Degree in Yogashastra
- Short-term courses in value-education
- M.A. in Sanskrit[62]

The V.H.P. operates 130 schools, 374 adult education programs, and 800 centers for informal education. The organization estimates that 20,000 students have learned to read and speak Sanskrit. The V.H.P. states about its informal centers: "With a view to inculcate moral education, character-building, patriotism and love for Hindu Society, Balbaris and Bal-Sanskar Centers have been started and about 20,000 children are attending these centers."[63]

An ambitious project of V.H.P. is eradication of illiteracy among the roughly one-third of the population that cannot read or write. Of course, the intent is also to instill Hindu nationalism. The V.H.P. program is called "Ekal Vidyalaya Yojana: One Teacher School."[64] The V.H.P. claims that the Indian government has failed to provide an adequate education for India's poor. The One Teacher Schools have primarily been organized in small villages among India's tribal groups. Besides teaching literacy and Hindu nationalism, the schools teach basic health care. The schools are supposedly "initiated by the Village People for Village Children and by the Village Youth."[65] V.H.P. states that goals of One Teacher Schools are:

- To provide moral education
- To provide non-formal education to children
- To create feeling of oneness and unity in the village (Social Equality)
- To teach sanitation and health care[66]

The local youth who are trained to operate these One Teacher Schools are to function as social workers and teachers. They combine Hindu nationalism with rural development projects. These local youth leaders are themselves given training "in basic education, methodology, moral education, patriotic songs, stories and lives of great men and saints, Yoga, rural games and sports, sanitation and health care."[67] V.H.A claims the existence of 7,360 One Teacher Schools and that: "Our experience has been that the schools became the focal point for various social and religious events for the entire village."[68]

As I have suggested, religious nationalism can lead to internal conflicts within countries. For example in Sri Lanka, the national government has struggled against the independence movement led by the Tamil Tigers who are mainly Hindu and Christian and represent an ethnic minority.

The Sri Lankan government is officially Buddhist. While claiming to protect the rights of other religions, the Sri Lankan Constitution states: "CHAPTER II — BUDDHISM: The Republic of Sri Lanka shall give to Buddhism the foremost place and accordingly it shall be the duty of the State to protect and foster the Buddha Sasana, while assuring to all religions the rights granted by Articles 10 and 14(1)(e)."[69] Inevitably, religion became a focal point of conflict in Sri Lanka. For example, in 2006 a giant white statue of Buddha was erected on a five-foot-high concrete platform near the market in a small Sri Lankan town. The Tamils considered this a provocative act by the ruling Sinhalese. The leader of the Tamil protest against the statue was killed while going to the bank. The bodies of five Tamil youths were found on a beach. In response, a bomb was set off in the market killing sixteen people. Then, Sinhalese Buddhists torched Tamil-owned stores, homes, and schools. In response, the Tamil Tigers set off a bomb in the capital. The Sinhalese Buddhist government responded with air strikes on Tamil villagers killing dozens.[70] Religious and ethnic violence continues in Sri Lanka.

## Sarvodaya: The Welfare of All

In contrast to the religious nationalism of the V.H.P. and the materialist goals of human capital doctrines, Indian leader Mohandas Gandhi offered a different vision of Hinduism and education based on pacifism and a rejection of industrialism. Gandhi led the struggle against British colonialism, social class differences, and the discriminatory distinctions of the Hindu caste system. Of particular concern to Gandhi was the plight of untouchables. In 1948, Gandhi was killed by a Hindu nationalist because of his willingness to seek reconciliation with Moslems. Unlike Hindu religious nationalists, Gandhi believed that there was a unity to all world religions. Gandhi wrote, that the "study of other religions besides one's own will give one a grasp of the rock-bottom unity of all religions and afford a glimpse also of the universal and absolute truth which lies beyond the 'dust of creeds and faiths'."[71]

Gandhi's religious ideas are still attractive to large numbers of the world's Hindu population and are considered an alternative to the religious nationalism preached in the *Hindutva*.[72] His doctrine of Sarvodaya or the welfare of all rejects the emphasis of human capital education on technological development and economic growth. Gandhi made a distinction between "standard of living" and "standard of life." Increases in the standard of living, he argued, simply means increased income and acquisition of material goods. Income and material goods are not indicators of the quality of life. In contrast, the concept of standard of life represented a major deviation from the dominant global commitment to economic growth as improving human lives. Gandhi wrote, "a rise in the standard of living might even lower the standard of life, by reducing man's physical, moral, intellectual and spiritual standards. Hence, the progressive development of Nature must be consistent with rise in the standard of life, and not of living."[73]

The "craze for machinery," as Gandhi referred to industrialism, he believed was primarily driven by greed. Consequently, the result has overworked laborers being exploited by the few owners of factories. "Scientific truths and discoveries," he asserted, "should first of all cease to be mere instruments of greed. Then laborers will not be over-worked and machinery, instead of becoming a hindrance will be a help."[74] From Gandhi's perspective, the goal of technological and economic development should be improving the standard of life for all people rather than improved industrial efficiency to profit the owners of production. Consequently, a major result of industrialism, Gandhi asserted, was greater social and economic inequality.

Gandhi's educational plan involved "Sarvodaya workers" reforming village life. Included in the agenda of Sarvodaya workers was making the spinning wheel and agriculture the center of productive and community life of villages. This was to be part of what Gandhi called "nation-building" to overcome the destructive effects of previous British colonialism. Sarvodaya workers were to be models of self-denial, voluntary poverty, and temperance. They were to be acquainted with all aspects of cloth-making including the use of spinning wheels. They were to be interested in the plight of untouchables. In this manner, Sarvodaya workers were to be models to guide the spiritual and moral life for villagers.

Sarvodaya workers were also teachers. First, Gandhi saw them spreading knowledge about sanitation and health which certainly is an important aspect of increasing the standard of life. Second, they were to impart orally useful information before actually teaching reading. Gandhi stated, "Lots of useful information on current affairs, history, geography, and elementary arithmetic can be given by word of mouth before the alphabet is touched. The eyes, the ears and the tongue come before the hand."[75] In Gandhi's curriculum reading was to be taught before writing, and learning the alphabet. However, the role of the scholar-teacher was to be secondary to being a model village worker: "He will not pose as a litterateur buried in his books, loath to listen to details of humdrum life. On the contrary, the people whenever they see him, will find him busy with the tools—spinning wheel, loom, adze, spade, etc.— and always responsive to their meanest inquiries."[76]

Gandhi's educational goal was self-governing and the development of independent villages or what he called complete republics. Villages were to be the basic governing unit of society. In these village republics activities were to be cooperative endeavor. The focus on cloth production would ensure, Gandhi hoped, economic independence for the villages. Education to the final basic course would be compulsory. Economic and social inequality would be banished, including discrimination against untouchables. "Here," Gandhi declared, "there is perfect democracy based upon individual freedom. The individual is the architect of his own government. The law of non-violence rules him and his government."[77]

In summary, Gandhi and his followers believed a truly spiritual life could be fostered by small republican villages focused on a simple life of farming and cloth making. The goal is a spiritual life of nonviolence and social and economic equality. Education will provide knowledge of sanitation, literacy, and basic knowledge of geography, current events, and history. Rather than seeking the good life through raising material standards of living, Gandhi stressed the importance of measuring the quality of living by a "standard of life." The value of technology would be determined by its contribution to the "standard of life" and not by how it might increase a company's profits or stimulate economic growth. By suggesting that all world religions shared similar spiritual messages, Gandhi avoided the conflictual religious nationalism expressed *Hindutva*.

Gandhi's form of Hinduism rejects the material goals of human capital theory. It also rejects the assumption of many progressive educators that education should promote equality of economic goods. Increased material goods might not contribute to an improved "standard of life." Reflecting an anti-materialist bias against the West, Gandhi proclaimed: "People in the West generally hold that the whole duty of man is to promote the happiness of the majority ... and happiness is supposed to mean only physical happiness and economic prosperity. If the laws of morality are broken in the conquest of this happiness [economic prosperity], it does not matter very much."[78] And from Gandhi's perspective, "The consequence of this line of thinking are writ large on the face of Europe."[79]

## Education and Liberation Theology

Liberation theology seeks to free humans from the spiritual vacuum caused by political and economic oppression. While liberation theology has been widely discussed and in some situations condemned by the leadership of the Roman Catholic Church it has been primarily practiced in Central and South America. As Samuel Huntington suggests "Latin America" can be considered a civilization where the role of Christian churches has been different from those in Europe and North America. In Europe, Marxist ideology was primarily atheist in its orientation. In

Central and South America, Marxist ideology was integrated into liberation theology which became a doctrine of Christian Catholicism. Jose Mariátegui, briefly discussed in chapter 1 regarding the global movement of educational ideas, was a leading figure in the integration of Marxism and Christianity. Often identified as the originator of South American Marxism, Mariátegui was born on July 14, 1894, and grew up in the small southern Peruvian coastal town of Moquegua. He is considered by many the originator of a Latin American form of Marxism that would influence Marxists throughout South and Central America, including the thinking of Che Guevara, Fidel Castro, and leaders of the Sandinistas. Marc Becker asserts, "He is widely regarded as being the first truly creative and original Latin American Marxist thinker."[80] In *Marxist Thought in Latin America*, Sheldon B. Liss concluded, "No Latin American Marxist receives more acknowledgments of intellectual indebtedness from fellow thinkers than José Mariatequi."[81]

Influenced by his devout Catholic *mestiza* mother, Mariátegui, by furnishing a role for the Catholic Church in his Marxist theories, provided an intellectual justification for liberation theology. Many Marxists in South and Central America blended socialist ideas with their religious faith. Liberation theology was formally proclaimed at the 1968 Medellin Bishops Conference which committed the Church to helping the poor and protecting human rights. Following the proclamation, a movement started called Christians for Socialism who believed, as stated by the Bishop of Cuernavaca, Mexico, Sergio Arceo that, "Only socialism can give Latin America the authentic development it needs... I believe that a socialist system is more in conformity with the Christian principles of brotherhood, justice, and peace."[82]

Besides being an early advocate of liberation theology, Mariátegui called for the mass political education of peasants and indigenous peoples as a necessary condition for the growth of Marxism in South America. Literacy should be taught with political content. Mass political education, Mariátegui believed, was necessary for adapting Marxism to South American conditions, particularly for the recruitment of peasants and indigenous peoples. Mariátegui argued, "The problem of Indian illiteracy goes beyond the pedagogical sphere. It becomes increasingly evident that *to teach a man to read and write is not to educate him.*" (author's emphasis)[83] He contended that Marxism should be adapted to South America's social and political conditions which included large peasant population and indigenous tribes.

Mariátegui believed that praxis, which influenced Paulo Freire's work (discussed in chapter 5), was necessary for creating a free as opposed to an authoritarian Marxist society. He defined praxis as a "dialectic interrelation between objective and subjective conditions."[84] In other words, people were to understand how their subjective beliefs determined their interpretation of the objective world and how the objective world informed their subjective views. This form of education, Mariátegui stated in a manner similar to Freire's later use of consciousness as a liberating force, would "spark the revolutionary consciousness that would accelerate the socialist revolution, and thus help to compensate for the underdeveloped nature of the nation."[85]

Mariátegui, who had Inca ancestry, believed that Marxism could be adapted to indigenous cultures. He envisioned the creation of an "Indo–American" socialism. In his most widely read and translated book, *Seven Interpretive Essays on Peruvian Reality*, Mariátegui rejected industrialization as a necessary condition for a socialist revolution among the Inca people and called for recognition of a traditional Inca-communist society. He argued that traditional Inca society was socialist. "Faith in the renaissance of the Indian is not pinned to the material process of 'Westernizing' the Quechua [Inca] country," he asserted. "The soul of the Indian is not raised by the white man's civilization or alphabet but by the myth, the idea, of Socialist revolution."[86] After noting how Chinese and Hindu societies were able to incorporate socialist ideas, he questioned those who did not see indigenous cultures as incorporating Marxist ideas: "Why should the Inca people, who constructed the most highly-developed and harmonious communistic system, be the only ones unmoved by the worldwide emotion? The consanguinity of the Indian movement with world revolutionary currents is too evident to need documentation."[87] Quoting indigenous peoples' advocate González Prada, Mariátegui emphasized the importance of revolution for changing the conditions of Native Americans, "the condition of the Indian can improve in two ways: either the heart of the oppressor will be moved to take pity and recognize the rights of the oppressed, or the spirit of the oppressed will find the valor needed to turn on the oppressors."[88]

Mariátegui provided the initial stimulus for members of the Catholic Church to look more closely at South America's social conditions and plan an educational and social program for uplifting peasant and indigenous populations. This work coalesced at the 1968 Conference of Latin American Bishops in Medellin, Columbia which proposed educational programs to carry out the work of liberation theology. Medellin Conference's declaration "Justice and Peace" stated, "The lack of political consciousness in our countries makes the educational activity of the Church absolutely essential, for the purpose of bringing Christians to consider their participation in the political life of the nation as a matter of conscience and as the practice of charity in its most noble and meaningful sense for the life of the community."[89]

The spirit of the conference was captured by the words Franic Split, one of the participants:

> If the workers do not become in some way the owners of their labor, all structural reforms will be ineffective. [This is true] even if the workers receive a higher salary in an economic system but are not content with these raises. They want to be owners, not sellers, of their labor... At present the workers are increasingly aware that labor represents a part of the human person. A person, however cannot be bought; neither can he sell himself. Any purchase or sale of labor is a type of slavery.[90]

The documents issued by the Medellin conference supported Paulo Freire's educational methods by emphasizing the importance of protecting cultures and by advocating "Concientización." The documents rejected violent revolution for peaceful methods. Similar to Freire, they advocate a cultural revolution through education. Using concepts of consciousness, the Medellin Conference's declaration "Justice and Peace" stated, "The lack of political consciousness in our countries makes the educational activity of the Church absolutely essential, for the purpose of bringing Christians to consider their participation in the political life of the nation as a matter of conscience and as the practice of charity in its most noble and meaningful sense for the life of the community."[91] This idea was reiterated in a section titled "Information and Concientización."

> We wish to affirm that it is indispensable to form a social conscience and a realistic perception of the problems of the community and of social structures. We must awaken the social conscience and communal customs in all strata of society and professional groups regarding such values as dialogue and community living within the same group and relations with wider social groups (workers, peasants, professionals, clergy, religious, administration, etc.).[92]

The Medellin Conference announced that the Church would actively work to raise the level of people's consciousness: "This task of 'concientización' and social education ought to be integrated into joint pastoral action at various levels."[93]

In addition to recognizing the educational role of the Church in raising political consciousness, "Justice and Peace" stressed the importance of recognizing cultural differences. "The lack of socio-cultural integration," the declaration argued, "in the majority of our countries, has given rise to the superimposition of cultures. In the economic sphere systems flourished which consider solely the potential of groups with great earning power. This lack of adaptation to the characteristics and to the potentials of all our people, in turn, gives rise to frequent political instability and the consolidation of purely formal institutions."[94]

Participants at the Medellin Conference believed that overcoming social and economic oppression was necessary for achieving Christian peace. The Conference refused to support armed revolution while recognizing that continued economic inequalities would disrupt peaceful relationships. "In the face of the tensions which conspire against peace, and even present the temptation of violence," the Conference declaration stated, "we believe that the Latin American Episcopate cannot avoid assuming very concrete responsibilities; because to create a just social order, without which peace is illusory, is an eminently Christian task."[95] The declaration went on to stress that pastoral work should include education, defending the rights of the poor and oppressed, denouncing economic inequalities, creating grass roots organizations, ending the arms race, and denouncing the unjust actions of world powers. Regarding education, it was declared, "To us, the Pastors of the Church, belongs the duty to educate the Christian conscience, to inspire, stimulate and help orient all of the initiatives that contribute to the formation of man."[96]

Liberation theology included a criticism of the ongoing efforts at economic "development." At the 1969 Campine, Switzerland, meeting of the World Council of Churches Peruvian theologian Gustavo Gutiérrez raised the question of "Why development? Why not liberation?" These ideas were later incorporated in Gutiérrez's 1971 book A Theology of Liberation.[97] "But it is not enough that we be liberated from," Gutiérrez wrote, "oppressive socio–economic structures; also needed is a personal transformation by which we live with profound inner freedom in the face of every kind of servitude, and this is the second dimension or level of liberation."[98] And finally, he argued there was liberation from sin as defined by the Catholic Church.

Similar to many other radicals, Gutiérrez urged the development of a social theory adapted to the special needs of Central and South America. He asserted that "one of the most creative and fruitful efforts implemented in Latin America is the experimental work of Paulo Freire, who has sought to establish a 'pedagogy of the oppressed'."[99] Gutiérrez cited the work of José Carlos Mariátegui who, as I previously discussed, urged the adaptation of Marxist theories to the needs of the indigenous peoples of South and Central America. "We must bring Indo-American socialism," Gutiérrez quoted Mariátegui, "to life with our own reality, in our own language."[100] Quoting Che Guevara, Gutiérrez emphasized the importance of a new theoretical approach: "One of the great dangers which threaten the building of socialism in Latin America—pressed as it is by immediate concerns—is the lack of its own solid theory, and this theory must be Latin American, not to satisfy a desire for originality, but for the sake of elementary historical realism."[101]

The educational efforts of advocates of liberation theology were primarily carried out by Base Ecclesial Communities (BECs). The formation of BECs were advocated by the bishops attending the 1968 Medellin meeting which called for "small communities," "grass-roots organizations," and "collaboration ... with non-Catholic Christian Churches and institutions dedicated to the task of restoring justice in human relations."[102] In his history of liberation theology, Christian Smith offered this summary of the BECs' work: "BECs offered not only a solution to the lack of clergy but also, for the liberation theology movement, a means of educating the masses at the grass roots. Pastoral workers, utilizing Paulo Freire's method of conscientization, taught community members how to do critical social analysis."[103]

Liberation theology's educational programs were practiced by the Sandinista National Liberation Front in Nicaragua which overthrew the dictatorship of the Somoza dynasty in 1979 and in neighboring El Salvador by the Farabundo Marti National Liberation Front which after a decade of civil war captured the government in 1989. The official director of the Nicaraguan Literacy Crusade was liberation theologian Father Fernando Cardenal who proclaimed at the beginning of the crusade, "Literacy is fundamental to achieving progress and it is essential to the building of a democratic society... You learn to read and write so you can identify the reality in which you live, so that you can become a protagonist of history rather than a spectator."[104]

In El Salvador, sociologist John Hammond concluded that liberation theology played major roles in supporting the armed struggle, "During the 1970s a political movement arose in the Salvadoran countryside that led to the decade-long revolt of the 1980s. Innovative church people inspired by liberation theology formed Christian base communities in rural parishes, and from these a new political consciousness emerged."[105] In one typical situation, Hammond described the use of the Bible as a thematic representation to explore local political and economic injustices.

In summary, liberation theology is sharply different from religious nationalism. Liberation theologists believed they were preaching universal religious values that were not linked to any particular nation. However, liberation theology did share with religious nationalism a concern that contemporary social movements were placed in a traditional religious context. For instance, both the V.H.P. and liberation theology combined religion and economic improvement in their educational campaigns. In the next section, I will examine a more traditional form of religious education.

## State Supported Islamic Education

Islamic education will be my example of the various supports given by governments to religious studies. While Islamic education can be associated with religious nationalism such as in Iran, I will focus on traditional elements in the passing on of Islamic religious knowledge. I would also like to remind the reader that my goal is to illustrate religious education models that are in potential conflict with human capital and progressive education models. In other words, religious education can counter the growth of uniform global education policies and practices. Also, in possible competition with global English, Islamic education requires learning Qur'anic Arabic to read the *Qur'an*.

In general, Islamic education has a holistic vision of knowledge and education. As I discuss in the next section, this holistic view of the world is different from that of many indigenous peoples. For Islam, holistic knowledge is directly related to the unity of God's knowledge. As the Creator, God's knowledge permeates humanity and the surrounding natural world. Consequently, a study of nature can lead to a knowledge about God. "A holistic education," writes Zahra Al Zeera author of *Wholeness and Holiness in Education: An Islamic Perspective*,[106] "should lead its followers through observation and reflection on nature to apprehend the unity that connects God's creation. A holistic education integrates and unites the spiritual and the physical."[107] As Al Zeera points out the Islamic concept of holistic knowledge is sharply different from that of Western support of human capital education and Western paradigms of knowledge. She argues that all the major paradigms in vogue in Western universities (positivist, post-positivist, critical theory, and constructivist) do not contain a spiritual dimension and they are grounded in secular and materialist reality.[108] From her perspective, Western education is not only lacking a holistic understanding of the interrelationship between God and the material world but also lacks any clear direction about how the world "ought to be." Driven by the quest for economic expansion and conquest of nature through science, Western education, in contrast to Islamic education, denies the ability of God's knowledge to enlighten humans and provide humans with a moral compass.

Consequently, Al Zeera supports a concept of holistic education that is quite different from most of those supported under the progressive models of education. Progressive models stress a holistic approach as a means of understanding the interrelationships between academic subjects. In contrast, a holistic approach to education within the Islamic model stresses the interrelationships between God, nature, and humans. She writes, "A holistic education should lead its followers through observation and reflection on nature to understand the unity that connects God's creation."[109] From this perspective, spirituality is a key component of holistic education: "A holistic education integrates and unites the spiritual and the physical."[110]

Despite this vision of holistic education, as described earlier in this chapter, the curricula of many state-supported schools in Islamic countries separate subjects by disciplines including special courses on Islam.

On the other hand, some countries support separate Islamic institutions. A description of traditional Islamic educational institutions provides background for understanding current government support of Islamic religious schools. Between roughly 1000 and 1500 A.C.E. Islamic *madrasas* were the primary sources of religious thought and education. They might be considered "colleges" in contrast to primary schools called *kuttabs*. In kuttabs, students recited and memorized the *Qur'an* while rocking back and forth. It was believed that the rocking motion aided memory. For most of these early years, there were no printed texts and instruction relied on oral instruction with students writing on slates. The first printed book used in Egyptian schools appeared in 1834. It was a printed version of a eighth-century legal commentary.[111] Memorization of the *Qur'an* can create a mental framework for interpreting life's events. A recalled verse of the *Qur'an* can serve to guide people in their social interactions and as a reminder of their duty to God.

A primary goal of madrasas of this period was to determine how to live a just and Godly life by studying the *Qur'an*, which required learning Arabic. Therefore, the subjects studied in these traditional madrasas were Qur'anic recitation, Arabic grammar, Qur'anic interpretation, jurisprudence, the sources of Sharia (Islamic canonical law), and moral instruction. Nonreligious subjects in some madrasas included arithmetic, astronomy, medicine, and poetry.[112] According to Robert Hefner, "A generation ago, historians of Islamic education concluded that the madrasa's classrooms, degrees (ijaza), professorships, and endowed properties were proof that madrasas were the Muslim equivalent of the medieval West's universities."[113]

Islamic scholars in these early madrasas focused their scholarship on theology and law. The *Qur'an* called for the creation of a society based on community, socioeconomic justice, and human egalitarianism. The goal of scholars was to achieve this type of society by formulating laws based on the *Qur'an* and the *Hadith*. The *Qur'an* is the very Word of God, while the *Hadith* is a collection of the sayings of Mohammed. Religious and legal scholars consulted both the *Qur'an* and the *Hadith* to determine how human relationships should be regulated.

In their search for just laws and a just society, madrasa scholars wrote commentaries on the *Qur'an* and the *Hadith*, and commentaries on the commentaries. Fazlur Rahman argues that this involved a deductive form of scholarship using the following method: "First one must move from the concrete case treatments of the *Qur'an*—taking the necessary and relevant social conditions of that time into account—to the general principles upon which the entire teaching converges. Second, from this general level there must be a movement back to specific legislation, taking into account the necessary and relevant conditions now obtaining."[114]

This scholarship formed the Sharia or Scared Law, which in the twentieth century was included in the constitutions of many Arab nations.

Under pressure from European colonialism and influence in the nineteenth century, Islamic scholars worried about how to protect Islamic values. One of these scholars, Muhammad 'Abduh (1849–1905 B.C.E.) had the greatest influence over Arab education. In Egypt, he stressed that the true goal of education was the cultivation of human character according to the principles of Islam. He objected to the foreign schools in Egypt with the declaration: "Let parents refrain from sending their children to foreign schools that tend to change their habits and religious faith."[115] Muhammad 'Abduh argued that national education systems should include religious education. Regarding Egyptian national education, 'Abduh wrote, "If one seeks to educate and improve the Egyptian nation without religion, it is as if a farmer would try to sow seed in unsuitable soil ... his efforts will be in vain."[116]

Of particular importance for 'Abduh was the use of Arabic as the medium of classroom instruction. While foreign schools used Euroamerican languages as the medium of instruction, many Arab schools used Turkish because of the influence of the Ottoman empire. 'Abduh advocated the use of Arabic for religious and nationalist reasons. First, knowledge of Arabic was essential for reading the *Qur'an*. Second, since culture and language were intimately bound together, preservation of Arab culture against the inroad of Euroamerican culture required the preservation of the Arab language.[117]

Indonesia and Malaysia provide examples of government support of contemporary madrasas. They represent attempts to combine human capital goals with Islamic morality. In Indonesia in 1997, the nation with the largest Islamic population, there were 1,770,760 students enrolled in Islamic *pesantrens* and 5,698,143 studying in madrasas out of a total national primary and secondary student population of 44,067,090.[118] Traditionally, pesantrens were three to four year boarding schools beginning at the ages of eleven or twelve for educating mosque leaders (*imam*) and religious teachers. However, government mandated reforms in the 1970s required pesantrens to include general education subjects (English, history, and mathematics). For private madrasas, the Indonesian government requires students to take 70 percent of their studies in general education and 30 percent in Islamic religious studies.[119] Madrasas exist as a subsystem to the general government educational system. In 1989, a government regulation defined madrasas as a "general school with an Islamic identity."[120]

In Malaysia madrasas became centers for resistance against British colonialism. In 1908, the first Malaysian madrasa was established with a curriculum that included the teaching of Malay, English, and Arabic.

After World War II, religion became a central issue as nationalist groups worked to finalize independence from the British. The 1957 constitution made Islam the official religion of Malaysia. Regarding educational institutions, the constitution declared, "Every religious group has the right to establish and maintain institutions for the education of children and provide therein instruction in its own religion."[121] One special clause allowed for government funding of Islamic schools: "federal law or State law may provide for special financial aid for the establishment or maintenance of Muslim institutions or the instruction in the Muslim religion of persons professing that religion."[122] Following the adoption of the constitution, the government made Islamic religious instruction compulsory for all Moslem students.

Islamic morality is now part of the Malaysian primary and secondary school curriculum. Islamic morality is embodied in the 1987 New Education Philosophy report issued by the Malaysian government: "Education in Malaysia is an on-going effort towards further developing the potential of individuals ... based on a firm belief in and devotion to God."[123] Under the New Education Philosophy, the teaching of Islamic values served the secular purpose of social control by the state. The school system was to educate good citizens with the following values:

- Have a firm belief in and obedience to God;
- Be knowledgeable;
- Possess living skills;
- Possess high moral standards;
- Be responsible to his self, society, and nation;
- Contribute to the well-being of society and nation;
- Have a balanced personality.[124]

Saudi Arabia is an example of an Islamic nation which provides government support to universities to counter Western influence. The three Islamic-oriented universities established by the Saudi government are the Islamic University of Medina, the Imam Muhammad ibn Saʻud Islamic University in Riyadh, and the Umm al-Qura University in Mecca. Saudi royal decree at the founding of the Islamic University of Medina illustrates the religious intent of these institutions: "the formation of scholars ('ulama) specializing in the Islamic and Arabic sciences ... and equipped with the forms of knowledge that would enable them to call others to Islam and to solve the problems that confront Muslims in their religious and worldly matters in accordance with the Book [of God], the normative example [of the Prophet] and the practices of the pious forbears."[125]

In Pakistan, the shortage of government schools aided the steady and rapid growth of madrasas since 1947.[126] Another important factor in the growth of Pakistani madrasas is that they provide free room and board, textbooks, and instruction through a combination of government subsidies and community. The Pakistani madrasas are famous throughout the Islamic world. They attract foreign students associated with fundamentalist Islamic movements including those who participate in the Taliban movement in Afghanistan.[127] The free room and board is particularly attractive to low income families. A.H. Nayyar writes,

> Madrasahs, unlike formal schools, are attractive because they are invariably boarding houses, providing free boarding and lodging, free books, and often even clothing... This is an important, perhaps, overriding, factor for many from the lower and lower–middle classes. Not only does it go to reduce the burden on the tight family budget, it also keeps the children away from loitering and street crime.[128]

Pakistani madarsas developed differently from that of Arab nations. The madrasas movement in nineteenth-century India provided the model for later madrasas in Pakistan. Nayyar states, regarding the madrasa revival in late-nineteenth century British India, "The founders of *madrasahs* were strongly anti-imperialist, and communicated this spirit to their students... They viewed the imperialism of the West more as that of Christendom, and the modern technology brought in by the imperialists as a tool in the hands of adversarial religious force."[129] The Pakistani madrasas focus on memorization of the *Qur'an* and discussion of the *Hadith*. They now serve the Islamic world in educating students for continued resistance to Western Christian values.

In summary, religious educational models offer striking contrasts to human capital and progressive educational models. However, religious content added to national systems of education might be nested in a more general goal of human capital development and used primarily as means of social control. On the other hand, spiritual teachings often run counter to the material desires needed to maintain an industrial consumer society. From that standpoint, Gandhi's Sarvodaya represents a radical break with assumptions that material prosperity is key to a higher standard of life. Liberation theology provides a spiritual attempt to overcome the oppression of economic and political systems. Religious nationalism, as exemplified in this section by *Hindutva*, lends support to Huntington's contention that present and future events will involve a clash of civilizations.

## Indigenous Models of Education

As discussed in chapter 1, the world's 370 million indigenous peoples are identified by a number of characteristics, including long-term occupancy

---

**Key Points: Types of Religious Education**

1. Religious content in national schools
    a. Religious values translated into secular values for public school instruction
    b. Used as a form of social control to ensure "good" behaviors among citizens which often occurs in public schools in Christian and Islamic countries
    c. Religious courses included in general curriculum of public schools
2. State supported religious schools
    a. Schools devoted to religious instruction
    b. Schools with religious instruction plus government mandated general curriculum
3. Religious Nationalism
    a. Nationalism and religion believed to be closely related, such as Hindu fundamentalism, some forms of Christianity, in the United States and religious groups in Japan
    b. Education involves creating a belief of the inseparability of religion from the identity of a particular nation
4. Globalized religious education
    a. Education to create international religious communities
    b. Often associate with the missionary work of Christians and Islamic forms of conversion
5. Religion and education for social justice
    a. Exemplified by Gandhi's Sarvodaya and the Christian Catholic Church's liberation theology

---

of the land, tribal organization, and subsistence-oriented production. Indigenous groups have a social and cultural identity distinct from dominant national societies. Similar to discussion of world religions it is not within the scope of this book to discuss all of the world's indigenous peoples. In chapter 1, I provided a generalized model of indigenous education.

Indigenous Education World Models
• Indigenous nations control their own educational institutions
• Traditional indigenous education serves as a guide for the curriculum and instructional methods
• Education is provided in the language of the indigenous nation
• Education reflects the culture of the indigenous nation

Most indigenous peoples have been subjected to attempts to eradicate their cultural traditions by colonial powers in the Americas, Europe, Russia, Australia, New Zealand, Africa, and the South Pacific. Some have faced cultural domination by an often hostile surrounding society such as in Russia, China, Japan, and India. As a result, many indigenous groups have attempted to rescue their educational traditions as a means of protecting or restoring their cultural traditions. In 2007, after many years of seeking United Nations' protection, this international body ratified the United Nations Declaration of the Rights of Indigenous Peoples. This Declaration specifies educational rights that are often in conflict with human capital, progressive, and religious global models. Article 14 of the UN Declaration states:

- Indigenous peoples have the right to establish and control their educational systems and institutions providing education in their own languages, in a manner appropriate to their cultural methods of teaching and learning.
- Indigenous individuals, particularly children, have the right to all levels and forms of education of the State without discrimination.
- States shall, in conjunction with indigenous peoples, take effective measures, in order for indigenous individuals, particularly children, including those living outside their communities, to have access, when possible, to an education in their own culture and provided in their own language.[130]

Numbers 1 and 3 of Article 14 are designed to protect and restore indigenous educational methods and languages. Article 14's number 2 is supposed to ensure that indigenous peoples have access to a nation's public school system.

Earlier in this chapter I outlined some of the basic characteristics of indigenous knowledges. Again, I should warn the reader that there is a danger in assuming that all indigenous peoples share the same educational and cultural characteristics. However, most attempts to summarize indigenous knowledge and educational practices emphasize the importance of holistic knowledge and educational practices. In the conclusion to the previous section, I suggested that Islamic thought and indigenous thought differed in their concepts of holistic knowledge and education. While both see all things permeated by the spiritual, Moslem people rely for guidance on the *Qur'an* and they believe creation is linked to a single God. In contrast, indigenous people tend to rely on guidance from nature, dreams, and intuition and often see the spiritual world as composed of many gods.

In contrast to indigenous knowledges, monotheistic religions consider humans to be the central focus of natural existence. Indeed, some world religions, including Judaism, Christianity, and Islam, believe only humans have souls and not other animals. In contrast, many indigenous peoples see humans as just one species among many others. For instance: "Islam sees man as the vice regency of God on earth... Gifted with intelligence in the true sense of the term, he alone of all creature is capable of knowing."[131] In contrast, Hinduism and Buddhism by believing in reincarnation see other animals as part of the same life cycle as humans.

Giving humans a privileged place in the natural order justifies human exploitation of other animals and nature. The assumption that only humans have souls leads to a supposition that all of earth was created by a god to benefit humans. Many indigenous peoples see themselves as sharing a spiritual life with animals and nature. Consequently, indigenous peoples are often romanticized in environmentalist literature. Indigenous animism can lead to seeking signs about the meaning of past, present, and future events in nature and often in dreams or visions.[132]

Learning through experience, traditional practices and the wisdom of elders is the basis for many forms of indigenous education. A examples of the many forms of indigenous education can be found in Maenette Benham and Joanne Cooper's *Indigenous Educational Models for Contemporary Practice: In our Mother's Voice*.[133] Many of these educational practices, in contrast to the use of the scientific method, study nature through careful observation and the learning of traditional knowledge. Knowledge of human social interactions utilizes accumulated wisdom about relationships which is passed on from generation to generation. Consequently, elders, who embody their own life experiences, are the keepers of tradition and assume the role of tribal educators.

The United Nations Declaration of the Rights of Indigenous Peoples gives indigenous peoples the right to control their own education and it provides protection against the loss of language. Of course, all tribal groups have been affected by outside forces and the influences of the world's knowledges. For many indigenous peoples, the hope is to preserve and restore languages and cultures while integrating influences from the global flow of cultures. Obviously, particularly after the ravages of colonialism and imposition of outside religions, indigenous peoples will never be able to restore their lives to the state that existed prior to the invasion of these outside forces. But for the purpose of this book's argument, indigenous movements are not only part of the global flow of educational practices and ideas but they are often critical of the crass materialism and exploitation of nature embodied in the goals of human capital education.

## Key Points: Characteristics of Ingidenous Education

1. Learning of traditional knowledge
   a. Usually taught by elders
   b. Elders' wisdom based on accumulated knowledge from the past
   c. Elders' wisdom based on accumulated personal experience
2. Careful observation of
   a. Nature
   b. Human interaction with nature
   c. Human interaction with other humans
3. Learning from spirits, dreams, and other prophetic signs
   a. Interpretation usually taught by elders
4. Holistic view of humans, nature, and spiritual world
5. Instruction of the interrelationship and interdependence of all humans, nature, and the spiritual world

## Conclusion: Rejecting the Industrial–Consumer Paradigm?

The existence of different knowledges suggests that there are global variations in course content despite global educational similarities in curricula and grade structures. Religion remains a central part of many people's lives and will continue to influence the way they think about the world and the values they hold. Consequently, the spiritual nature of religions creates a tension with the materialistic values embedded in human capital theory with its emphasis on economic growth and increasing personal income or, in the words of Gandhi, on raising the "'standard of living." Not only are there inherent tensions between religion and a consumer-oriented secular society, but there are also conflicts between religions that reduce the possibility of a uniform world culture. Religious nationalism and religious rejection of Western secular values gives support to Huntington's contention that the future involves a clash of civilizations rather than the sharing of common global values.

Those championing the restoration or maintenance of indigenous knowledges and culture cast a wary eye on the fruits of Western science and industrialization. Countering the influence of the secular–scientific global culture, indigenous educational programs stress the learning of traditional knowledge, careful observation of nature and human relations to others and nature, respect for the wisdom of elders, and the importance of the world of spirits. The hope is that indigenous education programs, as recognized by the United Nations Declaration of the Rights of Indigenous Peoples, will maintain indigenous cultures and languages while, at the same time, select from the world's knowledges useful information that will aid in the growth of the standard of life.

Will the globalization of educational practices and policies erode religious values and undermine indigenous cultures? Or is there some middle ground between education for human capital development and religious or traditional values? Will there be a continuing clash of civilizations or will all people adopt the similar ways of knowing and seeing the world?

## Chapter 7

# Global Migration and
# Language Policies

*[handwritten: multicultural education
language instruction]*

Global migration results in culture and language issues for both migrants and host countries. Global migration is accompanied by rural to urban migrations resulting in the majority of the world's peoples living in urban centers. In part, global and rural to urban migrations are prompted by hopes of better economic opportunities in other countries and urban centers. Often skilled and educated workers migrate from poorer to wealthier nations. This migration raises serious issues related to the effect on poorer nations of the loss of skilled and educated workers and how these migrant workers are integrated into the labor force of host nations. Global migration has made multicultural education and language instruction important issues for national school systems. What policies should public school systems adopt for the education of immigrant children who do not speak the dominant or national language? What cultural policies should national and local schools adopt when global migration results in multicultural populations? Is the global usage of English threatening local languages?

I will first describe the current pattern of global migration and the migration from rural to urban areas. Then, I will examine the educational issues facing the children of global migrants. In later sections, I will discuss *brain drain*, *brain gain*, *brain waste*, and *brain circulation*. Often global migration and rural to urban migration involve the movement of educated and skill workers from low-income nations and rural areas to more prosperous nations and/or urban centers. This is what is meant by *brain drain*. Some countries experience a *brain gain* by attracting immigrants with high levels of educational achievement. Sometimes migrants to other countries or urban areas are not able to obtain employment commensurate with their educational qualifications. This is called *brain waste*. Some migrants return to their home countries or become transnational with homes in different countries. This phenomenon is captured in the phrase *brain circulation*. Global migration and rural to urban migration has a direct affect on national supplies of educated workers and national school policies. Global migration raises

## Key Points: Global, International, and Rural to Urban Migration

1. Global migration
   a. Between 1960 and 2005, the number of international migrants more than doubled with 191 million in 2005
   b. The largest migration patterns are from poorer to wealthier nations
   c. A small number of countries host 75 percent of the world's international migration
   d. Immigrant populations have higher rates of unemployment due to
      i. Lack of networks to find jobs in host country
      ii. Lack of knowledge about the labor market in host country
      iii. Discrimination on basis of country of origin
2. Rural to Urban Migration
   a. In 2008 the majority of the world's population will live in urban centers
   b. By 2050, 80 percent of the world's population growth will be in urban centers
   c. In developing countries the poor constituted about half of the urban population
3. Brain Drain
   a. Many developing nations are experiencing a migration of their post-secondary educated populations
      i. This is seriously affecting health and education services and reducing the tax base in developing nations
   b. Many immigrants are over-qualified for the jobs resulting in brain waste

the issue of multilingual school policies, which may involve possible loss of some languages as a result of the spread of global English.

## Global Migration: International and National

Migration is both international and national. Migrations of populations within a country primarily involve population movement from rural to urban centers. International global migration has increased and apparently it will continue to do so. The largest migration patterns are from poorer to wealthier nations. While wealthier nations have only 16 percent of the world's workers, they have over 60 percent of global migrants.[1] The Report of the Global Commission on International Migration declared, "International migration has risen to the top of the global policy agenda … In every part of the world, there is now an understanding that the economic, social and cultural benefits of international migration must be more effectively realized, and that the negative consequences of cross-border movement could be better addressed."[2] Phillip Martin provided an official description of global migrants and general tally of the migration statistics for the Commission:

> Migrants are defined by the United Nations as people outside their country of birth or citizenship for 12 months or more. In a world of 190+ sovereign nation states, each of which issues passports and regulates who can cross its borders and stay in its sovereign territory, the UN's Population Division estimated there were 175 million migrants in 2000, including 65 million or 37 percent in "less developed" nations, which are those outside Europe and North America, Australia/New Zealand, Japan, and the ex-USSR "where it is presented as a separate area." The number of migrants in less-developed countries was stable in the 1990s, but the developing countries' share of the world's migrant stock fell with their rising population.[3]

Also, the United Nations' Population Division reports that "Between 1960 and 2005 the number of international migrants in the world more than doubled, passing from an estimated 75 million in 1960 to almost 191 million in 2005, *an increase of 121 million over 45 years*" (author's emphasis)[4] Prior to 1985, the number of international migrants in developing nations about equaled that in developed nations. After 1985, the international migrants to developed nations increased at a rapid rate while those in developing nations has remained about the same. Currently, the economic causes of migration reflect the rapid growth of migrant populations in developed nations. In 2005, only 7 percent of migrant population were refugees. The United Nations estimates that: "In 1960, 57 per cent of all migrants lived in the less developed regions but by 2005, just 37 per cent did so."[5]

In 2005, the following were the percentages of the population of each of the world's regions that were international migrants.

1. Oceania (15%)
2. North America (13%)
3. Europe (9%)
4. Africa, Asia, and Latin America and the Caribbean (less than 2%)[6]

The pattern of global migration becomes clearer when it is broken down by country. A small number of countries host 75 percent of the world's international migrants. In 2005, the United States had 20.2 percent of the total global migrants which is the world's highest national percentage. It should be noted that for the United States this was an increase of more than 5 percent since 1990.[7] The following is a list of the top eleven countries hosting the highest percent of the world's migrant population.

**Percentage of Global Migrants Hosted by a Nation in 2005**
1. United States          20.2%
2. Russian Federation     6.4
3. Germany                5.3  *immigration laws make*
4. Ukraine                3.6  *sense*
5. France                 3.4
6. Saudi Arabia           3.3
7. Canada                 3.2
8. India                  3.0
9. United Kingdom         2.8
10. Spain                 2.5
11. Australia             2.2[8]

It is important to note that the high percentage of global migrants in the Russian Federation and the Ukraine is a result of the 1991 disintegration of the Union of Soviet Socialist Republics (USSR). This is an example of how political changes can affect citizenship. The high percentage in these two countries is a result of the reclassification of citizens after the dissolving of the USSR. Prior to 1991, there were large numbers of internal migrants who moved from former parts of the USSR to what is now the Russian Federation and the Ukraine. After 1991 these formerly internal migrants were reclassified as international migrants.[9]

What countries are the sources of the world migrants? OECD has provided statistics for the sources of immigration into OECD European countries and into OECD countries outside of Europe. As discussed in chapter 3, OECD members include thirty of the richest nations in the world. Migration into OECD nations is often, but not always, a result of migrants seeking better economic opportunities. As indicated in the list below, many of the immigrants to European OECD nations are from poorer nations of the European Union, namely Poland and Romania. Also, the populations of some developed countries such as Germany, the United Kingdom, and France moved to other OECD countries. For instance, many retirees left the United Kingdom to live in Spain.[10]

**Ten Top Sources for Immigration in OECD Europe, 2005**
(from largest source to smallest source)
1. Poland
2. Romania
3. Morocco
4. Bulgaria
5. Germany
6. Ukraine
7. Turkey
8. United Kingdom
9. Russian Federation
10. France[11]

The statistics for sources of immigration outside of OECD Europe provides a broader view of the migration from developing to developed nations. However, there are exceptions in the list below. Some citizens of the United Kingdom and the United States simply seek to relocate or to retire to other countries.

**Ten Top Sources for Immigration to OECD Countries Outside of Europe, 2005**
(from largest source to smallest source)
1. China
2. Mexico
3. Philippines
4. India
5. United Kingdom
6. Korea
7. United States
8. Viet Nam
9. Russian Federation
10. Cuba[12]

Concurrent with increasing international migration is internal migration from rural to urban areas—humans are now primarily living in cities. A 2008 UN report predicted that, "During 2008, the population of the world will become, for the first time in human history, primarily urban, and is likely to continue to urbanize substantially over the coming decades."[13] The UN report also claimed that, "The shift of population from relatively low-productivity rural areas to higher productivity urban areas has been a major aspect if not a driver of economic progress."[14]

Below are a list of facts reported by the United Nations regarding global urbanization:

- Almost all of the world's population growth to 2050 will occur in urban areas of developing countries;
- In developing countries the poor constituted about half of the urban population;
- For a majority of developed countries, urban growth is a result of natural growth rather than rural-urban migration;
- Most of the urban population growth is in small cities (under 500,000);
- Large cities are growing at a relatively slow pace;
- The number of poor people is increasing faster in urban areas;
- Urbanization concentrates a large part of the population on a small surface of the earth;
- About 80 percent of the world's population growth to 2050 will be in urban areas in Asia and Africa;
- The growth of the world's rural population is expected to be *negative* by 2018;
- In 2007, 50 percent of all rural dwellers in the world lived in Asia, primarily in China, India and Indonesia.[15]

The report also noted that the rural to urban migrants tend to be young and to be better educated and have more skills than the rest of the rural population. In other words, there is a brain drain from rural to urban centers. In addition, as noted above, in developing countries the poor constitute half the urban population. This has strained social services including the provision of public education. Many of the rural to urban migrant poor have been forced "to invade and settle ("squat") on marginal lands, such as under bridges, on floodplains or on steep slopes."[16]

There is also the tragedy of illegal immigration into a country. National borders and passport controls can lead to tragedy as some people try to illegally enter countries to gain employment. The following are just a few examples of the tragedies associated with attempts to illegally cross national borders:

- In 2001 in Britain, fifty-eight illegal Chinese migrants died when they were crammed into a sweltering tomato truck.
- In 2002, Spanish authorities found the bodies of five illegal immigrant African men in the back of a refrigeration truck carrying vegetables from Morocco.
- In 2003, nineteen Latin American migrants died from overheating and suffocation inside a trailer truck as they illegally entered the United States.

- In 2008, Thai authorities reported the death of thirty-seven women and seventeen men being illegally smuggled from Myanmar to work in resorts serving foreign tourists in Phuket. The deaths resulted from 121 people being shipped inside an airtight seafood container that measured just twenty feet long and seven feet wide. These deaths were in addition to those in 2007 that included twenty-two illegal immigrants found floating in the ocean near the West Coast of Thailand and eleven illegal immigrants killed in truck crash as they were being smuggled.[17]

## The Children of Global Migrants in OECD Countries

OECD uses three classifications when discussing the children of immigrants:

1. Foreign-born who migrated at a young age (first generation);
2. Native-born children of foreign-born parents (second generation);
3. Native-born children with one foreign-born parent.

For foreign-born immigrant children, a major issue is the possible differences between the educational systems in the country of origin and the host countries. Is it easy for the school-age child to make the transition into the school system of the new country? Is there a similarity in the curricula between the two nations? Has the child received an education in several other countries before arriving in the new host country? What are the language issues for the new immigrant child? Does the host country have educational provisions for helping immigrant children learn the language used in local schools?

The above questions are important for considering the integration of migrants into the social and economic system of their host country. In OECD countries these questions are imperative because of the large percentage of youth ages twenty to twenty-nine with migrant backgrounds who are in the labor market. For instance, persons with migrant backgrounds account for almost 45 percent of the twenty- to twenty-nine-year-olds in Australia. In Canada the figure is close to 35 percent. In the United States the figure is about 25 percent, and in France it is around 24 percent.[18]

In general, first generation children do not obtain the same level of educational achievement as native-born children. The educational achievement of both the first and second generations is related to the educational achievement of their parents. Consequently, variations in achievement are related to the immigration policies of the host country. For instance, Australia and Canada select immigrants based on their education qualifications and the needs of their countries' labor markets. In these two countries the educational achievement of second-generation children is about the same or higher than other native-born children. In contrast, Germany and Belgium recruit low-skilled foreign workers. The educational achievement of the second generation in these two countries is significantly lower than that of other native-born children. In some countries, when the socio-economic status of immigrant parents is taken into account, second-generation children still have lower educational achievement levels compared to other native-born children particularly in Germany, Belgium, Switzerland, and Austria.[19]

There are significant gender differences in educational achievement among immigrants. Usually, women have lower levels of educational achievement among foreign-born and non-school age immigrants to developed OECD countries. However, this significantly changes for the second generation. This represents the cultural impact on family dynamics and female status of global migration. According to the OECD, "In all countries with the exception of the United States, native-born women with foreign-born parents have a higher educational attainment than their male counterparts."[20] In the United States education attainment is almost equal between second-generation men and women.[21]

Except for Canada, the United States, and Australia, first- and second-generation immigrants have higher rates of unemployment relative to native-born workers. Unemployment differences remain high even when the second generation has comparable educational attainment as other native-born workers. OECD provides the following reasons for the higher rates of unemployment:

- Lack of networks: OECD found that a significant proportion of jobs are found through friends and relatives;
- Lack of knowledge about the functioning of the labor market in host country;
- Discrimination on basis of country of origin.[22]

Language is the other factor affecting school achievement and employment opportunities. I will discuss language policies in more detail later in this chapter. However, there are important questions to consider regarding the language usage of first- and second-generation immigrants. Did the immigrant family know the language of the host country before immigrating? Do host countries have educational programs to help first generation children learn the language of the host country? Do immigrant families continue to speak their mother tongues when at home? According to OECD, "One factor specific to children of immigrants is that they often speak a language at home which differs from that of the host country. Such children tend to have lower [educational achieve-ment] outcomes than other children with a migration background."[23] Does the educational system in the host country try to maintain the languages of their immigrant populations? I will address these language issues in a later section.

## The Knowledge Economy: Brain Drain, Gain, and Circulation

One of the much studied aspects of the knowledge economy is the global migration of skilled and educated workers. The term "brain drain" was first used in the United Kingdom to describe the influx of Indian scientists and engineers.[24] In this situation, the United Kingdom had a brain gain while India lost educated workers. Now there is also focus on brain circulation where skilled and professional workers move between wealthy nations or return to their homelands after migrating to another country. The *Report of the Global Commission on International Migration* provided a justification for dropping brain drain in favor of brain circulation:

> Given the changing pattern of international migration, the notion of 'brain drain' is a somewhat outmoded one, implying as it does that a migrant who leaves her or his own country will never go back there. In the current era, there is a need to capitalize upon the growth of human mobility by promoting the notion of 'brain circulation', in which migrants return to their own country on a regular or occasional basis, sharing the benefits of the skills and resources they have acquired while living and working abroad.[25]

Brain circulation is aided by national efforts to bring back educated workers lost in the brain drain. In China returning knowledge workers are called "turtles" as explained in a 2007 issue of the *China Daily*: "Enticed by more opportunities in a blossoming economy, many overseas Chinese—or 'turtles'—are swimming home."[26] The Chinese government is offering special benefits to encourage turtles. Malaysia has developed a national strategy to bring scientists home.[27]

There is a great deal of debate about the effect of the movement of highly educated populations on the knowledge economies of nations. For instance, what is the long-term impact of the fact that "many Central American and island nations in the Caribbean had more than 50 percent of their university-educated citizens living abroad in 2000."[28]Nearly 40 percent of tertiary-educated adults have left Turkey and Morocco while Africa has lost 30 percent of its skilled professions.[29]

The problem of brain drain appears serious when you consider the statistics for other nations. In 2000, the number of post-secondary educated citizens emigrating from Guyana, Grenada, Jamaica was 89 percent, 85.1 percent, and 85.1 percent, respectively. The numbers emigrating from these countries is small because of their small populations. However, the problem is more serious for these countries when considered as a percentage of the total population. Sub-Saharan Africa, a region struggling with poverty, health problems, and wars has lost its educated population: Ghana (46.9%), Mozambique (45.1%), Sierra Leone (52.5%), Kenya (38.4%), Uganda (35.6%), Angola, (33.0%) and Somalia (32.7%). The same pattern is occurring in developing countries in Asia, such as Lao Peoples Democratic Republic (37.4%), Sri Lanka (29.7%), Vietnam (27.1%), Afghanistan (23.3%), and Cambodia (18.3%).[30]

A loss of such high percentages of educated workers from developing countries has devastating effects on health and education services. In part, this is a result of losses to the tax base as high-paid professional workers who migrate overseas.[31] For instance, 85 percent of Filipino nurses work overseas with many having migrated to the United Kingdom, Saudi Arabia, Ireland, and Singapore. Over half the graduates of Ghana's medical schools left the country within five years of graduation. Only 360 doctors out of 1,200 doctors educated in Zimbabwe in the 1990s remained in 2001. Twenty-one thousand doctors have left Nigeria to practice in the United States. Similar examples of the loss of medical personnel can be found for other developing countries.[32]

Another way of considering the brain drain are figures regarding the percentage of educated immigrants in a particular country, such as the United States. For instance, 83 percent of the immigrants over twenty-five years old from Nigeria in the United States have some form of post-secondary education. Other examples of the percentage of immigrants from a particular country to the United States who are over twenty-five with post-secondary education are: India (80%), Indonesia (75%), Egypt (78%), Sri Lanka (72%), and Pakistan (67%).[33]

Also, if a country invests money in educating a worker and that worker migrates to another country, then the country that provided the original education has lost its investment. For example, training a worker in India to be a data processing specialist in 2001 cost the Indian government from $15,000 to $20,000. If that worker migrates to another country, then India loses the cost of the training plus the worker's potential contribution to the Indian economy estimated at $2 billion.[34] This fact is important when one considers that in the 1970s, 31 percent of the graduates of one of India's most prestigious schools, Indian Institute of Technology Mumbai, migrated overseas. The overseas migration rate for graduates from India's most prestigious medical school, All India Institute for Medical Sciences, was 56 percent between

1956 and 1980 and 49 percent in the 1990s.[35] This represents a tremendous loss of talent and educational investments for India.

Some researchers claim positive effects for countries experiencing brain drain. One positive effect for nations losing educated people to wealthier nations are the remittances sent home with some of these remittances being used for education and health care.[36] Also, some researchers are suggesting the migration results in demands for greater government spending on education (brain gain) by populations in less developed countries wanting to migrate.[37] These researchers believe that this can result in a "net brain gain [for countries losing educated workers], that is, a brain gain that is larger than the brain drain; and a net brain gain raises welfare and growth."[38]

The argument that there is a net brain gain as a result of pressures for expanded educational opportunities might only apply to larger nations. The net brain gain argument does not apply to small developing countries that have difficulty maintaining their educational systems because of the loss of educational workers. Also, in the most recent study for the World Bank, Schiff concluded that previous studies had been overly optimistic about the positive effects of brain drain on countries experiencing the loss of educated workers. His conclusions for the World Bank study were: "the brain drain on welfare and growth is likely to be significantly greater, than reported.[39] Frustrated by the difficulty of determining the economic consequences of brain circulation, Vinokur argues that the debate over "who wins, who loses and how much" in brain circulation as being "irresolvable—analytically and empirically."[40]

Brain circulation is not always beneficial for developed nations such as members of OECD. In some cases jobs migrate rather than educated workers. According to some recent analysts, there is a movement of high skilled jobs from developed to developing countries. For instance, Brown and Lauder found software companies relocating from the United States and the European Union to India. In the United States, according to Brown and Lauder, software developers earned in 1997 from $49,000 to 67,500 as compared to $15,700 to 19,200 in India.[41] The implication of these findings is that rather than India experiencing a brain drain they could be experiencing a gain in brain related jobs. Or, in other words, the United States could experience a loss of jobs requiring highly skilled workers to countries with lower wages and an increasing number of college graduates.

What are the effects of educated and skilled migrants and foreign students to the destination country? Researchers find contradictory effects. In the most recent research for the World Bank, it was concluded that reducing the flow of students and skilled workers to the United States would have a strong negative impact on innovation in contrast to raising the number of foreign graduate students by 10 percent which would increase the number of patent applications by 4.7 percent.[42] On the other hand, researchers have found no significant increases in wages for college graduates in developed countries, such as the United States and Great Britain, except for those few entering at the top of the wage scale.[43] Two possible implications of these finding are that developed countries are experiencing an oversupply of college graduates, which would reduce wages, and that the brain gain from migration might be depressing wages for college graduates.

## Brain Waste

Is there a global oversupply of college graduates? Do host countries utilize the educational qualifications of their immigrants? Is there a global "brain waste?" According to OECD findings, well-educated immigrants have difficulty utilizing their educational training in OECD countries for the following reasons:

- Problems with the recognition of degrees in the country of origin
- Lack of human and social capital specific to the host country, such as proficiency in the language of the host country
- Local labor market conditions
- Various forms of discrimination[44]

Not surprisingly, given the above factors, OECD statisticians found that more immigrants were overqualified for their jobs than native-born workers. The over-qualification of immigrants varied between countries. In survey data for 2003–2004 for the workers aged fifteen to sixty-four, highest percentages of foreign-born who were overqualified were in Spain (42.9%), Greece (39.3%), Australia (24.6%), and Ireland (23.8%). The countries with smallest percentage of over-qualified foreign-born workers were Luxembourg (9.1%), Hungary (9.7%), Czech Republic (10.0%), and Switzerland (12.5%). In the United States, which as previously stated has 20.2 percent of the total global migrants, the percentage of over-qualified foreign-born workers was 18.1 percent.[45]

Examining similar statistics for the World Bank, Caglar Ozden stresses the importance of immigration laws and the nature of the labor market in determining the percentage of over-qualified foreign-born workers:

Despite the relatively large share of migrants from developing countries, migrants to the United States are relatively more educated. This selection effect might be the result of the relative ease with which highly educated people can migrate to the United States. The labor market and migration policies seem to favor the more educated in the United States, especially when compared to Europe.[46]

What about native-born workers? Is there brain waste or an over-education of the population? Of course, education has other benefits to the person and society than those related to employment. OECD provides national statistics on native-born workers who are overeducated for their jobs. Keep in mind that in every nation a higher percentage of foreign-born workers are overqualified for their jobs as compared to native-born workers. The countries that have the most native-born workers who are overqualified for their jobs are Spain (24%), Australia (19%), Ireland (15.7%), Belgium (15.6%), and the United Kingdom (15.3%).[47]

One measure of labor market discrimination against immigrant workers is the difference between the percentages of native-born workers who are over-qualified for their jobs as compared to immigrant workers. If there is no difference, then immigrant workers are being treated the same as native-born workers in the labor market. The greater the disparity in over-qualification between the two, the greater the degree of discrimination or difficulties for foreign workers entering the labor market. The highest ratios between over-qualified native-born workers and over-qualified foreign-born workers are in Greece, Italy, Luxembourg, Sweden, Austria, and the Czech Republic. In other words, these national labor markets are the most difficult for immigrants to find employment that utilizes their skills and education.[48]

A critical evaluation of the issue of brain waste might claim that large corporations are pressuring national governments to raise the educational attainment of their populations as a means of ensuring a cap or lowering of wages for educated workers. For instance, an oversupply of college graduates might reduce wages for the college educated. This would benefit the employer but not the employee. This argument is supported by the findings of Phillip Brown and Hugh Lauder. Regarding college graduates in the United States, they conclude that since 1973 "the vast majority of college graduates have received no additional 'premium' on their investments in their human capital [as promised by those arguing for human capital education for the knowledge economy] compared to college graduates in the 1970s."[49] For the United Kingdom, they argue that "the first jobs taken by young people today may have less income and status associated with them than when their fathers entered the labor market."[50]

There will be variations in the actual economic outcomes for individuals swept up in the rhetoric of human capital education. The paradigm of human capital education drives people to go to school to get well-paid jobs which might not exist after they graduate. Caught up in

*Corporations may be driving/supporting the over-abundance of those w/ degrees*

the global flow of well-educated migrant workers, the graduate might suffer the emotional pain of cultural change, loss of social and family relations, and a sense of being homeless. As I discussed in chapter 6, Gandhi warned that there is a difference between a "standard of living" and a "standard of life." The human capital model of education promises, but frequently does not deliver, a higher standard of living. There is no promise about improving the standard of life. Some global migrants might experience a declining standard of life through cultural and geographical dislocation and the possibility of being overeducated for jobs in their host countries.

## Remittances and Unskilled Labor

Global migration creates an interdependence on the global economy particularly as a result of the money (remittances) immigrants send back to their home countries. Economists suggest that countries experiencing brain drain to wealthier countries benefit from remittances. This has been particularly true for legal and illegal immigrants from Central and South America to the United States. Most of the migrant workers are unskilled, and their families that have been left behind depend on their remittances. However, the amounts of remittances are directly affected by economic conditions in the host country. This became starkly clear in 2008 when the United States economy began to erode and remittances began to decline to Central and South America. In 2008, Inter-American Development Bank reported that 50 percent of Latin American adults living in the 50 states and the District of Columbia in the United States sent remittances on a regular basis to their families. This percentage was lower than the 73 percent reported in 2006. This was after a steady growth in remittances since 2000. Normally, unskilled workers from Latin America earn an average of $1,600 a month and send an average of $160 of that pay back to their homelands. Remittances reached $1 billion in ten of the states of the United States with the largest coming from Nevada, Colorado, Washington, Massachusetts, and California.[51]

Why the decline in remittances? According to Donald Terry, General Manger of Inter-American Development Bank's Multilateral Investment Fund, the principal causes were the slowdown in the U.S. economy and more negative feeling towards immigrants by U.S. citizens. In 2008, 81 percent of the migrants from Central and South America found it more difficult to find a better paying job than in 2007. Sixty-eight percent reported that they were facing greater discrimination in contrast to 2001 when only 37 percent complained of discrimination.[52]

What will be the effect of declining remittances on economies of Central and South American countries? How does the effect of declining remittances demonstrate the interdependence of global economies? The answer to both questions can be found Donald Terry's dire warning, "If the current trend holds over the next year, we would expect millions of families throughout Latin America who until recently had been receiving remittances to fall below the poverty line."[53]

## Global Migration and Multicultural Education

A main concern of the Global Commission on International Migration is how nations maintain social cohesion with increasing multicultural populations. This is an important educational problem for wealthier nations facing an influx of immigrant cultures. The Commission declares the existence of nations containing a single cultural population a thing of the past:

> International migration is increasing not only in scale and speed, but also in terms of the number of countries and the range of people involved. Throughout the world, people of different national origins, who speak different languages, and who have different customs, religions and patterns of behavior are coming into unprecedented contact with each other. As a result, the notion of the socially or ethnically homogeneous nation state with a single culture has become increasingly outdated. Most societies are now characterized by a degree (and often a high degree) of diversity.[54]

Consequently, global migration is confronting national school systems with the problem of educating multicultural and multilingual populations. The Commission is concerned that unless immigrants are integrated into the social structures of their host societies, nations will face problems of social cohesion resulting in increased cultural conflicts between native-born and foreign-born populations. The Commission stresses under the heading "Strengthening social cohesion through integration" in its six "Principles of Action" that the integration of immigrants to national life "should be actively supported by local and national authorities, employers and members of civil society, and should be based on a commitment to non-discrimination and gender equity. It should also be informed by an objective public, political and media discourse on international migration."[55]

The problem of social cohesion resulting from global migration has stimulated many national responses to the issue of multicultural education. Multiculturalism also involves language issues. Sometimes national school systems provide little help in maintaining immigrant languages and either neglect language issues facing immigrant children or are primarily focused on ensuring that they learn the dominant language of the host country. Also some government leaders worry that the global use of English will undermine their national language. For example, worried about the effects of globalization, the Thai Ministry of Culture felt compelled to issue a small booklet of traditional nicknames compiled with help from language experts at the Royal Institute, the official authority on Thai language. The concern was that parents were no longer giving their children Thai nicknames like Shrimp, Chubby, and Crab but were using English nicknames such as Mafia or Seven—as in 7-Eleven—Tomcruise, Elizabeth, Army, Kiwi, Charlie, and God. Vira Rojpojchanarat, the permanent secretary of the Thai Ministry of Culture, declared that the booklet was necessary: "It's important because it's about the usage of the Thai language. We worry that Thai culture will vanish." On the other hand, Manthanee Akaracharanrya, a twenty-nine-year-old real estate contractor, whose nickname is the English word "Money," said that English nicknames were practical because foreigners had a hard time pronouncing Thai words.[56]

It is not possible in this book to describe all national forms of multicultural education. If readers are interested in particular national approaches to multicultural education, there are a number of works that can be consulted.[57] While I cannot describe all national multicultural educational programs, I can indicate international covenants related to multicultural education and provide a general outline of differing approaches. For instance in chapter 6, I discussed United Nations Declaration of the Rights of Indigenous Peoples, which protects the educational methods and languages and cultures of these peoples. The United Nations' 1960 Convention Against Discrimination in Education in Article 5, Section C provides clear protection of cultural and language minorities which would include immigrant children. Article 5, Section C states:

> (C) It is essential to recognize the right of members of national minorities to carry on their own educational activities, including the maintenance of schools and, depending on the educational policy of each State, the use or the teaching of their own language, provided however:
>
> i. That this right is not exercised in a manner which prevents the members of these minorities from understanding the culture and language of the community as a whole and from participating in its activities, or which prejudices national sovereignty;
>
> ii. That the standard of education is not lower than the general standard laid down or approved by the competent authorities; and
>
> iii. That attendance at such schools is optional.[58]

The first thing to note in Article 5, Section C of the United Nations' 1960 Convention Against Discrimination in Education is the assertion that national minorities should have the right to control and maintain their own schools in an effort to protect minority cultures and languages. If nations were to act on this aspect of the 1960 Convention, then immigrant minorities would be given the ability by governments to protect their immigrant cultures and languages. Of course, there is the danger that recognition of this right might result in children being excluded from the language and the culture of the host country. This could lead to discrimination. Consequently, Section C contains Clause i which stresses that this right should not result in the child not learning the majority language and culture. In other words, the protection of cultural and language rights of minority children should not result in them being excluded from the language and the culture of the majority. Also, attendance at schools operated by language and cultural minorities is presented as a right but not a requirement as stated in Section C, Clause iii.

What about cultural differences that include religious differences? A model for this issue can be found in the 1950 European Convention which was incorporated into the Treaty for the European Union. Currently, the European Union includes within its jurisdiction a variety of religions including Islam. The Convention declares, "the State shall respect the right of parents to ensure such education and teaching in conformity with their own religious and philosophical convictions."[59] If this right were followed by all national governments, then religious rights in education would be protected.

A world famous crusader for language rights, Tove Skutnabb-Kangas, has argued that languages are disappearing as quickly as living species. In part, she argues this a result of the spread of English, an issue I have discussed in previous chapters. It is also a result of nations not protecting minority languages and not using them as a medium of instruction in their educational systems. Skutnabb-Kangas proposes "A Universal Covenant of Linguistic Human Rights" which would protect the languages of national minorities and global migrants.

### A Universal Covenant of Linguistic Human Rights

Everybody Has the Right
- to identify with their mother tongue(s) and to have this identification accepted and respected by others
- to learn the mother tongue(s) fully, orally (when physiologically possible) and in writing
- to education mainly through the medium of their mother tongue(s), and within the state-financed educational system
- to use the mother tongue in most official situations (including schools).

q- does g ivn't fund that schools or is it private benefactors

## Other Languages

*   whose mother tongue is not an official language in the country
    where s/he is resident ... to become bilingual (or trilingual, if s/he
    has 2 mother tongues) in the mother tongue(s) and (one of) the offi-
    cial language(s) (according to her own choice).

## The Relationship Between Languages

*   any change ... [in] mother tongue ... [being] voluntary (includes
    knowledge of long-term consequences) ... [and] not imposed.

## Profit from Education

*   to profit from education, regardless of what her mother tongue is.[60]

Tove's language rights convention is designed to tackle a number
of issues. First is the problem of educational equality when classroom
instruction is presented in a language that is different from the family
language of the student. In this circumstance, the student is at a disadvantaged compared to pupils whose home language is the same as the
language of instruction. Tove's proposal would guarantee that children
could receive their education in their mother tongue. Of course, if students only learn their minority languages then they could be excluded or
discriminated against in the political and economic system. To correct
this situation, Tove stresses that children should learn the dominant language of the society in which they are living. Therefore, she argues, these
children should become bilingual or trilingual.

In *Globalization and Educational Rights*, I proposed language and
cultural rights articles that I believe should be included in national constitutions.[61] My intention in proposing these was to protect the language
and cultures of national minorities and immigrants. My list cultural and
language rights in education is based, in part, on existing human rights
conventions. Contrary to many others, I stress the importance of protecting religious cultures and religious languages. My list of cultural and
language rights in education include:

*   Everyone has a right to an education using the medium of their
    mother tongue within a government-financed school system when
    the number of students requesting instruction in that mother tongue
    equals the average number of students in a classroom in that govern-
    ment-financed school system.
*   Everyone has the right to learn the dominant or official language of
    the nation. The government-financed school system will make every
    effort to ensure that all students are literate in the dominant or offi-
    cial language of the country.

- Everyone has the right to instruction in a language used for religious purposes, such as Qur'anic Arabic or Hebrew, within a government-financed school system when the number of students requesting instruction in that language equals the average number of students in a classroom in that government-financed school system.
- The duty and right to an education includes the right to a secular or religious education financed by the government. No student will be forced to receive a religious education.
- The right of the parents to choose a government-financed school based on their philosophical convictions and/or cultural values includes the right for their philosophical convictions and/or cultural values to be reflected in the content and methods of instruction.[62]

In summary, there are several international covenants protecting the linguistic and cultural rights of minority groups within nations including those of immigrants. However, many nations, including many within OECD, are more concerned about assimilating minority and immigrant populations into the mainstreams of their societies. The fear is often of violence between dominant and minority groups and the loss of a sense of national community. On the other hand, some countries, such as Singapore, have reduced cultural tensions by creating an educational system where parents can chose to send their children to schools where classes are taught in the family's mother tongue. A sense of national community is supposedly achieved through a nationalistic curriculum and the learning of a common language, in addition to the mother tongues of its citizens, namely English.[63] In the next section, I will explore the range of possible national responses to multicultural and multilingual populations.

## Educational Responses to Multicultural and Multilingual Populations

There are a variety of possible educational responses by national governments to increasing multicultural and multilingual populations resulting from global migration. I am placing these responses on a scale from no effort by the educational system to preserve minority languages and cultures to strong effort to preserve. This scale is not meant to be judgmental with one end of the scale being considered negative and the other end positive. Of course, my proposal for an amendment to national constitutions indicates my own preference for preserving languages and cultures.

However, I am also realistic about special historical conditions that complicate multicultural issues. For instance, in Malaysia former British colonizers discriminated against Malay culture and language while importing workers from India and China. Today, the Malaysian government is trying to rectify this historical condition by giving special preferences to Malay language and culture over protests from the Indian and Chinese minorities. Complicating the issue in Malaysia are increased demands to learn English for global commerce.[64] The debates over language and cultural policies in Malaysia highlight the difficulty of developing any single multicultural educational plan for every nation. Each country must work out its own solutions to fit the particular conditions. My hope is that all national school systems in trying to resolve multicultural issues will keep in mind the global efforts to protect cultures and languages.

With the above qualifications to my scale, I would put at one end national school systems that provide no special help to linguistic and cultural minorities. In this situation, minority and immigrant students are immersed in the culture and language of the country without receiving any help. Now this might be a planned approach or, on the other hand, it could result from a lack of concern by educational leaders. If planned, then national leaders might have adopted a sink or swim attitude with a hope that minority cultures and languages will disappear. Students might be discouraged from speaking their mother tongues.

At the next step on the scale, government schools could provide special programs and classes to help minority and immigrant cultures assimilate to the dominant culture. This educational approach might be called planned assimilation. Students could be assisted in learning the national language including the use of bilingual education programs. These bilingual programs would not be for the purpose of preserving minority languages and cultures. The programs would only assist students to learn the majority language.

A variation to the above assimilation scenario might be a curriculum that stresses teaching about other cultures in hopes that this will result in fewer cultural conflicts. Teaching about other cultures is not the same as trying to maintain different cultures. The purpose would not be to preserve minority cultures but it would be to maintain social cohesion and reduce social tensions. The goal would be to maintain the dominant position of the majority culture and language.

The next step on the scale might involve educational attempts to maintain minority cultures and languages while at the same time creating unity through a shared culture and language. In this situation, bilingual education would be for the purpose of maintaining minority languages while also teaching the national language. Parents might have the choice of sending their children to schools where the family's mother tongue is used in classroom instruction. The schools using the mother tongue of the parents for instruction would center the curriculum on the cultural background of the students. Instruction would also be required in the national language and the curriculum would introduce students to the country's history, government, and cultures. This approach might be called unity through diversity where everyone feels united by sharing a learned national language and an understanding of the nation's attempt to maintain a multicultural society.

One variation on the above would be government support of religious schools where parents have a choice to send their children to a particular religious school. Consider a society with Christian, Hindu, and Moslem populations. One might assume that cultural traditions of the population are reflected in their religious practices. Choice of school based on religion might be a means of ensuring a multicultural society. Of course, language is still an issue. Would each religious school use the language of its particular religious culture for instruction? The answer is dependent on the circumstances of the various religions and whether or not there are cultural and language differences within each religious group.

The next step on the scale might involve each cultural group controlling their own schools and using the culture's language for instruction and traditional educational methods. This is the United Nation's proposal for protecting the rights of indigenous peoples. The school curriculum would reflect the culture of the group in control and would make every effort to maintain cultural traditions including religious traditions. In this scenario, the goal of the educational system is to maintain a multicultural and multilingual society.

Embodied in some of the above scenarios is the idea of choice, such as parents choosing to send their children to a school using their mother tongue or associated with their religious beliefs. Should educational choice be financially supported by the government? In most cases choices can only be meaningful if parents have the economic freedom to send their child to a particular type of school. Financed by the government, educational choice might be one way for schooling to maintain multilingual and multicultural societies.

There is also the issue of control. Should national governments control the content of instruction or should that be left to the school or local community? The reader will recall from chapter 6 that the Thai government wants to preserve "Thai Wisdom" in the school curriculum by maximizing local control. For indigenous groups the stress is on tribal control. What about religious schools? In Indonesia, the reader will recall from chapter 6, the government mandates a general curriculum for its religious schools. On the other hand, should the religious community associated with the school determine the curriculum?

Another option is what might be called education for cosmopolitanism. Rather than educating for submission to the will of a nation, students might be educated as global citizens where they learn to move easily among the world's peoples with an acceptance of differences in cultures and languages. In this case, education would not attempt to ensure allegiance to a particular nation-state but it would try to create an allegiance to humanity and a concern for the welfare of all people.

National discussions of multicultural education are beset with issues involving choice, local versus national control, the role of religion in education, and the desire by the majority to ensure that their language and culture remain dominant. How this will work out in the future is not clear. Those believing in the development of a global educational culture would argue that national policies will eventually become uniform regarding multilingual and multicultural populations. However, the differences in national histories and conditions would suggest that there may not be a single policy that can fit all circumstances. Each nation may have to find its own path in resolving the multicultural education issues in a world of mass global migrations.

## Conclusion: A World in Motion

The increasing migration of the world's peoples is part of our globalizing world. Education plays an important role in this process. Increasing schooling can result in brain drain from poorer countries. The skilled and well-educated in developing countries are increasingly moving to countries where they can have higher incomes. This phenomenon can cause an imbalance in the distribution of the world's educated population. Brain drain is matched by brain gain in richer countries. This type of global migration could exasperate the disparities between the rich and poor. In addition, rural to urban migrations in developing countries are increasing the plight and size of the urban poor while depleting rural areas of their educated populations. As a consequence, rural and developing nations are suffering a shortage of educated personnel in vital areas, such as health care and education.

Global migration is pushing the issue of multicultural education to the forefront of school agendas. Embedded in the issue of multicultural education is the preservation of the power of national elites. Dominant elites can feel threatened by minority cultures that continue to use their minority languages. Sometimes elites feel that their power will be protected if the schools protect their language and culture while trying to eradicate other languages and cultures. On the other hand, minority groups often demand some recognition and protection of their cultures and languages in schools. As I suggested above, there is no single solution for the issue of multicultural education because of the peculiar historical and cultural circumstances of each nation. Maybe this issue will be resolved in the future with a form of cosmopolitan education where each student is taught to hold allegiance to humanity rather than a nation-state.

## Key Points: Different Forms of Multicultural Education in a World of Mass Migrations

1. Immersion of children of minority cultures into the dominant culture and language of the nation
   a. No special help for linguistic and cultural minority students
   b. Minority students are discouraged from speaking their mother tongues
   c. Language of the classroom is the language of the majority population
   d. The curriculum reflects the history and culture of the majority population
2. Planned assimilation
   a. Special classes and programs to help students learn the majority language
   b. Bilingual programs to help students learn the majority language but not for the purpose of preserving minority languages and cultures
   c. Teaching about other cultures for purpose of maintaining social cohesion
3. Unity through diversity
   a. Educational efforts to maintain minority cultures and languages
   b. Classroom instruction using the mother tongue of the family
   c. The teaching of a shared culture and language
   d. Curriculum materials that include a variety of cultural perspectives
4. Religious schools
   a. Parents given choice of religious school
   b. Each religious school reflects the culture and language of the local members of that religion
5. Each national cultural group controls its own schools
   a. Each cultural group determines the content and methods of instruction
   b. Each cultural group determines the language of instruction

## Chapter 8

# Globalization and Complex Thought

## Is There a Theory of Educational Globalization?

Throughout this book I have provided examples supporting a number of theoretical perspectives regarding the globalization of education, including world education culture, postcolonial/critical, world system, and culturalist. Are they all right? I would argue, "No!" Are they all of wrong? Again my answer is, "No!" How can theories be both right and wrong?

I think people can be trapped by a form of techno-rational thought that assumes that humans can find, or that they have found, a theory to explain human behavior including interactions between humans in social settings. What we actually have are theories that serve as explanations for behaviors in certain contexts. In other words, the discussed theories are true for the examples provided but not for all other situations. The problem is that people sometimes assume that if they find a number of instances when a theory is true then it is true for all cases.

In the twenty-first century, scholars continue to grasp at theories that will open the door to truth. However, complex thinking suggests that life is filled with the unexpected and that we can only guess at the future. Scholars often forget that human actions are more driven by emotions and fantasies than by reason. French sociologist and philosopher Edgar Morin states that "We are infantile, neurotic, frenzied beings and yet we are rational. That is truly the stuff that human beings are made of."[1] Humans, he argues, often live in a world of fantasy and imagination combined with self-deception. Humans are often captured by the demonic, which drives them to folly and madness. This description of humanity applies to scholarly work which is a complex activity that might involve rational, infantile, neurotic, imaginative, self-deceptive, and demonic thought processes. Such a view of scholarly work and humanity leads to what Morin calls the "principle of rational uncertainty." Uncertainty and unpredictability is the condition of humanity. Despite using elaborate strategies to plan for the future, we can never be certain of the outcome of our actions. The desire for certainty and predictability Morin refers to as "an illness of our minds."[2] The principle of rational uncertainty, which Morin believes should be part of the education of children, means that rationality "must recognize the contributions of emotions, love, repentance" and that humans "must remain open to everything that disputes it; otherwise it closes itself into a doctrine and becomes rationalization."[3]

Human capital theory applied to education is a good example of an attempt to add certainty to the workings of society. Economists, who are the major proponents of human capital theory, are often inaccurate in their economic predictions. As Morin states, "economics, the most mathematically advanced social science is the most socially, humanly backward science because it has abstracted itself from the social, historical, political, psychological and ecological conditions inseparable from economic activity."[4] Consequently, economists have a poor track record about predicting and managing economies. Can we know what the labor market will be twelve to sixteen years after a child enters school? Is there certainty about the skills needed for entering a future labor market? Will people want to work in the type of economy predicted by human capital theorists or will their emotions and imagination cause them to drop out of society? Is it possible or desirable to plan an educational system to school workers into an unknown economy?

Morin suggests that our thinking is guided by blinding paradigms or, what I have called, wheels in the head.[5] The blinding paradigm gives privilege to particular logical operations and sets of assumptions in interpreting human action discourse. The blinding paradigm, according to Morin, "grants validity and universality to its chosen logic. Thereby it gives the qualities of necessity and truth to the discourse and theory it controls."[6]

The concept of blinding paradigms helps us to understand differences in interpretations of the globalization of education. World education culture theorists see globalization of education as a process originating in the spread of Western educational ideas and sustained by national leaders selecting best practices and research from a global flow of educational ideas. This spread of mass schooling, according to world culture theorists, is accompanied by Western ideas of human rights, democracy, free markets, and constitutional government. Schooling is thought of as a source of economic improvement and social advancement.

In contrast, world system and postcolonial/critical theorists work from the perspective that societies are in a constant struggle between the haves and have-nots. These theorists consider the central figures behind globalization to be those seeking the domination of the rich over the poor or the powerful over the powerless and those resisting this domination. As a result, these theorists contend, globalization is increasing inequalities between and within nations. Rather than considering the globalization of education as a positive spread of Western ideals, like the world education culture theorists, these theorists see it as a continuation of the exploitation by the few of the many. Consequently, the national adoption of an educational reform is often interpreted as another triumph for the power of the rich rather than, as world culture theorists might argue, adoption of a positive idea supported by concepts of justice and school improvement.

These differences in interpretation can be highlighted by a couple of quotes. In *National Differences, Global Similarities: World Culture and the Future of Schooling*, world educational theorists David Baker and Gerald LeTendre conclude, after reviewing the global spread of mass schooling, the growing uniformity of schooling, and the common use of educational research, "As the trends have led us to do throughout this book, we take a particularly bullish perspective on the future of mass education in general. Bullish in the sense that the institution, in a relatively short time, has become so dominant in most places in the world that we see little to suggest that it will not continue to be so into the near future."[7]

What is the blinding paradigm represented by the above quote? First, there is the assumption that mass schooling is good for humanity. Second, it is assumed that the common use of globally available educational research, which represents a form of techno-rational thought, will improve education and the lives of the world's peoples. This blinding paradigm leads world education cultural theorists to focus on examples of the spread of mass schooling and the development of global educational reform without considering the possibility that mass schooling might actually be bad for a society and that educational research and reform might actually be serving the interests of the rich and powerful and not the interests of the global poor and downtrodden.

Another part of this blinding paradigm is the assumption that people act in a rational manner. Educational research is viewed as a rational process in search of truth and that national education policy leaders think logically in selecting educational reform ideas and research from the global flow. Educational research embodies techo-rational thought where the belief is that research findings can be used to engineer the best learning situations. Students are viewed as brains on sticks to be manipulated to learn more and that learning more will improve the person and society.

My focus is on the blinding paradigm and, consequently, I'm avoiding the obvious questions about educational research, such as what is to be learned and for what purpose. Educational researchers, like other people, are also subject to the power of emotions and their own blinding paradigms. Emotions, desire for status and money, academic politics, and sources of funding play a fundamental role in shaping the nature and results of educational research. While they espouse techno-rational approaches to education, educational researchers often act to serve their own interests and those of their financial supporters and like others they can be dominated by emotions rather than reason. The same argument can be made about those who see national educational leaders making logical choices of the best educational practices. National political leaders are often driven by a lust for power and greed.

Secularism is another aspect of the blinding paradigm of world education theorists. This blindness to the importance of religion and the issue of religious education is shared by postcolonial/critical and world system theorists. Earlier in this book I quoted Eduardo Mendieta: "A theory of globalization that makes no room for religion has major theoretical flaws."[8] The lack of consideration of the role of religion in the globalization of education is a major deficit when wars of religion seem to dominate global politics and social movements since the late twentieth century. Often those trapped by techno-rational thought and secularism believe that religion stands in the way of social progress. Consequently, religious beliefs are something that will disappear with the spread of mass schooling or that religion can serve the purpose of regulating people's morality and acts as a form of social control. World culture theorists do not spend time examining education for the purpose of maintaining religious beliefs or the role of the spiritual in education and society.

In summary, the blinding paradigm of world culture theorists that obscures their world view includes the assumption that mass schooling is good, that mass schooling will result in a better society, that educational research is based on a techno-rational process, that national leaders utilize techno-rational processes in planning school systems, and that religious considerations are unimportant for educational planning.

Secularism is a value shared by world education cultural, postcolonial/critical, and world system theorists. When religion is discussed by postcolonial/critical and world system theorists, it is often treated as another instrument of domination by the rich and powerful or as a problem in maintaining a secular state. Exemplifying this flaw is the lack of any chapters on religion in the three major texts by postcolonialist/critical theorists on education and globalization, namely Nicholas Burbules and Carlos Torres (Eds.), *Globalization and Education: Critical Perspectives*; Michael Apple, Jane Kenway, and Michael Singh (Eds.), *Globalizing Education: Policies, Pedagogies, & Politics*; and Hugh Lauder, Phillip Brown, JoAnne Dillabough, and A. H. Halsey (Eds.), *Education, Globalization & Social Change*.[9]

The secular blindness to religion as a global education issue is exemplified not only by the lack of any chapters dealing with religion in the Burbules and Torres book, but by the total lack of discussion of the topic in *any* of the chapters. In the Apple, Kenway, and Singh book, a discussion does appear in Michael Apple's chapter "Are Markets in Education Democratic? Neoliberal Globalism, Vouchers, and the Politics of Choice."[10] Apple's discussion demonstrates the tendency of only mentioning religion when it is a threat to secularism or when it supports an economic ideology. Regarding the threat to secularism, Apple refers to "religious fundamentalists and conservative evangelicals who want a return to (their) God in all of our institutions."[11] And, referring to free market economics, he writes, "Still others will take the market road [supporting free markets] because for them God has said that this is 'His' road."[12] The issue is not that Apple is right or wrong in his comments—I tend to agree with him—but that these are the only comments in a book on globalization when the world has experienced centuries of religious struggles. In the Lauder, Brown, Dillabough, and Halsey book, the only article that I could find that discusses religion focuses on the threat to the secular state by Muslim women wearing head scarves to school.[13]

Secularism represents only one element of the blinding paradigm of postcolonial/critical theorists. Another is derived from the thinking of Adam Smith and Karl Marx. The assumption is that human actions can be explained as a self-interested pursuit of material rewards. Other human actions such as spiritualism, a return to indigenous cultural patterns, and rejection of industrialism are simply dismissed as delusional or a product of false consciousness. In fact, postcolonial/critical theorists often share the same assumptions as business leaders regarding human capital education. Business leaders are concerned that schools supply them with cheap labor. Postcolonial/critical theorists worry about human capital economics promoting greater economic inequality. These theorists want to ensure that schools promote economic equality. Both business leaders and postcolonial/critical theorists support an industrial consumer society and the material rewards it promises. The difference is in how the rewards are distributed.

The blinding paradigms of both world education culture and postcolonial/critical theorists might obscure the possibility that some people reject human capital theory because it despiritualizes humans and treats them as bloodless cogs to be fitted into the corporate and industrial global machinery. In discussions of human capital theory in my college classes, there are usually several students who react in abhorrence to the concept of humanity embedded in human capital theory; a concept of people that makes them simply natural resources to be molded by education to serve the economic system. World education culture theorists might applaud human capital education because it is supported by two organizations, the World Bank and OECD, which they consider engines of progress. On the other hand, the support by the World Bank and OECD might lead postcolonial/critical theorists to reject human capital economics because they see these two institutions as instruments that primarily serve the world's rich nations and people. However, there is little or nothing in the literature of these theorists about human capital education that expresses concern about the transformation of the traditional spiritual view of humanity, the effort to turn human society into a well-oiled machine, or to reduce human action to a techno-rational process.

Culturalists, such as the anthropologists and comparative education scholars discussed in chapter 1, provide a broad and complex view of globalization. Anthropologists search for ways in which cultures change as they interact with other cultures. Rather than seeing a developing uniformity to national and local schools, they see hybridity and new forms of education evolving. They also see competing educational models vying for dominance in the global arena. Missing from their work is the concern with economic inequalities and injustice that haunts the work of postcolonial/critical theorists. Their approach seems to blind them to the importance of power, wealth, and exploitation in shaping global culture. The borrowing and lending rhetoric of comparative educators creates a view of education as one of exchange rather than imposition though many comparative educators do recognize the educational impositions of former colonial powers. They also give recognition to the role of power and wealth in determining national policies. However, the traditional approach of comparative educators is a comparison of national schools systems to find ways by which school systems might be improved. Is the blinding paradigm of comparative educators the assumption that mass schooling operates for the benefit of humanity?

In summary, I think future research into the globalization of education should operate from Morin's principle of rational uncertainty. The world is a holistic and complex system that, at least at this point in time, cannot be encompassed in any single theory. Any theory of human action is only applicable to the examples that are used to prove it. The future is unpredictable. We can only make guesses, because humans are at the same time rational, emotional, and maniacal, and the effect of human interactions within the biosphere are uncertain. In other words, we should examine our own blinding paradigms as we try to describe the globalization of education.

Future research on the globalization of education should embrace Morin's principle of rational uncertainty. In chapter 2, I examined the policies and networks of the World Bank. Will future research show that the Bank's educational efforts had positive effects on local communities or will it, as I would suspect, show a mixed bag of results. In doing research on both the Bank and OECD, the scholar must carefully examine their own assumptions about what a "good education" means.

Chapters 2 and 3 demonstrate how the educational policies of the World Bank, OECD, and the United Nations are linked to the development of internet learning, games and television programs. In the future, will the Internet, video games, and television contribute to a global uniformity of educational policies and practices? In chapter 4, I examined the growth of the international marketing of tests, learning materials, and schools. Will these contribute to global uniformity of schooling? Chapters 5 and 6 discuss progressive and religious educational models that might be acting as countervailing influences to global educational uniformity. Also, civil society, as represented by international nongovernment organizations, might be countervailing powers to intergovernmental organizations like the World Bank and OECD. The complexity of the globalization of education is heightened by the findings of culturalists on how local communities and nations can change and adapt educational ideas in the global flow. And finally, as discussed in chapter 7, the image of globalization becomes even more complex when global migration is included. Based on their past histories, nations are developing their own educational responses to multicultural and multilingual populations. Given all these factors, the globalization of education should be researched from a holistic and complex perspective with a consideration of the dynamic conflicts and intersections of the following major players: intergovernmental organizations; global and local school leaders and citizens;, media and popular culture; international nongovernment organizations; multinational learning, publishing, and testing corporations; progressive and radical school agendas; religions; and the mass migration of the world's peoples.

# Notes

## Chapter I

1. Roger Dale and Susan Robertson, Editorial: Introduction to *Globalisation, Societies and Education* 1(1) 2003, pp. 3–11.
2. Nelly P. Stromquist, *Education in a Globalized World: The Connectivity of Economic Power, Technology, and Knowledge* (Lanham, MD: Rowman & Littlefield, 2003).
3. Dale and Robertson, p. 7.
4. For examples see Kathryn Anderson-Levitt, "A world culture of schooling?" in *Local Meanings, Global Schooling: Anthropology and World Culture Theory,* ed. Kathryn Anderson-Levitt (New York: Palgrave Macmillan, 2003), pp. 1–26.
5. Achieve Inc. & National Governors Association, "America's High Schools: The Front Line in the Battle for Our Economic Future" (Washington, D.C.: Achieve Inc. & National Governors Association, 2003), p. 1.
6. Ibid., p. 4.
7. European Commission, *Teaching and Learning: On Route to the Learning Society* (Luxemburg: SEPO-CE, 1998), p. 21.
8. See Ruth Hayhoe and Julia Pan, "A contribution of dialogue among civilizations," in *Knowledge Across Cultures: A Contribution to Dialogue Among Nations,* eds. Ruth Hayhoe and Julia Pan (Hong Kong: Comparative Education Research Centre, 2001), pp. 1–21; and Samuel Huntington, *The Clash of Civilizations and the Remaking of the World Order* (New York: Simon & Schuster, 1996).
9. Huntington, *The Clash of Civilizations.*
10. Michael Apple, Jane Kenway, and Michael Singh, eds., *Globalizing Education: Policies, Pedagogies, & Politics* (New York: Peter Lang, 2005).
11. Roger Dale, "Globalisation, Knowledge Economy and Comparative Education," *Comparative Education* 41(2) 2005, p. 123.
12. Martin Carnoy and Diane Rhoten, "What Does Globalization Mean for Education Change? A Comparative Approach," *Comparative Education* 46(1) 2002, p. 1.
13. Patricia Broadfoot, "Editorial. Globalisation in Comparative Perspective: Macro and Micro," *Comparative Education* 39(4) 2003, p. 411.
14. Dale, "Globalisation, Knowledge," pp. 117–149.
15. Steven Jordan and David Yeomans, "Meeting the global challenge? Comparing recent initiatives in school science and technology," *Comparative Education* 39(1) 2003, pp. 65–81.

16. Arjun Appadurai, *Modernity at Large: Cultural Dimensions of Globalisation* (Minneapolis: University of Minnesota Press, 1996).
17. Manuel Castells, *The Rise of the Network Society* (Oxford: Blackwell, 2000).
18. David Held, Anthony McGrew, David Goldblatt, and Jonathan Perraton, *Global Transformation: Politics, Economics, and Culture* (Palo Alto, CA: Stanford University Press, 1999).
19. Simon Marginson and Erlenwatin Sawir, "Interrogating Global Flows in Higher Education," *Globalisation, Societies and Education* 3(3) 2005, pp. 281–309.
20. See John Boli and George Thomas, eds, *Constructing World Culture: International Nongovernment Organizations Since 1875* (Palo Alto, CA: Stanford University Press 1999); Frank Lechner and John Boli, *World Culture: Origins and Consequences*. (Malden, MA: Blackwell, 2005); Francisco Ramirez (2003), "The Global Model and National Legacies," in *Local Meanings, Global Schooling: Anthropology and World Culture Theory*, ed. Kathryn Anderson-Levitt (New York: Palgrave Macmillan 2003), pp. 239–255; and Francisco Ramirez and John Boli, "The Political Construction of Mass Schooling: European Origins and Worldwide Institutionalization," *Sociology of Education* 60(1) 1987, pp. 2–17.
21. John Meyer, David Kamens, and Aaron Benavot, *School Knowledge for the Masses: World Models and National Primary Curricular Categories in the Twentieth Century* (Bristol, PA: Falmer Press, 1992) and David Baker and George LeTendre, *National Differences, Global Similarities: World Culture and the Future of Schooling*. (Palo Alto, CA: Stanford University Press, 2005).
22. Meyer, Kamens, and Benavot, *School Knowledge*, p. 2.
23. UNICEF, *The State of the World's Children 2006: Excluded and Invisible* (New York: UNICEF, 2005), pp. 114–117.
24. Meyer, Kamens, and Benavot, *School Knowledge*, p. 2.
25. Ibid., p. 51.
26. Ibid., p. 72.
27. Ibid.
28. Ibid., pp. 172–173.
29. Baker and LeTendre, *National Differences*, p. 3.
30. Ibid., p.12.
31. Ramirez, "The Global Model," p. 242.
32. Ibid., p. 242.
33. See Boli and Thomas, *Constructing World Culture*; Lechner and Boli, *World Culture*; Immanuel Wallerstein, *The Politics of the World-Economy: The States, the Movements, and the Civilizations* (Cambridge: Cambridge University Press, 1984); and Immanuel Wallerstein, *World-systems Analysis: An Introduction* (Durham, NC: Duke University Press, 2004).
34. Boli and Thomas, introduction to *Constructing World Culture*, p. 3.
35. John Meyer, John Boli, J., George Thomas, and Francisco Ramirez, "World Society and the Nation State," *The Globalization Reader,* eds. Frank Lechner and John Boli (Malden, MA: Blackwell, 2004), p. 90.
36. Kathryn Anderson-Levitt, "A World Culture of Schooling?" in Anderson-Levitt, *Local Meanings, Global Schooling*, p. 4.
37. Richard Tabulawa, "International Aid Agencies, Learner-Centred Pedagogy and Political Democratization: A Critique," *Comparative Education* 39(1) 2003, pp. 7–26; Wallerstein, *The Politics of the World-economy*; and Wallerstein, *World-systems Analysis*.

38. Hans Weiler, "Knowledge, Politics, and the Future of Higher Education: Critical Observations on a World Wide Transformation" in Hayhoe and Pan, *Knowledge across cultures*, pp. 25–45.

39. Michael Apple, "Are New Markets in Education Democratic" in *Globalizing Education*, pp. 209–230; Phillip Brown and Hugh Lauder, "Globalization, Knowledge and the Myth of the Magnet Economy," *Globalisation, Societies and Education* 4(1) 2006, pp. 25–57; David Gabbard, introduction to *Knowledge and Power in the Global Economy: Politics and the Rhetoric of School Reform,* ed. David Gabbard (Mahwah, NJ: Lawrence Erlbaum, 2000), pp. xiii–xxiii; Mark Olssen, "Neoliberalism, Globalization, Democracy: Challenges for Education," *Globalisation, Societies and Education* 2(2) 2004, pp. 231–275; and Weiler, "Knowledge, Politics," pp. 25–45.

40. Martin Carnoy, *Education as a Form of Cultural Imperialism* (New York: David McKay, 1974); Joel Spring, *Education and the Rise of the Global Economy* (Mahwah, NJ: Lawrence Erlbaum, 1998); Joel Spring, *Pedagogies of Globalization: The Rise of the Educational Security State* (Mahwah, NJ: Lawrence Erlbaum, 2006); and John Willinsky, *Learning to Divide the World: Education at Empire's End* (Minneapolis: University of Minnesota Press, 1998).

41. Gary Becker, "The Age of Human Capital" in *Education, Globalization & Social Change* (Oxford: Oxford University Press, 2006), pp. 292–295; Michael Crossley and Leon Tikly, "Postcolonial Perspectives and Comparative and International Research in Education: A Critical Introduction," *Comparative Education* 40(2) 2004, pp. 147–156; Robert Rhoads and Carlos Torres, eds., *The University, State, and Market: The Political Economy of Globalization in the Americas* (Palo Alto, CA: Stanford University Press, 2006); Spring, *Education and the Rise*; Stromquist, *Education in a Globalized World*; Nelly Stromquist and Karen Monkman, "Defining Globalization and Assessing its Implications on Knowledge and Education," in *Globalization and Education: Integration and Contestation Across Cultures,* eds. Nelly Stromquist and Karen Monkman (Lanham, MD: Rowman & Littlefield, 2000), pp. 3–25.

42. Daniel Schugurensky and Adam Davidson-Harden, "From Córdoba to Washington: WTO/GATS and Latin American Education," *Globalization, Societies and Education* 1(3) 2003, p. 333.

43. Crossley and Tikly, "Postcolonial perspectives," p. 148.

44. See Hayhoe and Pan, *Knowledge Across Cultures*; Angela W. Little, "Extended review. Clash of Civilisations: Threat or Opportunity?," *Comparative Education* 39(3) 2003, pp. 391–394; Majid Rahnema, "Science, Universities and Subjugated Knowledges: A Third World Perspective" in *Knowledge Across Cultures,* pp. 45–54; Zahra Zeera, "Paradigm Shifts in the Social Sciences in the East and West," in *Knowledge Across Cultures,* pp. 55–92.

45. National Commission on Excellence in Education, *A Nation at Risk* (Washington, DC: U.S. Government Printing Office, 2003).

46.David Berliner and Bruce Biddle, *The Manufactured Crisis: Myths, Fraud and the Attack on America's Public Schools* (New York: Perseus Books, 1995).

47. National Commission on Excellence in Education, p. 70.

48. See Spring, *Pedagogies of Globalization,* pp. 207–244.

49. David Phillips, "Toward a theory of policy attraction in education" in *The global politics of educational borrowing and lending*, ed. Gita Steiner-Khamsi (New York: Teachers College Press, 2004), pp. 54–65.
50. Anderson-Levitt, "A World Culture of Schooling," p. 2.
51. Ibid., p. 15.
52. Lesley Bartlett, "World Culture or Transnational Project? Competing Educational Projects in Brazil" in *Local Meanings, Global Schooling*, p. 196.
53. Anderson-Levitt, "A World Culture of Schooling," p. 9.
54. Ibid., p. 9.
55. Ibid.
56. Michael Apple, "Between Neoliberalism and Neoconservatism: Education and Conservatism in a Global Context" in *Globalization and Education*, pp. 57–58; Apple, Kenway, and Singh, *Globalizing Education*; Brown, and Lauder, "Globalization, Knowledge," pp. 25–57; Burbules and Torres, "Globalization and Education: An Introduction," in *Globalization and Education*, pp. 1–26; Crossley and Tikly, "Postcolonial Perspectives"; Dale, "Globalisation, Knowledge"; Gabbard, introduction; Olssen, "Neoliberalism, Globalization, Democracy," pp. 231–275; Michael Peters, James Marshall, and Patrick Fitzsimons, "Managerialism and Educational Policy in a Global Context: Foucault, Neoliberalism, and the Doctrine of Self–management" in, *Globalization and Education*" pp. 109–132; Stromquist, *Education in a Globalized World*.
57. Apple, "Are New Markets in Education Democratic," p. 214.
58. UN News Service, "United Nations Adopts Declaration on Rights of Indigenous Peoples." Retrieved on September 14, 2007, from http://www.un.org/news/printnews.asp?nid=23794.
59. George Dei, Budd Hall, and Dorothy Rosenberg, introduction to *Indigenous Knowledges in Global Contexts: Multiple Readings of Our World*, eds. George Dei, Budd Hall, and Dorothy Rosenberg (Toronto: University of Toronto Press, 2000), pp. 1–7.
60. The World Bank–Indigenous Peoples, "Key Concepts." Retrieved on April 18, 2006, from http://www.worldbank.org/WBSITE/EXTERNAL/TOPICS/EXTSOCIALDEVELOPMENT/EXTINDPEOPLE/0,,contentMDK:20436173~menuPK:906311~pagePK:148956~piPK:216618~theSitePK:407802,00.html.
61. Spring, *Education and the Rise*.
62. Carnoy, *Education as a Form of Cultural Imperialism*; Spring, *Education and the Rise*; Spring, *Pedagogies of Globalization*; and Willinsky, *Learning to Divide the World*.
63. Byron Marshall, *Learning to be Modern: Japanese Discourse on Education* (Boulder, CO: Westview, 1994), pp. 25–26.
64. "Preamble to the Fundamental Code of Education, 1872," in *Society and Education in Japan*, ed., Herbert Passin (New York: Teachers College Press, 1965), p. 210.
65. Gregory Starrett, *Putting Islam to Work: Politics and Religious Transformation in Egypt* (Berkeley: University of California Press, 1998), p. 26.
66. Philip Short, *Mao: A Life* (New York: Henry Holt, 1999), p. 52.
67. Paul Bailey, *Reform the People: Changing Attitudes towards Popular Education in Early 20th century China* (Vancouver: University of British Columbia Press, 1990), pp. 139–142.

68. Spring, *Education and the Rise*, pp. 37–69; and Spring, *Globalization and Educational Rights* (Mahwah, NJ: Lawrence Erlbaum, 2001), pp. 20–56.
69. I trace the global diffusion of progressive education ideas in Spring, *Pedagogies of Globalization*.
70. See Barry Keenan, B. (1977). *The Dewey Experiment in China: Educational Reform and Political Power in the Early Republic* (Cambridge, MA: Harvard University Press, 1977), and David Hall and Roger Ames, *The Democracy of the Dead: Dewey Confucius, and the Hope for Democracy in China* (Chicago: Open Court, 1999).
71. Keenan, pp. 14–15.
72. Larry Holmes, *Stalin's school: Moscow's Model School no. 25, 1931–1937* (Pittsburgh, PA: University of Pittsburgh Press, 1999), pp. 8–9. Also see Maurice Shore, *Soviet Education: Its Psychology and Philosophy* (New York: Philosophical Library, 1999).
73. Holmes, p. 10.
74. William Kilpatrick, *The Project Method* (New York: Teachers College Press, 1918).
75. Holmes, p. 11.
76. For a more detailed account of the evolution of the South American progressive education model see Spring, *Pedagogies of Globalization*, pp. 114–151.
77. Steiner–Khamsi, *The Global Politics*.
78. Sheldon Liss, *Marxist Thought in Latin America* (Berkeley: University of California Press, 1984), pp. 1–30.
79. José Mariátegui, *Seven Interpretive Essays on Peruvian Reality* (Austin: University of Texas Press, 1971), p. 122.
80. Ibid., p. 79.
81. Quoted in Ibid., p. 86.
82. Quoted in Ibid., p. 87.
83. Ibid., p. 88.
84. Ibid., p. 119.
85. Liss, pp. 272–273.
86. Ibid., p. 272.
87. Che Guevara, "Socialism and Man in Cuba," in *Global Justice: Liberation and Socialism*, ed. Maria Del Carmen (Melbourne, Australia: Ocean Press, 2002), p. 35. This book was published in cooperation with Che Guevara Studies Center in Havana, Cuba.
88. Ibid., p. 41.
89. For an intellectual autobiography of his writing of *Pedagogy of the Oppressed*, see Paulo Freire, *Pedagogy of Hope: Reliving Pedagogy of the Oppressed* (New York: Continuum, 2004).
90. Ibid., p. 55.
91. Paulo Freire, *Pedagogy of the Oppressed* (New York: Herder and Herder, 1970), p. 40.
92. In 1970 and 1971, I worked with Ivan Illich at the Center for Intercultural Documentation. It was there that I first met Paulo Freire.
93. The influences of CIDOC, Ivan Illich, and Paulo Freire are represented in my book, Joel Spring, *A Primer of Libertarian Education* (New York: Free Life Editions, 1975). The books coedited at CIDOC are Joel Spring and Jordan Bishop, *Formative Undercurrents in Compulsory Knowledge*

(Cuernavaca, Mexico: CIDOC, 1970) and *Roots of Crisis,* eds. Clarence Karier, Paul Violas, and Joel Spring (Chicago: Rand McNally, 1973).

## Chapter 2

1. Joel Spring, *Education and the Rise of the Global Economy* (Mahwah, NJ: Lawrence Erlbaum, 1998), pp. 159–189, and World Bank, *A Guide to the World Bank Second Edition* (Washington, D.C.: World Bank, 2007).
2. See Collete Chabbott, "Development INGOS" in *Constructing World Culture: International Nongovernment Organizations Since 1875,* eds. John Boli and George Thomas (Palo Alto, CA: Stanford University Press, 1999), pp. 222–248; and Leslie Sklair, "Sociology of the Global System" in *The Globalization Reader,* ed. Frank Lechner and John Boli ( Malden, MA: Blackwell, 2004), pp. 70–76.
3. For example Michael Goldman, *Imperial nature: The World Bank and Struggles for Social Justice* (New Haven, CT: Yale University Press, 2005); and Richard Peet, *Unholy Trinity: The IMF, World Bank and WT.* (London: Zed Books, 2003).
4. See Manuel Castells, *The Rise of the Network Society* (Oxford: Blackwell, 2000), 77–147, 216–247.
5. World Bank, *A Guide,* p. 3.
6. Spring, *Education and the Rise,* 179–182; and World Bank, *A Guide.*
7. Goldman, *Imperial nature,* p. 69.
8. World Bank, "About Us: Organization: Boards of Directors." Retrieved on July 17, 2007, from http://www.worldbank.org, para. 1.
9. The three other members of the World Bank Group are the International Finance Corporation, the Multilateral Investment Guarantee Agency, and the International Centre for Settlement of Investment Disputes.
10. World Bank, *A Guide,* pp. 9–19.
11. Ibid., pp. 18–19.
12. Ibid., pp. 14–16.
13. Ibid., pp. 11–12.
14. Ibid., p. 43.
15. UNESCO, "Education for all (EFA) International Coordination: The six EFA goals and MDGs." Retrieved on October 5, 2007, from http://www.portal.unesco.org/education/en/ev.php-URL_ID=53844&URL_DO=DO_TOPIC&URL_SECTION=201.html.
16. UNESCO, "Education for all (EFA) International Coordination: The EFA movement." Retrieved on October 5, 2007, from http://www.portal.unesco.org/education/en/ev.php-URL_ID=54370&URL_DO=DO_TOPIC&URL_SECTION=201.html.
17. UNESCO, "Education for all (EFA) International Coordination: Mechanisms involving international organizations." Retrieved on October 5, 2007, from http://www.portal.unesco.org/education/en/ev.php-URL_ID=47539&URL_DO=DO_TOPIC&URL_SECTION=201.html.
18. UNESCO, "Education for all (EFA) International Coordination: Collective Consultation of NGOs." Retrieved on October 5, 2007, from http://www.portal.unesco.org/education/en/ev.php-URL_ID=47477&URL_DO=DO_TOPIC&URL_SECTION=201&reload=114567740.
19. UNESCO, "Education for all (EFA) International Coordination: Public-Private Partnerships." Retrieved on October 5, 2007, from http://

wwwportal.unesco.org/education/en/ev.php-URL_ID=47544&URL_DO=DO_TOPIC&URL_SECTION=201.html.
20. Tiphaine Bertsch, Rebecca Bouchet, Joanna Godrecka, Kiira Karkkainen, and Tyra Malzy, *A Study for UNESCO: Corporate Sector Involvement in Education For All: Partnerships with Corporate Involvement for the Improvement of Basic Education, Gender Equality, and Adult Literacy in Developing Countries* (Paris: Fondation Naionale Des Sciences Politiques/Institut D'Etudes Politiques De Paris, 2005).
21. Ibid.
22. Ibid.
23. Ibid.
24. Ibid., p. 4.
25. Ibid., p. 71.
26. Discovery Channel Global Education Partnership, "Who We Are: Partners." Retrieved on October 8, 2007, from http://www.discoveryglobaled.org./who.html#oldtab3.
27. Discovery Channel Global Education Partnership, "Who We Are: Our Approach." Retrieved on October 8, 2007, from http://www.discoveryglobaled.org./who.html#oldtab1.
28. Discovery Channel Global Education Partnership, "What We Do: The Power of Television." Retrieved on October 9, 2007, from http://www.discoveryglobaled.org./what.html#oldtab1.
29. Ibid.
30. Discovery Channel Global Education Partnership, "DCGEP and the Coca-Cola Foundation Partner on Educational Initiative." Retrieved on October 9, 2007, from http://www.discoveryglobaled.org./news.html#oldtab1.
31. International Finance Corporation World Group, "EdInvest." Retrieved on July 18, 2007, from http://www.ifc.org/edinvest/.
32. International Finance Corporation World Bank Group, "Education." Retrieved on October 9, 2007, from http://www.ifc.org/ifcext/che.nsf/Content/Education.
33. Human Development Network, "About HDN." Retrieved on October 9, 2007, from http://www.hdn.org.ph/abouthdn.html.
34. Human Development Network, "What is sustainable development?" Retrieved on October 9, 2007, from http://www.hdn.org.ph/whatis.html.
35. World Bank, "Public-Private Partnerships in Education: Overview." Retrieved on October 9, 2007, from http://web.worldbank.org/WBSITE/EXTERNAL/TOPICS/EXTEDUCATION/0,,contentMDK:21317057~menuPK:282391~pagePK:64020865~piPK:51164185~theSitePK:282386,00.html.
36. International Finance Corporation World Bank Group, "SABIS school, Lebanon: Flagship of IFC Education Activities in MENA." Retrieved on October 9, 2007, from http://www.ifc.org/ifcext/che.nsf/Content/AttachmentsByTitle/Factsheet_SabisSchoolLebanon/$File/Sabis+School+Lebanon-Fact+Sheet.pdf.
37. Carl Bistany, "True partners in public-private partnerships" in *Mobilizing the Private Sector for Public Education: A View from the Trenches,* ed. Harry Patrinos and Shobhana Sosale (Washington, D.C.: World Bank, 2007), p. 31.
38. Ibid., p. 33.
39. World Bank, *Constructing Knowledge Societies: New Challenges for Tertiary Education* (Washington, D.C.: The World Bank, 2002).

40. Ibid., p. 7.
41. The World Bank Education, "Education for the Knowledge Economy." Retrieved on October 10, 2007, from http://web.worldbank.org/wBSTIE/EXTERNAL/TOPICS/EXTEDUCATION/0,,contentMDX:20161496~menuPK:540092~pagePK:148956~piPK:216618~theSitePK:282386,00.html.
42. Ibid.
43. See Brian Keeley, *Human Capital: How What You Know Shapes Your Life* (Paris: OECD Publishing, 2007), pp. 28–35; and Phillip Brown and Hugh Lauder, "Globalization, Knowledge and the Myth of the Magnet Economy," in *Education, Globalization & Social Change*, eds. Hugh Lauder, Phillip Brown, Jo-Anne Dillabough, and A. H. Halsey, (Oxford: Oxford University Press, 2006), pp. 317–340.
44. As quoted in Keeley, *Human Capital*, p. 29.
45. Gary Becker, *Human Capital* (New York: Columbia University Press, 1964).
46. Gary Becker, "The Age of Human Capital" in *Education, Globalization & Social Change* edited by Hugh Lauder, Phillip Brown, Jo-Anne Dillabough, and A. H. Halsey (Oxford: Oxford University Press, 2006), p. 292.
47. Ibid.
48. Daniel Bell, *The Coming of the Post–industrial Society* (New York: Basic Books, 1973).
49. Peter Drucker, *Post–capitalist Society* (London: Butterworth/Heinemann, 1993).
50. Robert Reich, *The Work of Nations: A Blueprint for the Future* (New York: Vintage, 1991).
51. Castells, *The Rise of the Network*, 77.
52. Ibid.
53. Ibid.
54. World Bank, *Constructing Knowledge Societies*, 9.
55. Ibid, 10.
56. World Bank, *Lifelong Learning in the Global Knowledge Economy: Challenges for Developing Countries* (Washington, D.C.: World Bank, 2003).
57. William Rideout, Jr., "Globalization and Decentralization in Sub-Saharan Africa: Focus Lesotho" in *Globalization and Education: Integration and Contestation Across Cultures*. eds. Nelly Stromquist, and Karen Monkman, (Lanham, MD: Rowman & Littlefield, 2000), pp. 255–274.
58. World Bank, "Topics: Education; Priorities & topics: Economics of education: Public-private partnerships in the education sector." Retrieved on July 18, 2007, from http:www.worldbank.org/education/.
59. Directorate-General for Education and Culture, *Education and Training in Europe: Diverse Systems, Shared Goals for 2010* (Luxembourg: Office for Official Publications of the European Communities, 2002), p. 7.
60. Commission of the European Communities, "Communication from the Commission, Mobilizing the Brainpower of Europe: Enabling Universities to Make Their full Contribution to the Lisbon Strategy" (Brussels: The European Commission, April 4, 2005).
61. Directorate-General for Education and Culture, *Education and Training in Europe*, p. 12.
62. World Bank, *Lifelong Learning in the Global Knowledge Economy*, p. 21.

63. Quoted by Stephen Stoer and António Magalhaes in "Education, knowledge and the network society," *Globalisation, Societies and Education* 2(3), p. 325.
64. For a summary of character traits in individualist and collectivist societies see Harry C. Triandis, "Individualism and Collectivism: Past, Present, and Future" in *The Handbook of Culture and Psychology*, ed. David Matsumoto (New York: Oxford University Press, 2001), pp. 35–50.
65. Shigehiro Oishi, "Goals as Cornerstones of Subjective Well–Being: Linking Individuals and Cultures," in *Culture and Subjective Well–Being*, eds. Ed Diener and Eunkook M. Suh (Cambridge: MIT Press, 2000), pp. 87–112, Ibid., p. 100. Puerto Rico is actually listed as the sixth most individualist society. However, Puerto Rico is not a country but a possession of the United States and it has been influenced by U.S. culture since the early twentieth century.
66. Ibid., p. 100.
67. World Bank, *Lifelong Learning in the Global Knowledge Economy*, p. 22.
68. Ibid., p. 22.
69. Ibid., pp. 3–4.
70. Hassan M. Fattah, "Saudis Rethink Taboo on Women Behind the Wheel," *New York Times* (September 28, 2007). Retrieved on September 28, 2007, from *New York Times* on the Web http:www.nytimes.com.
71. Organization for Economic Cooperation and Development, "Adult Literacy." Retrieved on October 16, 2007, from http: www.oecde.org/dataoecd/27/24/2345257.pdf.
72. Ibid.
73. World Bank, *Lifelong Learning in the Global Knowledge Economy*, p. 23.
74. Ibid., p. 25.
75. Ibid.
76. Ibid.
77. Ibid., p. 32.
78. Ibid.
79. Ibid., p. 33.
80. Ibid.
81. Ibid., p. 36.
82. Ibid., p. 43.
83. See Carmel Borg and Peter Mayo, "The EU memorandum on Lifelong Learning. Old Wine in New Bottles?," *Globalisation, Societies and Education* 3(2005), pp. 203–225 and Spring, *Education and the Rise*.
84. World Bank, *Lifelong Learning in the Global Knowledge Economy*, p. xix.
85. CEC, Commission Staff Working Paper. *A Memorandum on Lifelong Learning* (Brussels: The European Commission) p. 3.
86. Kai Ming Cheng and Hak Kwong Yip, *Facing the knowledge society: Reforming secondary education in Hong Kong and Shanghai* (Washington, D.C.: World Bank, 2006), p. 34.
87. Cedefop and Eurydice, *National Actions to Implement Lifelong Learning in Europe* (Brussels: Eurydice, 2001), p. 31.
88. Lynn Olsen, "Ambiguity About Preparation for Workforce Clouds Efforts to Equip Students for Future," *Education Week* 25(2006), 1, 18–20.

89. Achieve Inc. & National Governors Association, *An Action Agenda for Improving America's High Schools: 2005 National Summit on High Schools* (Washington, D.C.: Achieve, Inc. & National Governors Association, 2005).
90. Brown and Lauder, "Globalization, Knowledge," p.320.
91. Ibid., p.323.
92. Ibid., p. 324.
93. Ibid., 329.
94. Frédéric Docquier and Abdeslam Marfouk, "International Migration by Education Attainment, 1990–2000" in *International Migration, Remittances & the Brain Drain*, eds. Çaglar Özden and Maurice Schiff, 175–185 (New York: Palgrave Macmillan, 2006).
95. Çaglar Özden, "Educated Migrants," p. 238.
96. World Bank, *Constructing Knowledge Societies*, p. 11.
97. Ibid.
98. Ibid.
99. Peet, *Unholy Trinity*, p. 120.
100. Ibid.

## Chapter 3

1. Explore *Panwapa, Cyberschoolbus*. Retrieved on November 6, 2007, from http://www.cyberschoolbus.un.org.
2. International: Sesame Street Workshop. Retrieved on November 6, 2007, from http://www.sesameworkshop.org/international/.
3. OECD, Internationalization of Higher Education (Paris: OECD, 1996), p. 2.
4. OECD, "About the OECD." Retrieved on November 7, 2007, from http://www.oecd.org.
5. Ibid.
6. OECD, "Education: About." Retrieved on November 7, 2007, from http://www.oecd.org/about/0,3347,en_2649_37455_1_1_1_1_37455,00.html.
7. Ibid.
8. Fazal Rizi and Bob Lingard, "Globalization and the changing nature of the OECD's educational work," in *Education, Globalization & Social Change*, eds. H. Lauder, P. Brown, J. Dillabough, and H. Halsey,(Oxford: Oxford University Press, 2006), p. 259.
9. Malcolm Skilbeck, "Book Reviews," in *Globalisation, Societies and Education* 1(1) 2003, p. 114.
10. Rizi and Lingard, p. 248.
11. OECD, "Centre for Educational Research and Innovation." Retrieved on July 19, 2007, from http://www.oecd.org/department/0,3355,en_2649_35845581_1_1_1_1_1,00.html.
12. OECD, "Programme on Institutional Management in Higher Education (IMHE), para. 1. Retrieved on July 19, 2007, from http://www.oecd.org/department/0,3355,en_2649_35961291_1_1_1_1_1,00.html.
13. OECD, "Programme on Educational Building (PEB)," para. 1. Retrieved on July 19, 2007, from http://www.oecd.org/department/0,3355,en_2649_35961311_1_1_1_1_1,00.html.
14. OECD Directorate for Education, "UNESCO Ministerial Round Table on Education and Economic Development: Keynote Speech by Angel Gurr'a,

OECD Secretary-General Paris, 19 October 2007." Retrieved on November 13, from http://www.oecd.org/document/19/0,3343,en_2649_33723 _1_1_1_1,00.html.
15. Brian Keeley, *Human Capital: How What You Know Shapes Your Life* (Paris: OECD Publishing, 2007), p.14.
16. Ibid., pp. 10–11.
17. Ibid., p. 10.
18. Ibid., p. 11.
19. Ibid.
20. Ibid., p. 103.
21. Ibid., p. 45.
22. As quoted in Ibid., p. 46.
23. Ibid., p. 56.
24. Ibid., p. 82.
25. Ibid., p. 81.
26. OECD, *The Pisa 2003 Assessment Framework–Mathematics, Reading, Science and Problem Solving, Knowledge and Skills* (Paris: OECD, 2003), p. 14.
27. David Baker and Gerald LeTendre, *National Differences, Global Similarities: World Culture and the Future of Schooling* (Palo Alto, CA: Stanford University Press, 2005), p. 150.
28. OECD, *PISA–The OECD Programme for International Student Assessment* (Paris: OECD, 2007), p. 4.
29. Ibid., p. 5.
30. Ibid., p. 6.
31. OECD Programme for International Student Assessment (PISA), "What PISA Assesses." Retrieved on November 13, 2007 from http://www.pisa.oecd.org/pages/0,3417,en_32252351_32235918_1_1_1_1_1,00.html.
32. Ibid., p. 7.
33. OECD, *The Pisa 2003 Assessment*, p. 108.
34. Ibid., p. 24.
35. Ibid., p. 133.
36. Ibid.
37. Madhu Singh, "The Global and International Discourse of Lifelong Learning from the Perspective of UNESCO" in *Lifelong Learning: One Focus, Different Systems*, eds. Klaus Harney, Anja Heikkinen, Sylvia Rahn, and Michael Shemmann (Frankfurt am Main: Peter Lang, 2002), p. 18.
38. Edgar Faure et al., Learning To Be: The World of Education Today and Tomorrow (Paris: UNESCO, 1972).
39. Ibid., p. vi.
40. Ibid.
41. Ibid.
42. Ibid., p. xxv.
43. Ibid.
44. Ibid., xxvi–xxvii.
45. Ibid., p. xxix.
46. Ibid., pp. xxxi–xxxii.
47. Jacques Delors, *Learning: The Treasure Within: Report to UNESCO of the International Commission on Education for the Twenty-First Century* (Paris: UNESCO, 1996).
48. William Gorham (United States), President of the Urban Institute in Washington, D.C.; Aleksandra Kornhauser (Solvenia), Director, International

Centre for Chemical Studies; and Rodolfo Stavenhagen (Mexico), Professor at the Centre of Sociological Studies, El Colegio de Mexico.

49. In'am Al Mufti (Jordan), former Minister of Social Development; Isao Amagi (Japan) Adviser to the Minister of Education; Roberto Carneiro (Portugal), former Minister of Education and Minister of State; Fay Chung (Zimbabwe), former Minister of Education; Marisela Quero (Venezuela), former Minister of the Family; Karan Singh (India), several times Minister for Education and Health; Myong Won Suhr (Republic of Korea); former Minister of Education; and Zhou Nanzhao (China), Vice-President, China National Institute for Educational Research.

50. Other members, in addition to Jacques Delors, are Bronislaw Geremek (Poland), Member of Parliament; Michael Manley (Jamaica), Prime Minister (1872–80); and Marie-Angelique Savane (Senegal), member of the Commission on Global Governance and Director, Africa Division, UNFPA.

51. International Commission on Education, p. 11.

52. Ibid.

53. Ibid., p. 19.

54. Ibid., pp. 86–97.

55. Ibid., p. 21.

56. Ibid.

57. Ibid.

58. Ibid., p. 17.

59. Ibid.

60. Ibid.

61. UNESCO, "International Implementation Scheme (IIS)." Retrieved on November 17, from http://portal.unesco.org/education/en/ev.php-URL_ID=23280&URL_DO=DO_TOPIC&URL_SECTION=201.html.

62. Ibid.

63. UNESCO, *Education for Sustainable Development United Nations Decade 2005–2014: Highlights on ESD Progress to Date April 2007* (Paris: UNESCO, 2007), p. 2.

64. UNESCO, "International Implementation Scheme (IIS)."

65. Ibid.

66. Cyberschoolbus, "Mission Statement." Retrieved on November 21, 2007 from http://www.cyberschoolbus.un.org/miss.html.

67. Recommendation can be found on the Cyberschoolbus Web site. Retrieved on November 21, 2007, from Information about International Society for Technology in Education's can be found on their Website. Retrieved on November 21, 2007, from http://www.iste.org.

68. The statement appears as the lead on "About" section of the International Society for Technology in Education's Web site. Retrieved on November 21, 2007, from http://www.iste.org/AM/Template.cfm?Section=About_ISTE.

69. Cyberschoolbus, "Mission Statement."

70. Ibid.

71. Ibid.

72. Cyberschoolbus, "About Poster Contest." Retrieved on November 21, 2007, from http://www.cyberschoolbus.un.org/poster/exhibit/about.asp.

73. Ibid.

74. Cyberschoolbus, "Infonation." Retrieved on November 22, 2007, from http://www.cyberschoolbus.un.org/infonation3/menu/advanced.

75. Ibid.

76. Cyberschoolbus, "Infonation: Country Grouping Glossary." Retrieved on November 22, 2007, from http://cyberschoolbus.un.org/infonation3/glossay.html.
77. Cyberschoolbus. Retrieved on November 22, 2007 from http://cyberschoolbus.un.org.
78. Office of the United Nations High Commissioner for Human Rights, *ABC: Teaching Human Rights—Practical Activities for Primary and Secondary Schools* (New York and Geneva: United Nations, 2004).
79. *Sesame Street Workshop, Welcome to Panwapa! A Place to Inspire and Empower Young Children to Become Responsible Global Citizens* (New York: Sesame Workshop, 2007), p. 2.
80. Clinton Global Initiative, "Education Commitments: Sesame Street Afghanistan, 2007." Retrieved on November 24, 2007, from http://www.commitments.clintonglobalinitiative.org/projects.htm?mode=view&rid=209668.
81. Sesame Street Workshop, *Welcome to Panwapa*, p. 1.
82. Sesame Street International Co-Production Home, "*Sesame Street* Around the World." Retrieved on November 24, 2007, from http://www.sesameworkshop.org/international/portal.php.
83. Sesame Street Workshop, *Welcome to Panwapa*, p. 4.
84. Ibid.
85. Panwapa, "Educational Framework for Program Leaders, Teachers, Parents, and Caregivers." Retrieved on October 28, 2007, from http://www.panwapa.com.
86. Sesame Street Workshop, *Welcome to Panwapa*, p. 4.
87. Panwapa, "Educational Framework.".
88. Ibid.
89. Lloyd Morrisett, introduction to *Children and Television: Lessons from "Sesame Street,"* Gerald S. Lesser (New York: Vintage, 1975), p. xxi.
90. Lesser, *Children and Television*, p. 23.
91. Information provided in *The World According to Sesame Street: A Global Documentary of Local Proportions*, DVD, produced and directed Linda Goldstein Knowlton and Linda Hawkins Costigan (New York: Participant Productions, 2006).
92. Lesser, *Children and Television*, pp. 24–25.
93. Ibid., pp. 254–255.
94. Sesame Workshop International, "Sesame Street Around the World." Retrieved on November 13, 2007, from http://www.sesameworkshop.org/international/portal.php.
95. Sesame Workshop International, "Meet the *Ulita Sezam* Characters," Retrieved on November 13, 2007, from http://www.sesameworkshop.org/international/ru/eng/characters.php.
96. Sesame Workshop International, "Meet the *Alam Simsim* Characters." Retrieved on November 13, 2007, from http://www.sesameworkshop.org/international/eg/eng/characters.php.
97. For a documentary on the South African production see *The World According to Sesame Street*.
98. Sesame Workshop International, "About *Takalami* Sesame." Retrieved on November 13, 2007, from http://www.sesameworkshop.org/international/za/home.php.
99. For a documentary on the Bangladesh production see *The World According to Sesame Street*.

100. Sesame Workshop International, "About *Sisimpur.*" Retrieved on November 13, 2007, from http://www.sesameworkshop.org/international/ba/ eng/home.php.

## Chapter 4

1. Dubai Knowledge Village, "About Dubai Knowledge Village." Retrieved on December 18, 2007, from http://www.kv.ae/en/cms/showcontent.asp? menu=side&menuid=69&DocumentID=8.
2. There are many histories of the international trade in educational services. For an introduction to different aspects of the field see John Willinsky, *Learning to Divide the World: Education at Empire's End* (Minneapolis: University of Minnesota Press, 1998); Theodore Vestal, *International Education: Its History and Promise for Today* (Westport, CT: 1994; Joel Spring, *Pedagogies of Globalization: TheRise of the Educational Security State* (Mahwah, NJ: Lawrence Erlbaum, 2006), and Joel Spring, *Education and the Rise of the Global Economy* (Mahwah, NJ: Lawrence Erlbaum, 1998).
3. Daniel Schugurensky and Adam Davidson-Harden, "From Córdoba to Washington: WTO/GATS and Latin American education," *Globalization, societies and education* 1(3) 2003, p. 322.
4. World Trade Organization, *WTO Legal Texts: The Uruguay Round Agreements: Annex 1B General Agreement on Trade in Services (GATS)*, p. 302. Retrieved on November 28, 2007, from http://www.wto.org/english/docs_e/legal_e/legal_e.htm#finalact.
5. Jane Knight, "Higher Education and Trade Agreements: What are the Policy Implications?" in *Universities and Globalization: Private Linkages, Public Trust*, eds. Gilles Breton and Michel Lambert, 81–106 (Quebec, Canada: UNESCO, 2003), pp..
6. Ibid., p. 87.
7. Christopher Arup, *The New World Trade Organization Agreements: Globalizing Law Through Services and Intellectual Property* (Cambridge: Cambridge University Press, 2000), pp. 177–213.
8. Jane Knight, "Higher Education and Trade Agreements: What are the Policy Implications?" in *Universities and Globalization*, pp. 87–89, and Arup, *The New World Trade*, pp. 95–214.
9. Gary Rhoads and Sheila Slaughter, "Academic Capitalism and the New Economy: Privatization as Shifting the Target of Public Subsidy in Higher Education," in *The University, State, and Market: The Political Economy of Globalization in the Americas*, eds., Robert Rhoads and Carlos Torres, 103–104 (Palo Alto, CA: Stanford University Press, 2006).
10. Helen Raduntz, "The Marketization of Education within the Global Capitalist Economy" in Michael Apple, Jane Kenway, and Michael Singh (Eds.), *Globalizing Education: Policies, Pedagogies, & Politics* (New York: Peter Lang, 2005), pp. 231–245.
11. World Trade Organization, "Understanding the WTO: The Organization: Whose WTO is it anyway?" Retrieved December 5, 2007, from http:// www.wto.org/english/thewto_e/whatis_e/tif_e/org1_e.htm.
12. World Trade Organization, "Understanding the WTO: Basics: The Case for Open Trade." Retrieved December 5, 2007, from http://www.wto.org/ english/thewto_e/whatis_e/tif_e/fact3_e.htm.

13. Ibid.
14. Arup, *The New World Trade* p. 97.
15. Ibid.
16. Educate, Inc. (2007). About us. Retrieved on July 15, 2007, from http://www.educateinc.com/aboutus.html.
17. Stephen Burd, "Promises and Profits: A for-profit college is under investigation for pumping up enrollment while skimping on education," *Chronicle of Higher Education*, January 13, 2006. Retrieved on January 18, 2008, from http://chronicle.com/weekly/v52/i19/19a02101.htm.
18. Goldie Blumenstyk, "Why For-Profit Colleges Are Like Health Clubs: They spend more on recruiting and less on instruction than their nonprofit counterparts do, a scholar's model shows, *Chronicle of Higher Education*, May 5, 2006. Retrieved on January 18, 2008, from http://chronicle.com/weekly/v52/i35/35a03501.htm.
19. Educate, Inc. (2007). About us. Retrieved on July 15, 2007, from http://www.educateinc.com/aboutus.html.
20. Muckety, Listings, Edge Acquisition, LLC. "Edge Acquisition, LLC full screen relationship." Retrieved on January 3, 2007, from http://www.muckety.com/Edge-Acquisition-LLC/5016495.muckety?full=true.
21. Ibid.
22. Ibid.
23. Ibid.
24. Ibid.
25. Laureate Education Inc. "About Laureate." Retrieved on July 12, 2007, from http://www.laureate-inc.com.
26. Laureate Education Inc. "Global post-secondary education market." Retrieved on July 15, 2007, from http://www.laureate-inc.com/GPSEM.php.
27. Laureate Education Inc. "Investors relations: News and information. University of Liverpool and Laureate International Universities Announce expanded international collaboration." Retrieved on July 12, 2007, from http://www.phx.corporate-ir.net/phoenix.zhtml?c=91846&p=irol-newsArticle&ID=993862&highlight=.
28. Goldie Blumenstyk, "The Chronicle Index of For-Profit Higher Education," *The Chronicle of Higher Education* (August 17, 2007). Retrieved on January 18, 2007, from http://www.chronicle.com/weekly/v54/i11/fptest.htm.
29. Samuel Trosow and Kirsti Nilsen, *Constraining Public Libraries: World Trade Organization's General Agreement on Trade in Services* (Lanham, MD: Scarecrow Press, 2006).
30. Ibid., p. 89.
31. Ingram, "Welcome to Ingram Book Group," Retrieved on January 7, 2008, from http://www.ingrambook.com.
32. Ingram Library Services, "Programs & Services." Retrieved on January 7, 2008, from http://www.ingramlibrary.com/progserv/default.asp.
33. Coutts, "Welcome to Coutts." Retrieved on January 7, 2008, from http://www.couttsinfo.com.
34. Ibid.
35. Ibid.
36. Bertelsmann, "Corporate Divisions." Retrieved on July 8, 2007, from http://www.bertelsmann.com; HCIRN, "Human–Computer Interaction Resource Network." Retrieved on July 13, 2007, from http://www.hcirn.

com; HCIRN, "Kluwer Academic Publishers." Retrieved on July 13, 2007, from http://www.hcirn.com/res/kap.php; Informa, "About." Retrieved on July 14, 2007, from http://www.informa.com; Informa, "Divisions: Taylor and Francis." Retrieved on July 14, 2007, from http://www.informa.com/corporate/divisions/academic_scientific/taylor_francis.htm; Holtzbrinck Publishers. "Who We Are." Retrieved on July 13, 2007, from http://www.holtzbrinckus.com/about/about_who.asp; Pearson Education. "About Pearson Education." Retrieved on July 16, 2007, from http://www.pearsoned.com; Reed Elsevier, "About Us." Retrieved on July 17, 2007, from http://www.reed-elsevier.com; The McGraw-Hill Companies. "Education. Financial Services. Information & Media." Retrieved on July 13, 2007, from http://www.mcgraw-hill.com; Thomson, "About Scientific." Retrieved on July 13, 2007, from http://scientific.thomson.com/aboutus.

37. Bertelsmann: Media Worldwide, "One Company–Six Divisions." Retrieved on January 6, 2008, from http://www.bertelsmann.com/bertelsnann_corp/wms41/brn/index.php?ci=99&language=2.
38. HCIRN, "Kluwer Academic Publishers." Retrieved on July 13, 2007, from http://www.hcirn.com/res/kap.php.
39. Verlagsgruppe Georg Von Holtzbrinck, "The Company." Retrieved on January 7, 2008 from http://www.holtzbrinck.com/artikle/778433&s=en.
40. Holtzbrinck Publishers, "Employment Opportunities." Retrieved on January 7, 2008, from http://www.holtzbrinckusa-jobs.com.
41. Informa, "Divisions: Taylor and Francis." Retrieved on July 14, 2007, from http://www.informa.com/corporate/divisions/academic_scientific/taylor_francis.htm.
42. Pearson, "Live and Learn." Retrieved on January 7, 2008, from http://www.pearson.com.
43. Pearson, "About Us." Retrieved on January 7, 2008, from http://www.pearson.com/index.cfm?pageid=2.
44. The McGraw-Hill Companies, "About Us, Overview." Retrieved on January 8, 2008, from http://www.mcgraw-hill.com/about us/overview.shtml.
45. The McGraw-Hill Companies, "Information & Media, Overview." Retrieved on January 8, 2008, from http://www.mcgraw-hill.com/ims/default.shtml.
46. The McGraw-Hill Companies, "Education, Overview." Retrieved on January 8, 2008, from http://www.mcgraw-hill.com/edu/default.shtml.
47. Springer Science+Business Media, "Developing Countries Initiatives." Retrieved on July 23, 2007, from http://www.springer-sbm.com.
48. International Association for the Evaluation of Educational Achievement, "Brief History of IEA." Retrieved on January 28, 2008, from http://www.iea.nl/brief_history_iea.html.
49. Ibid.
50. Ibid.
51. Ibid.
52. Ibid.
53. International Association for the Evaluation of Educational Achievement, "Mission Statement." Retrieved on January 28, 2008, from http://www.ies.nl/mission_statement.html.
54. Pearson Vue, "About Pearson VUE: Company History." Retrieved on January 9, 2008, from http://www.pearsonvue.com/about/history.
55. Pearson Vue, "Welcome to the New Pearson Vue." Retrieved on January 9, 2008, from http://www.pearsonvue.com.

56. Pearson Vue, "Pearson VUE Renews Global Test Delivery Contract with Association for Financial Professionals." Retrieved on January 9, 2008, from http://www.pearsonvue.com/about/release/07_12_17_afp.asp.

57. Pearson Vue, "Kaplan Test Prep and Admissions and Pearson VUE Renew Exckysuve Agreement to Deliver GMAT Ultimate Practice Test," Retrieved on January 9, 2008, from http://www.pearsonvue.com/about/release/07_12_17_Kaplan.asp.

58. Ruby Chua, "Pearson VUE Testing." E-mail received on February 5, 2008, from Technology Training Center, Queens College.

59. Ibid.

60. Thomas Wailgum, "Testing 1, 2, 3: Kurt Landgraf of ETS has all the Right Answers," *Continental* (January, 2008), p. 59.

61. ETS. (2007). ETS global. Retrieved July 12, 2007, from http://www.ets.org/portal/site/ets/menuitrn.435c0bd0ae7015d9510c3921509/?vgnextoid=d04b253b164f4010VgnVCM10000022f95190RCRD.

62. ETS, "ETS Global." Retrieved on January 7, 2008, from http://www.ets.org.

63. ETS, "News: G2nd Systems Group Named ETS Preferred Vendor." Retrieved on January 8, 2008, from http://www.ets.org/portal/site/ets/menuitem.c988ba0e5dd572bada20bc47c3921509/?vgnextoid=aacabafbdc86110VgnVCM10000022f9510RCRD&vgnextchannel=.

64. G2ndSystems, "News & Press Releases." Retrieved on January 8, 2008, from http://www.g2nd.com/public_systems?News%20and%20Press%20Releases.thm.

65. G2ndSystems, "Intercultural English–A New Global Tool." Retrieved on January 8, 2008, from http://www.g2nd.com/public_systems/courses/Intercultural%20English%20A%20New%20Global%20Tool.htm.

66. Ibid.

67. Apollo Group, Inc. "About Apollo Group." Retrieved on July 15, 2007, from http://www.apollogrp.edu/About.aspx.

68. Craig Swenson, "New Models for Higher Education: Creating an Adult-Centred Institution" in *Universities and Globalization: Private Linkages, Public Trust*, eds. Gilles Breton and Michel Lambert (UNESCO: Paris, 2003), p. 196.

69. Ibid.

70. Ibid.

71. Apollo Group, Inc. "History." Retrieved on January 6, 2008, from http://www.apollogrp.edu/History.aspx.

72. Swenson, "New Models for Higher Education," p. 202.

73. Ibid., pp. 204–206.

74. Ibid., p. 208.

75. "Fraud by University Owner is Found, January 17, 2008." Retrieved on January 17, 2008, from the New York Times on the Web http://www.nytimes.com.

76. Apollo Group, Inc. "Management." Retrieved on January 6, 2008, from http://apollogrp.edu/Management.

77. UNESCO, "World Declaration on Higher Education for the Twenty-First Century: Vision and Action." Retrieved on January 10, 2008, from http://www.unesco.org/education/educprog/wche/declaration_eng.htm#world%20declaration.

78. Daniel Schugurensky, "The Political Economy of Higher Education in the Time of Global Markets: Whither the Social Responsibility of the

University?," in *The University, State, and Market: The Political Economy of Globalization in the Americas*, eds. Roberts Rhoads and Carlos Torres (Palo Alto: Stanford University Press, 2006), pp. 301–320.

79. Ibid.
80. UNESCO, "World Declaration on Higher Education".
81. UNESCO, "Higher Education: Milestone-World Conference on Higher Education." Retrieved on January 11, 2007, from http://www.portal.unesco.org/education/en/ev.php-URL_ID=DO_Topic&URL_SECTION=201.html.
82. UNESCO, "World Declaration on Higher Education."
83. OECD, Higher Education and Regions: Globally Competitive, Locally Engaged (Paris: OECD, 2007).
84. Ibid., p. 11.
85. Ibid., p. 15.
86. Ibid., p. 16.
87. Ibid.
88. Eugene McCormack, "Worldwide Competition for International Students Heats Up, November 16, 2007," *Chronicle of Higher Education*. Retrieved on January 18, 2008, from http://www.chronicle.com/weekly/v54/i12/12a03401.htm.
89. Ibid.
90. Ravinder Sidhu, *Universities and Globalization: To Market, To Market* (Mahwah, NJ: Lawrence Erlbaum, 2006).
91. For a history of schools, advertising, and brand names see Joel Spring, *Educating the Consumer-Citizen: A History of the Marriage of Schools, Advertising, and Media* (Mahwah, NJ: Lawrence Erlbaum, 2003).
92. Ibid., p. 91.
93. Ibid., p. 106.
94. Ibid., p. 130.
95. Ibid., pp. 131–132.
96. Ibid., p. 135.
97. Ibid., p. 134.
98. Jan Currie, "Australian Universities as Enterprise Universities: Transformed Players on a Global Stage," in *Universities and Globalization: Private Linkages, Public Trust*, eds. Gilles Breton and Michel Lambert (Quebec, Canada: UNESCO, 2003), pp. 185.
99. Sidhu, p. 202.
100. As quoted in Ibid., p. 206.
101. Dubai Knowledge Village, "About Dubai Knowledge Village."
102. Ibid.
103. Ibid.
104. SAE Institute, "Mission Statement." Retrieved on December 18, 200, from http//www.sea.edu/mission_statement.
105. Emirates College for Advanced Education, "Mission and Vision." Retrieved on December 19, 2007, from http://www.ecae.ac.ae/English/Mission.aspx.
106. "Corporate Developments: Senior NIE Staff Helms Emirates College for Advanced Education," *News* (October 2007) No. 62, p. 4.
107. Ibid.
108. Corporate Developments, "Education Deans Form Worldwide Alliance," *News* (October 2007) No. 62, p. 3.

109. Press Release, "NYU to Open Campus in Abu Dhabi, Friday, Oct. 12, 2007." Retrieved on January 8, 2008, from http://www.nyu.edu/public. affairs/rreleases/detail/1787.
110. Ibid.
111. Emirates College for Advanced Education, "Bachelor of Education." Retrieved on December 19, 2007, from http://www.ecae.ac.ae/English/ CourseBachelor.aspx.
112. Philip Altbach, "The Imperial Tongue: English as the Dominating Academic Language," *International Higher Education* (Fall 2007) No. 49, pp. 2–5. Retrieved on December 19, 2007, from http://www.bc.edu/bc_ org/avp/soe/cihe/newsletter/Number49/p2_Altbach.htm.
113. Ibid., p. 2.
114. Ibid., pp. 2–4.
115. Ibid., p. 3.
116. Ibid., p. 4.
117. Ibid., p. 5.
118. A good example of the development of bicultural perspectives by cross-cultural psychologists is Richard Nisbett's *The Geography of Thought: How Asian and Westerners Think Differently ... and Why* (New York: Free Press, 2003).
119. International Association of Universities, "General Information." Retrieved on January 18, 2008, from http://www.unesco.org/iau/assoca-tion/index.html.
120. International Association of Universities, "International Association of Universities: Palgrave Macmillan Ltd Prize in Higher Education Policy Research." Retrieved on January 18, 2008, from http//www.uhnesco.org/ iau/scientifcpub/prize_HEP_2008.pdf.
121. Center for International Education, "Welcome." Retrieved on January 22, 2008, from http://www.bc.edu/bc_irg/avp/soe/cihe/welcome.htm.
122. Ibid.
123. International Network for Higher Education in Africa, "Welcome." Retrieved on January 22, 2008, from http://www.bc.educ/bc_org/avp/ soe/cihe/inhea/index.htm.
124. Philip G. Altbach, "Globalization and Forces for Change in Higher Education," *International Higher Education* 50 (Winter 2008), p. 1.
125. Ibid.
126. Ibid.
127. "Realizing the Global University," Conference, 15th November, 2007, Thistle Marble Arch Hotel London. Retrieved on January 20, 2007, from http://www.wun.ac.uk/theglobaluniversity/conference.html.
128. The Observatory on Borderless Higher Education, "About the Observatory." Retrieved on January 18, 2008, from http://www.obhe.ac.uk/ aboutus/.
129. "Realizing the Global University."
130. "Realizing the Global University." Home. Retrieved on January 20, 2008, from http://www.wun.ac.uk/theglobaluniersity/index.
131. Ibid.
132. Graham Spanier, "Internationalizing Today's Universities." Paper delivered at the Conference on Realizing the Global University, London, November 15, 2007. Retrieved on January 20, 2008, from http://www. wun.ac.uk/theglobaluniversity/conference.html.

133. Eric Thomas, "Defining A Global University." Paper delivered at the Conference on Realizing the Global University, London, November 15, 2007. Retrieved on January 20, 2008, from http://www.wun.ac.uk/theglobal-university/conference.html.
134. Ibid.
135. Ibid.
136. Worldwide Universities Network, "About Us." Retrieved on January 21, 2008, from http://www.wun.ac.uk/aboutus.php.
137. Ibid.
138. Worldwide Universities Network, "Contemporary China Center Video Seminars." Retrieved on January 21, 2008, from http://www.wun.ac.uk/chinacenter/documents/poster_USletter.pdf.
139. Universitas 21: The International Network of Higher Education, "About Us." Retrieved on January 21, 2008, from http://www.universitas21.com/about.html.
140. Universitas 21: The International Network of Higher Education, *Universitas 21 Strategic Plan 2007–2012*, p. 5. Retrieved on January 21, 2008, from http://www.universitas21.com/StrategicPlan.pdf.
141. Universitas 21: The International Network of Higher Education, "Shanghai Declaration on Universitas 21 Student Mobility." Retrieved on January 21, 2008, from http://www.universitas21.com/shanghaideclaration.html.
142. Universitas 21: The International Network of Higher Education, *Universitas 21 Strategic Plan*, p. 10.

## Chapter 5

1. These two collections are Kathryn Anderson-Levitt, ed. *Local Meanings, Global Schooling: Anthropology and World Culture Theory* (New York: Palgrave Macmillan, 2003) and Gita Steiner-Khamsi, ed. *The Global Politics of Educational Borrowing and Lending* (New York: Teachers College Press, 2004).
2. Kathryn Anderson-Levitt, "A World Culture of Schooling?" in *Local Meanings*, p. 1.
3. Ibid.
4. Gita Steiner-Khamsi, "Blazing a Trail for Policy Theory and Practice," in *Global Politics*, pp. 202–203.
5. Kathryn Anderson-Levitt, p. 9–12.
6. Ibid., p. 13.
7. Ibid., p. 14.
8. Gita Steiner-Khamsi, "Globalization in Education: Real or Imagined" in *Global Politics*, p. 4.
9. Ibid., p. 4.
10. Steiner-Khamsi, "Blazing a Trail," p. 203.
11. Ibid., pp. 204–207.
12. Ibid., p. 206.
13. Ibid, p. 207.
14. David Phillips, "Toward a Theory of Policy Attraction in Education" in *Global Politics*, pp. 54–74.
15. Ibid., p. 55.

16. Susan Jungck and Boonreang Kajornsin, "'Thai Wisdom' and Globalization: Negotiating the Global and Local in Thailand's National Education Reform," in Kathryn Anderson-Levitt, "A World Culture of Schooling?" in Kathryn Anderson-Levitt (Ed.), *Local Meanings*, p. 28.
17. Quoted in Ibid., p. 29.
18. Quoted in Ibid., p. 31.
19. Quoted in Ibid.
20. Quoted in Ibid., p. 32.
21. Quoted in Ibid., p. 33.
22. Ibid., pp. 38–39.
23. Iveta Silova, "Adopting the Language of the New Allies" in *Global*, p. 80.
24. Martin Fackler, "Losing an Edge, Japanese Envy India's Schools (January 2, 2008)." Retrieved on January 2, 2008, from New York Times on the Web, http://www.nytimes.com.
25. Ibid.
26. Ibid.
27. See Barry Keenan, *The Dewey Experiment in China: Educational Reform and Political Power in the Early Republic* (Cambridge, MA: Harvard University Press, 1977), and the story of the Soviet use of the Dalton method and Stalin's reaction in the 1930s can be found in Larry Holmes, *Stalin's School: Moscow's Model School No. 25, 1931–1937* (Pittsburgh, PA: University of Pittsburgh Press, 1999).
28. The Portuguese manuscript was completed in 1968 and it was published in the United States as Paulo Freire, *Pedagogy of the Oppressed* (New York: Herder and Herder, 1970).
29. Jürgen Schriewer and Carlos Martinez, "Constructions of Internationality in Education," in *Global Politics*, pp. 29–52.
30. Ibid., p. 45.
31. Ibid.
32. For a general study of the internationalization of progressivism and other educational ideas see Joel Spring, *Pedagogies of Globalization: The Rise of the Educational Security State* (Mahwah, NJ: Lawrence Erlbaum, 2006).
33. Keenan, pp. 30–33.
34. Quoted in Ibid., p. 78.
35. See Philip Short, *Mao: A Life* (New York: Henry Holt and Company, 1999), pp. 1–133.
36. Freire, p. 40.
37. Ibid., p. 82.
38. Ibid., p. 40.
39. The best general summary of global wars of liberation is Daniel Moran's *Wars of National Liberation* (London: Cassell, 2001).
40. Sheldon Liss, *Fidel! Castro's Political and Social Thought* (Boulder, CO: Westview, 1994), p. 137.
41. Ibid., p. 139.
42. Che Guevara, "Socialism and Man in Cuba," *Global Justice: Liberation and Socialism* (Melbourne, Australia: Ocean Press, 2002), p. 35. This book was published in cooperation with Che Guevara Studies Center in Havana, Cuba.
43. Paulo Freire, *Pedagogy of Hope: Reliving Pedagogy of the Oppressed* (New York: Continuum, 2004), p. 43.

44. Freire, *Pedagogy of the Oppressed*, p. 77.
45. Ibid., p. 83.
46. This is footnote #10 on p. 83 of Freire's *Pedagogy of the Oppressed* which is cited as from the *Selected Works of Mao-Tse-Tung*, Vol. III. 'The United Front in Cultural Work' (October 30, 1944) (Peking, 1967), pp. 186–187.
47. See Sheryl Hirshon with Judy Butler, *And Also Teach Them to Read: The National Literacy Crusade of Nicaragua* (Westport, CT: Lawrence Hill & Company, 1983); and John L. Hammond, *Fighting to Learn: Popular Education and Guerilla War in El Salvador* (New Brunswick, NJ: Rutgers University Press, 1998).
48. Schriewer and Martinez, p. 43.
49. Lesley Bartlett, "World Culture or Transnational Project?: Competing Educational Projects in Brazil," in *Local Meanings*, pp. 183–197.
50. John Boli and George M. Thomas, eds., *Constructing World Culture: International Nongovernmental Organizations Since 1875* (Palo Alto, CA: Stanford University Press, 1999).
51. John Boli and George Thomas, "INGOs and the Organization of World Culture" in *Constructing World Culture*, p. 43.
52. John Boli, Thomas A. Loya, and Teresa Loftin, "National Participation in World-Polity Organization," in *Constructing World Culture*, p. 53.
53. Ibid., p. 56.
54. Dana Burde, "International NGOs and Best Practices: The Art of Educational Lending" in Education," in *Global Politics*, p. 174.
55. Ibid., p. 183.
56. Ibid.
57. Akira Iriye, *Global Community: The Role of International Organizations in the Making of the Contemporary World* (Berkeley: University of California Press, 2002).
58. Ibid., p.3.
59. Ibid., p. 14.
60. For instance see World Bank, "Environment and Development: Partnerships & Initiatives." Retrieved on February 11, 2008, from http://www.worldbank.org/WBSITE/EXTERNAK/TOPICS/ENVIRONMENT/0,,menuPK:17651~pagePK:149018~piPK:149093~theSitePKPK244381,00.html.
61. Boli and Thomas, "INGOs and the Organization of World Culture," p. 23.
62. Margaret E. Keck and Kathryn Sikkink, *Activists Beyond Borders* (Ithaca, NY: Cornell University Press, 1998), p. 11.
63. Joel Spring, *How Educational Ideologies Are Shaping Global Society: Intergovernmental Organizations, NGOs, and the Decline of the Nation-State* (Mahwah, NJ: Lawrence Erlbaum, 2004), pp. 68–71.
64. Canadian Human Rights Foundation, *Module: The Global Human Rights Context* (Montreal: Canadian Human rights Foundation, 2002), p. 10.
65. Ibid., p.14.
66. Ibid., p. 16.
67. Ibid., p. 19.
68. Ibid., p. 23.
69. Ibid., p. 25.
70. Betty Reardon, *Educating for Human Dignity: Learning About Rights and Responsibilities: A K-12 Teaching Resource* (Philadelphia: University of Pennsylvania Press, 1995).

71. Ibid., pp. 189–191.
72. Ibid., p. 192.
73. Ibid.
74. Ibid., p. 193.
75. Ibid., p. 194.
76. Ibid., pp. 33–35.
77. Ibid., p. 35.
78. *Human Rights Here & Now: Celebrating the Universal Declaration of Human Rights* (Minneapolis: Human Rights Educators' Network, Amnesty International USA, Human rights Resource Center, 1998). The copy of the book I used is available online at http://www.hrusa.org/hrh-and-n/ and it has unnumbered pages.
79. Second World Conservation Strategy Project, *Caring for the Earth: A Strategy for Sustainable Living* (Gland, Switzerland: The World Conservation Union/United Nations Environment Programme/World Wide Fund For Nature, 1991), p. 77.
80. "Principle 10 of the Report of the United Nations Conference on Environment and Development: Rio Declaration on Environment and Development (12 August 1992), http://www.un.org/documents/ga/conf151/aconf15126-1annex1.htm; and Paul Pace, "From Belgrade to Bradford–20 Years of Environmental Education," in *A Sourcebook for Environmental Education: A Practical Review Based on the Belgrade Charter,* eds. W. Leal Filho, Z. Murphy, and O'Loan (Pearl River, NY: The Parthenon Publishing Group, 1996), p. 18.
81. Ibid., p. 19.
82. The Global People's Forum, "Civil Society Declaration." Retrieved on March 12, 2003, from http://www.worldsummit.org.za/.
83. Ibid.
84. Ibid.
85. EELink: A Project of the North American Association for Environmental Education, "Perspectives: Foundations of EE." Retrieved on January 5, 2005, from http://eelink.net/perspectives-foundationsofee.html.
86. A four part table of the World Wildlife Fund's emerging forms of education is given in William B. Stapp, Arjen E. J. Wals, and Sheri L. Stankorb, *Environmental Education for Empowerment: Action Research and Community Problem Solving* (Dubuque, IA: Kendall/Hunt Publishing, 1996), p. 6. This publication is copyrighted by the Global Rivers Environmental Education Network.
87. WWF, "A History of WWF." Retrieved on December 15, 2002, from http://www.panda.org/about_wwf/who_we_are/history.
88. Earth First!, "Direct Action Gets the Goods," Retrieved on January 7, 2003, from http://www.earthfirstjournal.org.
89. Edward Abbey, *The Monkeywrench Gang* (New York: Perennial, 2000).
90. Earth First!, "Monkeywrenching: What's up with that?," Retrieved on January 15, 2003, from http://www.earthfirstjournal.org.
91. Dave Foreman and Bill Haywood, *ECODEFENSE: A Field Guide to Monkeywrenching* (Chico, CA: Abbzug Press, 1993).
92. Quoted in Christopher Manes, *Green Rage: Radical Environmentalism and the Unmaking of Civilization* (Boston: Little, Brown, 1990), p. 167.
93. Ibid., p. 170.
94. Ibid., p. 190.

95. Ingrid E. Newkirk, "Week 4: Veganize Your Cafeteria" (New York: Lantern Books, 2003).
96. Newkirk, "Week 11: Cut Out Dissection."
97. Newkirk, "Week 2: Make a Library Display."
98. Elizabeth Becker, "Animal Rights Group to Sue Fast-Food Chain," *New York Times* (7 July 2003), p. A11.
99. Ibid.

## Chapter 6

1. Eduardo Mendieta, "Society's Religion: The Rise of Social Theory, Globalization, and the Invention of Religion," in *Religions/Globalizations: Theories and Cases*, eds. Dwight N. Hopkins, Lois Ann Lorentzen, Eduardo Mendieta, and David Batstone (Durham, NC: Duke University Press, 2001), p. 47.
2. George J. Sefa Dei, Budd L. Hall, and Dorothy Goldin Rosenberg, introduction to *Indigenous Knowledges in Global Contexts: Multiple Readings of Our World*, eds. George J. Sefa Dei, Budd L. Hall, and Dorothy Goldin Rosenberg (Toronto: University of Toronto Press, 2000), p. 4.
3. Paul Wangoola, Mpambo, "The African Multiversity: A Philosophy to Rekindle the African Spirit," in *Indigenous Knowledges*, p. 273.
4. Ibid.
5. Sefa Dei, Hall, and Goldin Rosenberg, in *Indigenous Knowledges*, p. 3.
6. Richard E. Nisbett, *The Geography of Thought: How Asians and Westerners Think Differently ... and Why* (New York: Free Press, 2003).
7. Quote from unnumbered front matter to Nisbett, *The Geography of Thought*.
8. Ibid.
9. Ibid.
10. Marlene Brant Castellano, "Updating Aboriginal Traditions of Knowledge" in *Indigenous Knowledges*, pp. 23–24.
11. Ibid., p. 26.
12. Ibid., p. 26.
13. Ibid., p. 29.
14. Ibid., p. 30.
15. Ibid.
16. Ibid.
17. Wangoola, p. 265.
18. Mahia Maurial, "Indigenous Knowledge and Schooling: A Continuum Between Conflict and Dialogue" in *What is Indigenous Knowledge? Voices from the Academy*, eds. Ladislaus M. Semali and Joe L. Kincheloe (New York: Falmer Press, 1999), p. 63.
19. George J. Sefa Dei, "African Development: The Relevance and Implications of 'Indigenousness'," in *Indigenous Knowledges*, p. 73.
20. Ibid.
21. Ibid., 74.
22. Ibid., p. 75.
23. For a summary of character traits in individualist and collectivist societies see Harry C. Triandis, "Individualism and Collectivism: Past, Present, and Future" in *The Handbook of Culture and Psychology*, ed. David Matsumoto (New York: Oxford University Press, 2001), pp. 35–50.

24. Samuel P. Huntington, *The Clash of Civilizations and the Remaking of World Order* (New York: Simon & Schuster, 1996).
25. Ibid., p. 41.
26. Ibid., p. 47.
27. Gabriel Almond, R. Scott Appleby, and Emmanuel Sivan, *Strong Religion: The Rise of Fundamentalisms Around the World* (Chicago: University of Chicago Press, 2003).
28. Mark Juergensmeyer, "The Global Rise of Religious Nationalism," in *Religions/Globalizations*, pp. 73–74.
29. Almond et al., p. 91.
30. Huntington, p. 45.
31. V.D. Savakar, *Hindutva Second Edition* (New Delhi, 2005). Also see Almond et al., pp. 135–140.
32  Almond et al., pp. 40–45.
33. For an introduction to current strand of Russian nationalism see Andrew Meier, "Putin's Pariah," *New York Times Magazine* (March 2, 2008). Retrieved on March 3, 2008, from http://www.nytimes.com.
34. For examples of violent religious confrontations including Western Christianity see Almond et al., pp. 145–191.
35. Huntington, p. 46.
36. Almond et al., p. 114.
37. Regarding the Zapatista movement see Lois Ann Lorentzen, "Who is an Indian? Religion, Globalization, and Chiapas" in *Religions/Globalizations*, pp. 84–102. Regarding the Indigenous political movement in Bolivia see Simon Romero, "Protestors in Bolivia Seek More Autonomy" (December 16, 2007). Retrieved on March 3, 2008, from http://www.nytimes.com.
38. Fouad Ajami, "The Summoning: 'But They Said, We Will Not Harken'," in *Samuel P. Huntington's The Class of Civilizations?: The Debate* (New York: Council on Foreign Relations, 1996), p. 27.
39. Robert L. Bartley, "The Case for Optimism," in *Samuel P. Huntington's The Class of Civilizations*, p. 44.
40. Jeane Kirkpatrick, "The Modernizing Imperative," in *Samuel P. Huntington's The Class of Civilizations*, p. 53.
41. Gerard Piel, "The West is Best," in *Samuel P. Huntington's The Class of Civilizations*, p. 55.
42. Richard Osmer and Friedrich Schweitzer, *Religious Education between Modernization and Globalization: New Perspectives on the United States and Germany* (Grand Rapids, MI: William Eerdmans, 2003), p. 11.
43. See Joel Spring, *The American School: From the Puritans to No Child Left Behind Seventh Edition* (New York: McGraw–Hill, 2008), pp. 110–115, 459–478.
44. "Saudi Arabia–Constitution." Retrieved on March 4, 2008, from http://www.the-saudi.net/saudi-arabia/saudi-constitution.htm.
45. Ibid.
46. "Constitution of the Arab Republic of Egypt," Retrieved on March 4, 2008, from http://www.uam.es/otrocentros/medina/egypt/egypolcon.htm.
47. Ibid.
48. Ibid.
49. Ibid.
50. Ibid.
51. Ibid.

52. Leslie S. Nucho, ed., *Education in the Arab World Volume I: Algeria, Bahrain, Egypt, Jordan, Kuwait, Lebanon, Morocco* (Washington, D.C.: AMIDEAST Publications), p. 150.
53. Gregory Starrett, *Putting Islam to Work: Politics and Religious Transformation in Egypt* (Berkeley: University of California Press, 1998), p. 78.
54. Ibid., 131–132.
55. Almond et al., pp. 135–140.
56. Ibid., pp. 156–157, 140–142.
57. Neela Banerjee, "Clashing Over Church Ritual and Flag Protocol at the Naval Academy Chapel (March 8, 2008)." Retrieved on March 8, 2008, from http://www.nytimes.com.
58. Savakar, p. 18.
59. Ibid., p. 113.
60. See Human Rights Watch, "'We Have No Orders To Save You': State Participation and Complicity in Communal Violence in Gujarat." Retrieved on March 7, 2008, from http:/hrw.org/reports/2002/india; and "11 More Churches Torched in Orissa," *The Times of India* (27 December 2007). Retrieved on March 7, 2008, from http://timesof india.indiatimes.com/articlesshow/2654765.cms.
61. Vishva Hindu Parishad: Hindi Home Page, "K.J.Somaiya Bhartiya Sanskriti Peetham: An Institution for Training Teachers Cultural & Research Institute." Retrieved on March 5, 2008, from http://www.vhp.org/englishsite/d.Dimensions_of_VHP/qvishwa%20Samanvya/scholarship_for_overseas_student.htm.
62. Ibid.
63. Vishva Hindu Parishad: Hindi Home Page, "In The Field of Education." Retrieved on March 5, 2008, from http://www.vhp.org/englishsite/d.Dimensions_of_VHP/aSewa/NSNS/intheserviceof poor.htm#in.
64. Vishva Hindu Parishad: Hindi Home Page, "One Teacher School (OTS)." Retrieved on March 3, 2008, from http://www.vhp.org/englishsite/d.Dimensions_of_VHP/bekal%20vidyalya/ekalvidyalayayojana.htm.
65. Ibid.
66. Ibid.
67. Ibid.
68. Ibid.
69. Sri Lanka: The Constitution, "Chapter II-Buddhism." Retrieved on March 8, 2008, from http://www.priu.gov.lk/Cons/1978Constitution/Chapter_02_Amd.html.
70. Somini Sengupta, "Sri Lankan City Mired in Ethnic Violence (May 15, 2006)." Retrieved on March 8, 2008, from http://www.nytimes.com.
71. M. K. Gandhi, *Sarvodaya: The Welfare of All* (Ahmedabad, India: Jovanji Dahyabhai Desai Navajivan Press, 1954), p. 27.
72. For instance, see Viniti Vaish's discussion of Gandhi and Sarvodaya in Viniti Vaish, *Biliteracy and Globalization: English Language Education in India* (Clevedon, England: Multilingual Matters Ltd., 2008).
73. Gandhi, p. 194.
74. Ibid., p. 43.
75. Ibid., p. 128.
76. Ibid.
77. Ibid., p.132.
78. Ibid., p. 7.
79. Ibid.

80. For a study of his lasting influence, see Marc Becker, *Mariátegui and Latin American Marxist Theory* (Athens: Ohio University Center for International Studies, 1993).
81. Sheldon B, Liss, *Marxist Thought in Latin America* (Berkeley: University of California Press, 1984), p. 129.
82. Ibid., p. 284.
83. José Carlos Mariátegui, *Seven Interpretive Essays on Peruvian Reality* (Austin: University of Texas Press, 1971), p. 122.
84. Becker, p. 38.
85. Ibid., p. 37.
86. Mariátegui, *Seven Interpretive Essays*, p. 28.
87. Ibid., p. 29.
88. Ibid., p. 25.
89. Medell'n Conference. (1968). *Medell'n Conference Documents: Justice and Peace*. Retrieved on November 20, 2004, from the Latin American Studies Program of Providence College Web site: http://www.providence.edu/las/documents.htm#Medell'n%, p. 3.
90. Quoted in Paulo Freire, *Pedagogy of the Oppressed* (New York: Herder and Herder, 1970), pp. 139–140.
91. Medell'n Conference (1968), *Medell'n Conference Documents: Justice and Peace*, Latin American Studies Program of Providence College. Retrieved on November 20, 2004, from, http://www.providence.edu/las/documents.htm#Medell'n%, p. 3.
92. Ibid., pp. 3–4.
93. Ibid.
94. Ibid., p. 1.
95. Ibid., p. 10.
96. Ibid., p. 10.
97. Christian Smith, *The Emergence of Liberation Theology: Radical Religion and Social Movement Theory* (Chicago: The University of Chicago Press, 1991), pp. 15–21.
98. Gustavo Gutérrez, *A Theology of Liberation; 15th Anniversary Edition* (Maryknoll, New York: Orbis Books, 1988), p. xxxviii.
99. Ibid., p. 57.
100. Ibid., p. 56.
101. Ibid., p. 56.
102. Smith, p. 19.
103. Ibid., p. 107.
104. Quoted in Sheryl Hirshon with Judy Butler, *And Also Teach Them to Read: The National Literacy Crusade of Nicaragua* (Westport, CT: Lawrence Hill & Company, 1983), p. 5.
105. John L. Hammond, *Fighting to Learn: Popular Education and Guerilla War in El Salvador* (New Brunswick, NJ: Rutgers University Press, 1998), p. 25.
106. Zahra Al Zeera, *Wholeness and Holiness in Education* (Herndon, VA: International Institute of Islamic Thought, 2001).
107. Zahra Al Zeera, "Paradigm Shifts in the Social Sciences in the East and West" in *Knowledge Across Cultures: A Contribution to Dialogue Among Civilizations*, eds. Ruth Hayhoe and Julia Pan (Hong Kong: Comparative Education Research Center, 2001), p. 70.
108. Al Zeera, *Wholeness and Holiness*, pp. 25–53.
109. Ibid., p. 68.

110. Ibid., p. 68.
111. Gregory Starrett, *Putting Islam to Work: Politics and Religious Transformation in Egypt* (Berkeley: University of California Press, 1998), p. 27.
112. See Robert Hefner, "Introduction: The Culture, Politics, and Future of Muslim Education" in *Schooling Islam: Culture and Politics of Modern Muslim Education*, eds. Robert Hefner and Muhammad Qasim Zaman (Princeton, NJ: Princeton University Press, 2007), pp. 1–39.
113. Ibid., p. 8.
114. Fazlur Rahman, *Islam & Modernity: Transformation of an Intellectual Tradition* (Chicago: University of Chicago Press, 1982), p. 20.
115. A. L. Tibawi, *Islamic Education: Its Traditions and Modernizations into Arab National Systems* (London: Luzac & Company, 1972), p. 71.
116. Bassam Tibi, *Arab Nationalism: Between Islam and the Nation-State* (New York: St. Martin's Press, 1997), p. 93.
117. Tibawi, p. 74.
118. Azyumardi Azra, Dina Afrianty, and Robert Hefner, "Pesantran and Madrasa: Muslim Schools and National Ideals in Indonesia," in *Schooling Islam*, pp. 178–179.
119. Ibid., 186.
120. Ibid., p. 187.
121. "Constitution of Malaysia ratified on August 31, 1957," Retrieved on January 25, 2005, from http://www.confinder.richmond.edu/local_malaysia.html.
122. Ibid.
123. Hashim, p. 130.
124. Ibid., p. 131.
125. Muhammad Qasim Zaman, "Epilogue: Competing Conceptions of Religious Education," in *Schooling Islam*, p. 253.
126. A. H. Nayyar, "Madrasah Education Frozen in Time," in *Education and the State: Fifty Years of Pakistan*, ed. Pervez Hoodbhoy (Karachi: Oxford University Press, 1998), pp. 228, 229, 232.
127. Ibid., p. 230.
128. Ibid., p. 233.
129. Ibid., p. 226.
130. United Nations General Assembly, *Report of the Human Rights Council: United Nations Declaration on the Rights of Indigenous Peoples, Article 14* (New York: United Nations, 2007), p. 6.
131. Al Zeera, p. 71.
132. See Joel Spring, *How Educational Ideologies Are Shaping Global Society: Intergovernmental Organizations, NGOs, and the Decline of the Nation-State* (Mahwah, NJ: Lawrence Erlbaum, 2004), pp. 100–130.
133. For examples of indigenous forms of education see *Indigenous Educational Models for Contemporary Practice: In our Mother's Voice*, eds. Maenette Benham and Joanne Cooper (Mahwah, NJ: Lawrence Erlbaum, 2000).

## Chapter 7

1. See Phillip Martin, "Migrants in the global labor market" and John Parker, "International migration data collection." Both papers were prepared for the policy analysis and research programme of the Global Commission

on International Migration. Geneva: Global Commission on International Migration and were utilized in the Report of the Global Commission on International Migration, *Migration in an Interconnected World: New Directions for Action*. Geneva: Global Commission on International Migration, 2005.

2. Report of the Global Commission on International Migration, p. vii.
3. Martin, p. 7.
4. United Nations, Department of Economic and Social Affairs: Population Division, *Trends in Total Migrant Stock: The 2005 Revision* (New York: United Nations Population Division, 2006), p. 1.
5. Ibid., p. 2.
6. Ibid.
7. Ibid., p. 3.
8. Ibid.
9. Ibid., p. 2.
10. OECD, *International Migration Outlook: Annual Report 2007 Edition* (Paris: OECD, 2007), p. 39.
11. Ibid., p. 38
12. Ibid.
13. United Nations, Department of Economic and Social Affairs, Population Division, *United Nations Expert Group Meeting on Population Distribution, Urbanization, Internal Migration and Development New York, 21–23 January 2008* (New York: United Nations, 2008), p. 3.
14. Ibid.
15. Ibid., pp. 3–4.
16. Ibid., pp. 5–9.
17. Seth Mydans, "Migrants Perish in Truck to Thailand." New York Times on the Web (April 11, 2008) and Emma Daly, "World Briefing: Spain: Immigrants Found Dead in Truck." New York Times on the Web (October 12, 2002). Retrieved on April 15, 2008, from http://www.nytimes.com.
18. OECD, *International Migration Outlook*, p. 79.
19. Ibid., pp. 79–80.
20. Ibid., p, 81.
21. "Annex Table I.A1.3: Education levels for immigrants, the second generation, and other native-born, 20–29 and not in education, by gender, latest available year," in OECD, *International Migration Outlook*, pp. 92–93.
22. Ibid., p. 85.
23. Ibid., p. 80.
24. Annie Vinokur, "Brain migration revisited." *Globalisation, Societies and Education* 4(1) 2006, pp. 7–24.
25. Report of the Global Commission on International Migration, p. 31.
26. R. Jiaojiao, "The Turning Tide," *China Daily* (2007, May 30), p. 20.
27. Susan Robertson, "Editorial: Brain Drain, Brain Gain and Brain Circulation," *Globalisation, Societies and Education* 4(1) 2006, pp. 1–5.
28. Caglar Ozden and Maurice Schiff, "Overview," in *International Migration, Remittances & the Brain Drain*, eds. Caglar Ozden and Maurice Schiff (Washington, D.C.: The World Bank, 2006), p. 11
29. Robertson, pp. 1–5.
30. Frederic Docquier and Abdeslam Marfouk, "International Migration by Educational Attainment, 1990–2000," in *International Migration*, pp. 175–185.

31. See Devesh Kapur and John McHale, *Give Us Your Best and Brightest: The Global Hunt for Talent and Its Impact on the Developing World* (Washington, D.C.: Center for Global Development, 2005).
32. Ibid., pp. 25–29.
33. Ibid., p. 17.
34. Vinokur.
35. Kapur and McHale, pp. 21–22.
36. Richard Adams, "Remittances and Poverty in Guatemala" in *International Migration*, pp. 53–80; and Jorge Mora and J. Edward Taylor, "Determinants of Migration, Destination, and Sector Choice: Disentangling Individual, Household, and Community Effects" in *International Migration* (pp. 21–52).
37. O. Stark, "Rethinking the brain drain," *World Development* 32(1) 2004, 15–22.
38. Maurice Schiff, "Brain Gain: Claims about Its Size and Impact on Welfare and Growth are Greatly Exaggerated," in *International Migration*, p. 202.
39. Ibid., p. 203.
40. Vinokur, p. 20.
41. Phillip Brown and Harold Lauder, "Globalization, Knowledge and the Myth of the Magnet Economy," *Globalisation, Societies and Education* 4(1)2006, pp. 25–57.
42. Gnanaraj Chellaraj, Keith Maskus, and Aadotya Mattoo, "Skilled Immigrants, Higher Education, and U.S. Innovation," in *International Migration*, pp. 245–260.
43. Lawrence Mishel and Jared Bernstein, *The State of Working America 2002/2003* (Ithaca, NY: Cornell University Press, 2003).
44. OECD, *International Migration Outlook*, p. 132.
45. Ibid., p. 137.
46. Caglar Ozden, "Educated Migrants: Is There Brain Waste?" in *International Migration*, pp. 236–237.
47. OECD, *International Migration Outlook*, p. 137.
48. Ibid., p. 137.
49. Brown and Lauder, p. 37.
50. Ibid., p. 37.
51. Inter-American Development Bank, "Fewer Latin Americans sending money home from the United States, survey finds" (April 30, 2008). Retrieved on May 1, 2008, from http://www.iadb.org/News/articledetail.cfm?artid=4595&language=En.
52. Ibid.
53. Ibid.
54. Report of the Global Commission on International Migration, p. 42.
55. Ibid., p. 4.
56. T. Fuller, "In Thai Cultural Battle, Name-Calling Is Encouraged." New York Times on the Web (August 23, 2007). Retrieved on August 23, 2007, from http://www.nytimes.com.
57. For global perspectives on multicultural education see: James Banks, ed. *Diversity and Citizenship Education: Global Perspectives* (New York: Jossey-Bass, 2007); Carl Grant and Joy Lei, eds.*Global Constructions of Multicultural Education; Theories and Realities* (Mahwah, NJ: Lawrence Erlbaum, 2001); Iris Rotberg, ed. *Balancing Change and Tradition Global Education Reform* (Lanham, MD: ScarecrowEducation, 2004);

Stephen Stoer and Luiza Cortesao, "Multiculturalism and Educational Policy in a Global Context," in Nicholas Burbules and CarlosTorres(Eds.), *Globalization and Education: Critical Perspectives* (New York: Routledge, 2000), pp. 253–274.
58. "Convention Against Discrimination in Education, 1960," in *Basic Documents on Human Rights Third Edition,* ed. Ian Brownlie (New York: Oxford University Press, 1994), pp. 320–321.
59. "European Convention on Human Rights and Its Five Protocols," in *Basic Documents,* p. 342.
60. See Tove Skutnabb-Kangas, *Linguistic Genocide in Education or Worldwide Diversity and Human Rights?* (Mahwah, NJ: Lawrence Erlbaum, 2000), pp. 567–638.
61. Joel Spring, *Globalization and Educational Rights* (Mahwah, NJ: Lawrence Erlbaum, 2001).
62. Ibid., pp. 161–162.
63. For a discussion of Singapore and a general picture of multiculturalism in a global society see Joel Spring, *How Educational Ideologies are Shaping Global Society* (Mahwah, NJ: Lawrence Erlbaum, 2004), pp. 1–28.
64. For an introduction to the problems caused by the multicultural legacy of British colonialism, including Malaysia, see Joel Spring, *Pedagogies of Globalization: The Rise of the Educational Security State* (Mahwah, NJ: Lawrence Erlbaum, 2006), pp. 152–189.

## Chapter 8

1. Edgar Morin, *Seven Complex Lessons in Education for the Future* (Paris: UNESCO, 2008), p. 48.
2. Ibid., p. 75.
3. Ibid., pp. 20–21.
4. Ibid., p. 34.
5. Morin, pp. 21–23 and Joel Spring, *Wheels in the Head: Educational Philosophies of Authority, Freedom and Culture from Confucianism to Human Rights, Third Edition* (New York: Routledge, 2008).
6. Morin, p. 22.
7. David Baker and Gerald LeTendre, *National Differences, Global Similarities: World Culture and the Future of Schooling* (Palo Alto, CA: Stanford University press, 2005), p. 174.
8. Eduardo Mendieta, "Society's Religion: The Rise of Social Theory, Globalization, and the Invention of Religion," in *Religions/Globalizations: Theories and Cases,* eds. Dwight N. Hopkins, Lois Ann Lorentzen, Eduardo Mendieta, and David Batstone (Durham, NC: Duke University Press, 2001), p. 47.
9. Nicholas Burbules and Carlos Torres, eds. *Globalization and Education: Critical Perspectives* (New York: Routledge, 2000); Michael Apple, Jane Kenway, and Michael Singh, eds., *Globalizing Education: Policies, Pedagogies, & Politics* (New York: Peter Lang, 2005); and Hugh Lauder, Phillip Brown, JoAnne Dillabough, and A. H. Halsey, *Education, Globalization & Social Change* (Oxford: Oxford University Press, 2006).
10. Michael Apple, "Are Markets in Education Democratic? Neoliberal Globalism, Vouchers, and the Politics of Choice" in *Globalizing Education,* pp. 209–231.

11. Ibid., p. 211.
12. Ibid., pp. 210–211.
13. Seyla Benhabib, "Multiculturalism and Gendered Citizenship" in *Education, Globalization*, pp. 154–155.

# Index